PEACEMAKING IN YOUR NEIGHBORHOOD:

REFLECTIONS
ON AN EXPERIMENT
IN COMMUNITY MEDIATION

Jennifer E. Beer

Friends Suburban Project

Foreword by Elise Boulding

new society publishers

philadelphia, pa

ISBN: Hardcover 0-86571-072-4
ISBN: Paperback 0-86571-071-6

Printed in the United States of America

Cover Design by Barbara Benton
Book Design by Nina Huizinga and Jennifer E. Beer
Artwork by Jay Miller

For more information about Friends Suburban Project, write or phone:
FSP
Box 462
Concordville, PA 19331
215-459-4770

New Society Publishers is a project of the New Society Educational
Foundation and a collective of the Movement for a New Society. New Society
Educational Foundation is a nonprofit, tax-exempt, public foundation.
Movement for a New Society is a network of small groups and individuals
working for fundamental social change through nonviolent action. To learn
more about MNS, write: Movement for a New Society, 4722 Baltimore
Avenue, Philadelphia, PA 19143. Opinions expressed in this book do not
necessarily represent positions of either New Society Educational
Foundation or Movement for a New Society.

Foreword

If you have felt discouraged about prospects for world peace lately (and who hasn't), this is a wonderfully affirming book to read. It talks about where peace begins—in one's own neighborhood. It recounts how one group launched a peacemaking project in that most unpromising of all settings, the fringes of a city, and saw that project take root there.

Conflict, we know, is everywhere. It is in our own inner being, it is present in our relationships even with those we love most. Wherever human beings are in relationship—in the home, at work, in civic affairs, in political decisionmaking, and in the macro-institutions of state and world—they to some degree clash with each other. Each *I* has unique wants, needs, interests, and perceptions, as does each social group, in a conglomerate of uniquenesses which is staggering to the mind if we think of the number of conflictual interactions taking place at any one moment on the planet. Out of this conflict can come human growth and development, or destruction. The quality of any human group, institution, or society depends on how that conflict is handled.

Mostly, human beings handle their daily conflicts pretty well—or society would fall apart. We make peace a hundred times a day, with our family, with our co-workers, in a myriad of public and private encounters. But our overall record as peacemakers in the twentieth century is a very mixed one. We have learned a lot about human development and nurturant interaction. We know a lot about creative problem-solving and how to turn zero-sum games, in which there is only one winner, into positive-sum games, in which all participants gain something. But we have also experienced the profound alienation induced by a technological civilization opaque in its complexity, a civilization which divides rich from poor and turns individuals into social security numbers. The answering escalation of interpersonal and international violence belies our gains in human understanding. Feelings of individual helplessness are pervasive, even among well-educated persons engaged in ostensibly significant professional work.

We have lost our sense of the whole, of how things connect. Peacemaking at the neighborhood level is one important way of regaining the sense of the whole in that it involves taking a torn and fragmented set of local relationships and creating the conditions for their repair and renewed wholeness. That experience of local healing is empowering on many levels, both for the participants and for the mediators. It reduces the sense of helplessness and makes people feel that they can do something about the world around them.

All this is testified to in this book. The story of the development of a local mediation service is really the story of the development of mediation and conflict resolution capacities for society as a whole. Of course no one will pretend that a successful neighborhood mediator could take on arms control negotiations between the Russians and the Americans. Nevertheless it is also true that a society which has not developed the capacity to make those small yet psychologically huge leaps of faith and trust which dispute settlement between individual adversaries always requires will not be able to take the comparably small but psychologically huge steps of trust which international negotiation requires. Cultures are not created in the halls of parliaments and presidential palaces; they are created locally and only later drawn on nationally. Therefore the cultures of mediation and peacemaking must begin locally.

Jennifer Beer's story of a neighborhood mediation project is the story of a new national movement which is contributing to the growth of this much-needed culture of peace in our time. At present there are 1000 national institutes and services which provide research, training, and services in dispute settlement according to the *Dispute Resolution Program Directory* for 1984. The American Bar Association identifies about 300 individual mediation services specifically oriented to community mediation, and there are hundreds of local enterprises providing a range of special services. Mediation professionals with advanced training are just the tip of the iceberg. The majority of mediators have been apprentices to other mediators and serve on a volunteer basis. That is why one can speak of a movement. These volunteer mediators represent the generation after the flower children, after the Vietnam anti-war demonstrators, a generation which has turned from love-ins and sit-ins to practical problem-solving where conflict festers. They are not simply pragmatists, however. Beer's research on these mediators reveals that they are idealistic community activists who are involved in a number of other civic enterprises besides mediation. They worry about larger problems of social justice and sometimes fear the band-aid effect of mediation, which may delay the addressing of the larger problems. These dilemmas are real and must be faced.

The story of the volunteer mediators which Beer tells is an inspiring one, albeit told with care for realistic detail about the problems and shortcomings of mediation. Beer and her colleagues have spent a great deal of time going over office records to make the story complete. As a sociologist I welcome this excellent documentation of an important new social development. But Beer does more than present data. She presents a vivid story of people in action, of an institution in the making. The story of the suburban Delaware County project is set in the national context. One of the most interesting facts about these local mediators is that they also feel they are a part of this national and international context. They know they are contributing to peace in the larger sense. Many readers will want to go and do likewise, and this book will help focus their intentions and actions.

The development of an apparently simple two-hour mediation sequence for local disputes from a more complex set of labor mediation protocols is an amazing story—the more amazing because over and over again it *works*. The advice of a third party helping people solve conflicts is as old as the oldest historical records of our species. New are the assumptions that 1) most people can in fact be trained to serve in that third party role and 2) the third party is not the peacemaker but the empowerer, enabling adversaries trapped in their own anger to get a handle on their conflict and to make their own peace.

The role of a mediator is demanding and exhausting. Most of them are unpaid volunteers. Why do they do it? For the joy of seeing people liberated from being immobilized by their own hostilities, says Beer. The term peace*making* is misleading because, as Beer makes clear, mediators are not *making* peace for the adversaries. Rather, the mediator is the "outsider in the middle" who structures interaction for disputants so they become their own peacemakers.

The concepts and protocols for this remarkable type of peacemaking do not come out of the blue. While certainly owing much to the techniques of labor mediation, it is no accident that the project was developed under Quaker auspices. The historic peace churches generally have had much to do with the new mediation movement. Another interesting discussion centers on the role of women's peace culture in the movement, since two thirds of the mediators in the Community Dispute Settlement program are women.

A striking feature of Beer's discussion of the mediation process is the emphasis on the importance of appropriate assertiveness on the part of the mediator, of willingness to be firm, to rule certain behaviors out of bounds, to exhibit what is felicitously called "tough love" in family therapy circles. This raises an interesting point in regard to both Quakerism and women: The Quaker way and the woman's way have suffered in the past century from an obscuring of that type of realistic, common-sense assertiveness which is native to both, so that Quakers and women have endured a partly self-imposed and ahistorical cult of false gentleness. False gentleness does not work in the turbulence of mediation. Coming to terms with the need for assertiveness has been an important growing experience for Quaker mediators, for women mediators, and perhaps most of all for Quaker women mediators! I venture to hope that this type of development will help to right the imbalances that have developed in Quakerism in the quietist period and in women as a result of industrialization.

The second part of Peacemaking in Your Neighborhood deals with organizational/structural problems. Beer does not minimize the difficulties in creating a workable and efficient community mediation service. Oddly, the supply of mediation services has developed faster than the demand. People are suspicious of outside involvement in their conflicts. The new culture of peacemaking has yet to catch on for the average man or woman, the average neighborhood. Class differences between mediators and users of mediation are troubling. Much remains to be done. The honesty with which the problems are discussed is part of the excellence of the book itself. The fine bibliography at the end provides a valuable tool for the reader who would go further.

Letting the reader in on the whole process, as Beer has done, has been in my view a highly successful strategy. The book leaves us with an overpowering impression of hope, of dynamism, of having found the beginning of an exciting new road. This road is certainly one of the surer paths into the twenty-first century, and one which every reader of this book will want to contemplate for themselves personally.

Elise Boulding
Dartmouth College

Acknowledgements

David Albert   Rebecca Kratz Mays
Frances Beer   Jay Miller
Barbara Benton   Melva Mueller
Betty Corry   Anne Richan
T. L. Hill   Carol Smith
Nina Huizinga   Brenda Wolfer

The Thomas H. and Mary William Shoemaker Foundation

The Chace Fund Committee

Philadelphia Yearly Meeting of the Religious Society of Friends

Goshen, Kennett, and Media Monthly Meetings

Friends Suburban Project Committee

To the two full-time staff members of Friends Suburban Project, my special thanks:

Charles C. Walker, mentor and friend.

Eileen M. Stief, whose energy, whimsy, and astute practicality have sustained our working partnership. As Community Dispute Settlement's first director, her ideas and innovations shaped that program's organization and philosophy. The observations and reflections presented in this book are as much hers as mine.

Jennifer E. Beer
24 September 1985

Publisher's Note

A long time ago, or so the story goes, people set up laws and legal institutions and governments to help them handle the conflicts which arose in the context of their daily lives. The same story says that we live in an age of progress where human understanding advances steadily, and with it come advances in legal systems, governments, social justice, and international peace.

But New Society Publishers is located in a West Philadelphia neighborhood where the Mayor orders the police to drop incendiary devices on men, women, and children whose lifestyles he doesn't approve of. We live in a state where funds cannot even be found to distribute dairy products provided to the state for free to the poor, the hungry, and the homeless, much less to provide decent legal counsel to those who can't afford it. We live in a country where not only are more than three new atomic weapons produced every day, but where instruments of torture are fabricated and shipped to scores of "free world" nations. And we live in a world which has as little open conflict as it does only because the hungry and dispossesed don't even have the strength to ask for what should be theirs by birthright.

And the story goes on. Community mediation won't change the script. But it does give us a glimpse of a way in which we as citizens can claim a sense of unity and community with our neighbors, and then perhaps as nations and, ultimately, beyond them.

Such glimpses are all too rare, and make us feel quite giddy. What I most appreciate about *Peacemaking in Your Neighborhood* is its concreteness, its wealth of detail, and its sense of what a struggle it is to take even one small but effective step toward this community.

I think that no peace or social change activist should leave or change the focus of her/his ongoing work without carefully evaluating the effectiveness of her/his contribution and finding an appropriate means of sharing it with others. Jenny Beer's study of her work with the Community Dispute Settlement Program is an outstanding model, one I hope will be emulated often. With this in mind, New Society Publishers is proud to publish *Peacemaking in Your Neighborhood: Reflections on an Experiment in Community Mediation*.

David H. Albert
for New Society Publishers
2 January 1986

Contents

Mediating in pairs
The Facts
Consensus or compromise?
Outcomes
Empowerment

Part II

An overview of the CDS program
The new idea
Different program models
Major program decisions
Staffing
Referrals and constituency
Intake
Records and confidentiality
Evaluating mediators
Survival

The professional community
The legal community
The police
Officials, agencies, schools, and churches
Mediation's place in the suburban neighborhood
Rules and social norms
Isolation and independence
Choosing: Rules or relationships?
Spreading the skills

Alternative to the criminal justice system
Protection, access, and coercion
Pacification and control
Social change
Looking back
Future directions
A kernel of radical change?
Conclusions?

Introduction

"Every morning, I wake up and think, 'I've got to face this again today,'" the woman said. It was a hot day. She stood on her small front porch, looking over the fence at her neighbor's house. "Whenever my kids play outside, he curses at them. He steals their balls. My Mom has had to take my kids most days. I can't keep them indoors all the time, can I? Half the time I'm scared to answer the door for fear its going to be him or the police again."

She wasn't finished. "You know, we don't have much money but we paid for this house. They think this street is their private property! For five years we've tried to be good neighbors. All I want is to live in peace."

We went next door. The husband was eager to talk. "Don't let her fool you. That woman lies through her teeth! To hear her, you'd think her kids were floating around with a couple of halos. Look where they smashed our fence. They run all over our vegetable garden. Once my wife told them to get out, and she says, 'Oh, Jimmy, don't listen to that old bag.' So he sticks out his tongue." The man jabbed his finger towards the fence. "They're like animals, those people."

His wife spoke up. "We've lived here for 24 years and never had trouble like this, ever. Every weekend it's loud parties, cars in and out till all hours.... We don't want trouble. I call the police and let them take care of it." Her face had been expressionless but now her voice caught. "We just want to be left alone to live out our last years in peace."

* * *

2 / PEACEMAKING IN YOUR NEIGHBORHOOD

Small troubles, we may think to ourselves, but for these neighbors the desperate edge to the frustration is real. In spite of their attempts to make the situation better, little incidents have grown into looming thunderclouds. A few days before we talked to them, the young mother had received a summons. She had to put down $300. The charge? She didn't know.

Neighbors who are having problems with each other often have few ways to resolve them. When they can no longer ignore the aggravation, they may try to talk matters over. If that ends in an angry shouting match, they usually turn to public officials—the police, the council representative, the judge.

The Community Dispute Settlement (CDS) program in suburban Philadelphia was started as an alternative step between private and public forums. Disputants have a chance to speak directly to each other and to work out some solutions within a structured setting. The young mother and the retired couple of our story were sent to the program by the local magistrate. Using a simple mediation format, two trained volunteers sat down with them for two hours. As we will hear later, the neighbors eventually came to an amicable agreement.

This book by Friends Suburban Project, the Quaker group which founded Community Dispute Settlement, describes in detail its experiment in community mediation. What were our hopes for this program? What actually happened? Our answers raise a host of implications for other groups who are turning to mediation as a way of peacemaking in their communities.

Beginnings

In 1976 Friends Suburban Project (FSP) was looking for a new project. Over the years it had started many programs addressing community peace and justice issues in Delaware County, the region just south and west of Philadelphia's city line. They wanted another community experiment which would follow their three customary program guidelines: *nonviolence*, *alternatives*, and *empowerment*. The ideal project would have an impact on the whole county and interest other activists working in neighborhoods across the country.

At the time this search began, three women in FSP's Youth Advocates program, Betsey Leonard, Eileen Stief, and Emily Sontag, were working with teenagers in trouble. The women were in the bad graces of a local police department and the county schools for delinquents. They had seen too much and were asking too many public questions.

Betsey Leonard recalls attending school conferences where, "the adults would sit around focusing on 'this naughty child' instead of what *they* had to do with it." It became apparent that just helping one person was not likely to resolve a difficult situation.

They were also spending long hours in the courtrooms. What they saw disturbed Eileen Stief: "Many people got short shrift in the poorer courts.... Judges were put in impossible situations of deciding who was lying, who was wrong, especially with neighbors. The judges were the first to admit it; it frustrated them." It seemed common sense that people could have made better decisions themselves.

The idea of neighborhood mediation was beginning to surface in community organizing newsletters and conferences. Another Quaker organization, the American Friends Service Committee, started a clearinghouse on the subject. The three women believed that mediation might give families and neighbors a better way to resolve conflicts than calling the police or going to court. With negotiation training from the American Arbitration Association under their belts, they decided to ask FSP to sponsor their plan for a community mediation program.

The three guidelines for all of FSP's work seemed to fit such a project well.

1) Community dispute settlement would be an experimental *alternative* to suing family members or neighbors in court.

2) Early intervention in community conflicts would *decrease* the potential for *violence* and provide a model for handling future troubles.

3) Because disputants construct their own agreements, mediation would *empower* people to take control of their own problems.

The Friends Suburban Project committee (equivalent to a board of directors) approved. Eileen Stief was hired to organize the new Community Dispute Settlement (CDS) program. FSP set about connecting with agencies and judges who could send cases. A core of volunteer mediators formed quickly. Interest was high, disputants seemed satisfied. Nevertheless, CDS stayed small. For six years, FSP's staff operated the program from the FSP office. In 1982, following FSP's custom of spinning off successful projects, CDS incorporated as an organization independent of the Quakers and moved to a storefront in Darby, PA, a municipality close to the Philadelphia boundary. (Please see the note at the end of the bibliography if the difference between FSP and CDS is confusing.)

The mediations

Both the purpose and the format of the mediation model

developed during the first years have remained much the same. In the low-key Community Dispute Settlement mediation procedure, a pair of CDS volunteers help the disputants talk with each other about what has been happening. Mediators begin with an opening explanation of what to expect. Next, each person has a turn to speak. The subsequent arguments over points of tension eventually give way to problem-solving. If this is successful, an agreement is written out. With this simple outline, even new mediators are able to help most people reach workable resolutions.

Neighbor disputes are by far the most common cases. For some local judges the words "barking dogs" and "common driveways" have become synonymous with Community Dispute Settlement. Almost every case involves harassment. That can mean anything from constant taunts and namecalling to having five pizza services deliver at one time next door. (Yes, it happened!) Property lines, children, and noise are frequent areas of dispute. Every so often, an organization with internal tensions will ask for mediation services. The program also mediates between couples or within families. In the early years CDS frequently handled difficulties between teenagers and parents. The usual mediation involves two to ten disputants.

Today, more than nine years later, the now autonomous Community Dispute Settlement Program still offers mediation to anyone in Delaware County. After several years of month-by-month financing, the program has an established funding base. The number of mediations has risen to about four a month. Total referrals, that is all cases where at least one party has called CDS, number over 300 a year. CDS has gained an accepted place among the county's human services organizations.

An overview of the book

CDS's growth has been paralleled across North America by a surge of interest in dispute resolution. Institutes and professional societies are growing rapidly. The National Conference on Peacemaking and Conflict Resolution has drawn hundreds of attenders. Several states have instituted a system of mediation programs. Law schools have put alternative dispute resolution and negotiation skills into their curricula. Chief Justice Warren Burger and other high officials call publicly for more mediation and arbitration. Among mediators, the mood is upbeat.

Despite the energetic expansion of mediation and conciliation, some commentators wonder whether this trend towards informal justice will last. Because it provides a mirage of justice, the burgeoning movement only harms those it sets out to help, these writers say, and the low caseload of voluntary programs like CDS indicates that the ordinary person senses this.

Both advocates and critics often seem to speak to themselves, as their different bibliographies reveal. Mediation proponents write about running programs and improving mediation techniques. Evaluations focus on the quality of service: Do people reach agreements? Do they stick? They look at whether a mediation program gives less expensive, quicker results than the court system. Their literature is filled with enthusiasm and activity. Critics, meanwhile, scarcely look at the dynamics of mediation sessions. They are more interested in why political leaders are suddenly pushing conciliation. Mediation is liberalism's latest panacea for the problems of our courts, they say. Claims that mediation is better, cheaper, more efficient, and often more appropriate are seen as rationales which screen a more devious agenda. They see informal programs as a reaction to the liberal tenet of equality. By hindering people's access to the courts, complaints of civil rights violations are shoved aside. By offering an easy new solution to the devastating problems of the justice system—acknowledged by all sides—mediation programs divert attention from serious flaws in our economic and legal system. Critics also point to the distinct lack of community involvement in these avowedly "community" programs as another sign that they are a tool of suppression.

This book crosses the bounds between practitioners and critics, examining the CDS experience in light of the concerns and questions of both. Each chapter is an essay which looks at a different facet of the mediation program.

Part I. We begin by looking at the core of any dispute settlement program: what happens during the mediation session itself. The next two chapters discuss the disputant and the mediator. Who are they? What brings them to mediation? From there we examine the mediator's role both as outsider and as the person in control. What influences have helped define this role in CDS? An evaluation of the framework of CDS mediation culminates in a discussion of outcomes. Do disputants truly get what they want? Are the agreements fair? The first half of the book ends with a look at "empowerment," a concept dear to CDS but one that is hard to define and harder to document.

Part II. The second section discusses mediation in its wider community context. Program models across the country are still very much in the experimental stages; there are many forms and few standard answers. We review the choices and the changes CDS has made over the years. The Community chapter surveys the program's relations to different segments of the community. CDS disputes reveal much about suburban life and some unsettling observations about the potential place of mediation in suburban communities. The last chapter addresses the hard questions. FSP's fond dreams for social change lead to troubling issues about the part community mediation plays in our criminal justice system. We look at CDS's experience in light of the critiques about the use and misuse of mediation. What directions can CDS and other programs choose for the future? For those who are consciously working towards a more just and peaceful society, mediation holds both promise and danger.

Sources. FSP reviewed about 500 case files from 1977 till the present. Many mediators and other people connected with the program were interviewed. We collected comments from disputants during intake, mediation sessions, and follow-up. Fortunately, the program records had been well organized from the beginning, and several historically-minded staff members had saved files of memos and minutes. Input from other programs has also been important. Over the years CDS has benefited from visits to more than a dozen of these centers. We have used the publications or spoken with staff from many others (See sources list in the bibliography).

Although names and any peculiar details which could identify a particular disputant have been changed, examples and quotes in this book are all drawn from CDS material. Any hypothetical cases are so indicated. Direct quotes are usually attributed or set off in italics. One-liner remarks which explain a point, on the other hand, are composites of refrains we hear from many people. FSP trains and consults for other community programs besides CDS; occasionally, examples are cited from these groups as well.

FSP has been too involved in its CDS experiment to produce a disinterested study, but we attempt to observe our experience honestly. This review is not easy. For years we have "sold" mediation to referral sources, to disputants, to trainees. We speak about mediation in necessarily general and sometimes idealistic terms. Holding to what has actually happened requires vigilance, and the reader will certainly find places where myth has again overtaken us! Description is dry without reflection; reflections are empty without historical and sociological research. We have tried to combine these approaches for a many-sided look at one suburban community mediation project.

Visions of peacemaking

We called this book *Peacemaking in Your Neighborhood* because ultimately it is not the particular tool of mediation but the interplay of conciliation and confrontation which interests us. Whether a mediator takes on quarrelling neighbors, warring gangs, or hostile nations, the goal is a cooperative one of searching for some common ground for new directions. Often the mediation is a process of reaffirming good intentions that have disappeared behind the drama of accusation and retaliation. Other times it seems impossible to find a fair give-and-take solution. Dispute resolution tries to balance the desire for harmonious relations with our visions of justice. That tension seems to lie at the heart of mediation's limitations and its usefulness.

When Friends Suburban Project entered the mediation field, it articulated a distinct agenda for social change which would include both justice and conciliation. Nine years later the record is mixed. The individual mediations often succeed in moving people towards genuine settlement. Mediators have learned valuable skills which they have used within their own circles. The program has not come close to realizing its hopes for social change and community empowerment, however. Its experience substantially supports the critics of dispute resolution. Nevertheless, using a third party is a widespread tradition—because it often works and is deemed more promising than alternatives. What society does not have go-betweens or facilitators? Mediation is a process too powerful to dismiss. The final issue is not whether but *how* we choose to use it—and how well we can make it work.

Part I

One: The Session

The simple mediation framework CDS has developed divides the session into stages. The disputants may not be aware of all these divisions; they mostly serve as guides for the mediators.

Opening Statement

Uninterrupted Time

The Exchange

Building the Agreement

Writing the Agreement

Closing Statement

To illustrate what may happen in each stage, we will walk step by step through the events of a real case. Names and personalities have been changed, as have some terms of the agreement.

Opening Statement

The parents come in as one unit. Terry follows a few yards behind, her long dark hair hiding her as if she has drawn a curtain. James and Kay, the two mediators, welcome them to the small blue church social room. Kay looks at Terry. Yes, it is just beginning to show; she is probably about four months pregnant. Her face still looks innocent, like a child's. After shy hellos, everyone takes a seat at the table.

The mediators begin with the Opening Statement. Kay, the more experienced mediator, tells them what they can expect, then explains the Community Dispute Settlement policies of confidentiality and voluntary participation. The second mediator, James, compliments the Fabio family on their courage to try out something new. No one has questions. Probably they are too preoccupied with their own anxious thoughts to take in much of what the mediators are saying.

* * *

The Opening Statement is crucial to setting the tone of the mediation. Mediators strive for a friendly, informal atmosphere which at the same time dispels disputants' worries that the meeting will get out of hand. The introduction, therefore, includes words of encouragement (as James gave the Fabios) and clear explanation of procedures. In the *Mediator's Handbook* (Beer, et al., 1982), a CDS mediator is asked to cover:

Welcome and words of encouragement. In addition to introducing themselves to each disputant, the mediators ask how people want to be addressed. They note the locations of the water fountains and bathrooms, and they explain the smoking regulations.

Mediators compliment the disputants on their courage to try something new. Often disputants enter the room tense, frustrated, and skeptical. Mediation is an unknown for them. Neighbors find themselves sitting across the table from people they do not like. People will be talking about their own faults and mistakes. Open acknowledgement by the mediators of the disputants' willingness to experiment with a new process helps start the session on a positive note.

The purpose of the session and the mediators' role. Everyone is present to talk about the situation and to try to reach some agreement about how things will be from now on. The participants will make those decisions. Mediators will not be judges but will direct the discussion.

What will happen. Mediators explain that everyone will have Uninterrupted Time, followed by discussion and writing an agreement. Anyone may ask for time to meet separately with another person or call for a stretch break.

Mediators' promise of confidentiality and policy on notetaking. Affirmation that people are willing to continue with the mediation, that the mediators are acceptable.

Opening Statements vary considerably—CDS mediators have different styles, different emphases. One woman talks about "mediation as a working session"; another is concerned that participants be there in good faith; a third talks about reconciliation, and so on. These individual slants seem to make little impact on the direction of the mediation. One of CDS's more disconcerting discoveries has been that disputants rarely take in much of what the mediators say at this point. They are too preoccupied with what they are going to do when their turn comes and with avoiding eyes across the table. For this reason, setting an atmosphere of ease and control appears to be the critical function of this opener. Information can be repeated; commitment to working things out can be explored later. As one experienced mediator remarked when program trainees were concerned about a disputant's reluctance to participate, "I say make it short. The faster you can get them started talking, the better. After they start talking they forget about their reluctance."

CDS mediators have found it wise to divide the five to ten minute introduction between themselves because when only one mediator speaks the disputants thereafter persistently address that person as lead mediator.

Uninterrupted Time

Moving into the Uninterrupted Time segment of the mediation session, Kay asks each person in turn to explain what is happening and how he or she feels about it.

Terry does not want to go first, so Mrs. Fabio starts. Terry will not talk to them. She cries; she goes out for long walks alone late at night; worse, she has started cutting school. "Furthermore," says Terry's mother, "I raised two children and have no intention of raising another one." Terry looks at her hands. Then her father takes his turn. He does not want an illegitimate grandchild in his house. Terry's education is more important than this pregnancy. He will pay for an abortion. He also wants no more sullen behavior. His wife interrupts him several times. James asks her to hold her comments and assures her that there will be plenty of time to talk after everyone has spoken. She says it is hard to stay quiet but agrees to try.

It is Terry's turn. She says only, "I haven't decided what to do." Her shrug indicates that she does not wish to discuss her feelings with her parents. James asks her a few questions but does not press. She will probably feel more comfortable later.

* * *

"Thank goodness for Uninterrupted Time," says one mediator. "It gives mediators as well as disputants something structured to do at the outset." The effectiveness of this simple technique is obvious to anyone who has worked with conflicts; this part of the mediation framework is found in nearly every kind of mediation program.

Uninterrupted Time allows each party and the mediators to hear every person's story. In spite of themselves, participants find themselves listening to each other. Often this is the first time each person has been able to explain what has been happening from their point of view with minimal interruption and fear of attack.

Disputants are trying to win the approval of the mediators. Their Uninterrupted Time statements are often carefully crafted to show good will, to put themselves and their positions in the most favorable light. A truer picture is more likely to emerge later during free discussion. Uncovering the facts, then, is not a primary purpose.

For this reason, CDS has changed its Uninterrupted Time period so that it differs from many other programs in one way: mediators are also expected to respect the disputants' time. Of course, they still intervene when other parties interrupt. Otherwise they only break in to gently encourage fearful or reluctant talkers, as with young Terry, or to stop an abusive or long-winded person. Questions which fill in gaps of information are left till the Exchange time. This change allows CDS mediators to model paying attention and to establish more easily the appearance of impartiality.

The Exchange

Mrs. Fabio erupts when Uninterrupted Time is over, spontaneously jumping into the volatile Exchange period. She is angry. "Why don't you talk? How can we deal with a kid who sulks and hides and doesn't even take care of her own safety? How can you be a mother when you aren't anything but a child yourself?" No answer. "If you think I'm going to go through that whole thing again, forget it. I'll throw you out first."

Kay steers the discussion away from Mrs. Fabio's threats, then prods Terry a bit more. What really bothers her? "Well, she's always looking at ads for apartments and leaving bride magazines around. Then she tells me not to marry Brian because he is a jerk and doesn't treat me right." She shoots a defiant glance at her parents. The mediators sit back. Terry has opened up. For the next half hour the discussion gets hotter and hotter. Accusations and threats are tossed back with denials and counter charges. "My daughter a slut! I won't have it." "Why shouldn't I cut school. Do you want everyone to know?"

Mrs. Fabio cries briefly, then starts shouting again. She brings up the apartment and getting married for the fourth time.

"Give up will you, Mom?" Terry lapses into silence and won't say anything more. The Exchange is winding down; no one has anything new to say.

Usually at this point, mediators and disputants begin to think that nothing will ever work out! To help the Fabios move into a problem-solving discussion, the mediators ask to meet separately with the parties. Kay takes Terry aside to see if she has any ideas about what she would like to do. "I don't want to marry Brian, but I've got to talk to him and find out what he is going to do. But my folks won't let me near him. I wish they'd just leave me alone."

Meanwhile James is confronting Mrs. Fabio's wishful thinking. "I don't hear Terry saying that she is considering marriage. I think we need to ask Terry frankly if that is an option." He then presses the parents to talk for a few minutes about other possibilities acceptable to them.

* * *

Facilitating the Exchange has been likened to a rodeo rider outlasting a bucking horse. During this time, disputants respond to issues, accusations, and questions. Both the mediators and the parties have a chance to get the information they need. The most noticeable characteristic of this phase is the release of strong feelings. Polite masquerades drop away. Names fly. There are tears and pointing fingers. For some people this is merely performing a well-rehearsed fight for a new audience. Others, less used to showing emotion in public, surprise themselves with their own vehemence. Couples often tell each other to calm down, not to get excited, to remember their high blood pressure. Most often they are embarrassed at their own frankness. They apologize for crying or trembling. When the mediators reassure them that this is part of what happens during mediation, they seem relieved; the mediators' easy acceptance of emotional outbursts often results in a turning from outrage to discussion.

Though many mediators believe that this venting of feelings is critical to effective resolution of a conflict, CDS is strict about the difference between allowing a limited amount of such behavior and encouraging it. The *Handbook* states: "Many feelings will come up: jealousy, resentment, hatred, fear, grief, outrage. Do not press people to talk about these emotions. Although airing feelings helps the mediation process, the mediators are present to guide people towards specific agreements about changing behavior, not to provide catharsis or therapy."

CDS mediators, when asked how much they restricted or favored venting emotions, said that they encouraged it within "somewhat tolerable limits" as long as the session kept moving. Abusive anger or "poor-me" victim feelings were examples of emotions mediators reported cutting off. Because neighbor and family mediations are significantly different in degree and range of emotion, mediators reported keeping tighter rein on permissible topics and expression during family mediations. "Otherwise, all the garbage of the past fifteen years is dragged out." Everyone agreed that drawing the line was difficult, especially in cases where they could not predict the direction the discussion would take.

Building the Agreement

Back together again, the mediators ask for a statement from the parents. Silence. "Look, Terry," says Mr. Fabio finally, grinding out his cigarette, "We really don't want you to get married." His wife nods. "I think we all agree on that." After reaching that understanding, the three relax somewhat, and the mediators no longer need to help Terry speak out.

During this Building the Agreement phase, discussion turns to practical considerations: Should Terry have the child? Where is the money to come from? Should she talk to the baby's father about this? How can she finish high school? With the baby due in 6 months, they feel more urgent about settling the future than do disputants who are involved in drawn-out quarrels with no deadlines. The longest part of the mediation, this phase is calmer. Emotions have cooled, and now the Fabios each have to decide what they personally are willing to contribute towards a satisfactory solution. There is some reluctance and yet a sense of excitement. After all those arguments, finally they are moving on this!

* * *

At last disputants are ready to hammer out specifics. Out of the barrage of complaints, a few large issues have floated to the top. The mediators check for accuracy and completeness of the issues: Is this what people want to work on? The mediators will work to draw out ideas and alternatives. Nothing is too detailed. Who makes the phone call to the obstetrician? What time will Terry be in? The mediators hold back from making suggestions, encouraging the participants to come up with proposals.

At the core of this stage is a model of consensual decision-making which tries to incorporate the needs and opinions of all participants. Although we will discuss this process in more detail later, it is important to understand that the mediators' job is not to find answers, but to help the disputants find their own.

Several times during discussion the mediators will stop and check: Does everyone feel able to live with each point of the contract? As one writer notes, the agreement needs to be an "acceptance rather than a retreat" (Wall, 1981: 166). The process of building the agreement through repeated suggestion and adjustment across the table is the surest way to reach a solution which will hold long after the mediation is over.

The Agreement

After forty-five minutes, James reads back the points of the agreement which have been tentatively accepted during the past hour. Each person is asked to suggest changes. Mr. Fabio wants to add something about a curfew and his willingness to pay medical and tutoring expenses. Terry wants it clear that they agreed she will make the final decision about abortion. Final dickering and changing takes nearly a half hour. The family agrees that meeting again in a few weeks would be useful.

Everyone, including James and Kay, signs the preliminary contract. It will be tacked up in the Fabios' kitchen until the next meeting. Everyone will give it a try.

1) Mr. Fabio agrees to talk Monday morning to the school district office about home tutoring. He is willing to pay for the tutor.

2) Terry agrees to call her mother's obstetrician for an appointment tomorrow afternoon. Cost will be discussed at the next two meetings. Everyone agrees that Terry will have the final decision about whether or not to have the baby.

3) All agree that no one will talk about marriage.

4) Terry agrees to take walks alone only before dark.

5) The family agrees to meet with Brian and his family next week. The mediators will call Brian and also arrange the time and place for this meeting.

6) The family agrees to meet with the mediators again on May 14, 7:00, same place.

* * *

The ideal agreement marks the conclusion of a dispute and serves as the blueprint for what will replace it. Even in situations like the Fabios' where the tension is likely to build again, that piece of paper serves as a cease fire. One mother told us that three years after their mediation, she and her sons still "rattle the contract" when the fighting starts.

Much as mediators talk about process, relationships, and emotions, the visible measure and culmination of a "successful" mediation is the agreement. That contract defines what each party can expect from the others and what they themselves promise to do. In other words, the agreement draws from the ideal worlds pictured by each disputant those pieces which are realizable. Mediation is the art of the possible; the agreement is a practical, often blunt, expression of those hopes for and limits on the future.

Good agreements are usually a surprise to disputants. "I never thought she'd agree to anything." If court charges have been dropped, there is relief at circumventing potential expense and public embarrassment. For most people that piece of paper means simply that the other party is finally off their backs.

Agreements are less likely to surprise mediators, who find the same terms worked out mediation after mediation. Most CDS agreements typically lay out patterns for future communication: "The W's and the L's agree to speak politely to each other." "N will call Mrs. J after she gets home from work if there are any problems."

"The parents agree to let the children try to work things out themselves first." "H agrees to phone Mr. E before she calls the police." Specific problems of driveways, dogs, and stereo noise also have predictable outcomes. The common drive is left open, the dogs come inside when they start barking, the stereo or the doghouse is moved to the far side away from the neighbors. Quiet hours are set. If a case is pending, usually the complainant agrees to drop charges.

Here are examples of actual agreements from CDS mediations:

This neighbor quarrel had lasted over a decade but produced a short, typical contract:

1) Both families agree not to speak to the other or harass them.

2) Bart and Joe agree to talk if any problems come up.
[Bart and Joe were the two fathers, and the least involved in the dispute.]

The mediators in this case pointed out that "not speaking to each other" was going to be difficult. What if there was an emergency? Or if they met on the sidewalk? The parties were not swayed in their determination, however, so it was written as they requested.

Here is one between two teenage boys, one who wanted to be friends, the other who didn't:

1) P and E agree to stop fighting and agree to treat each other courteously.

2) They may occasionally include each other in group or other activities.

3) P and E agree to tell their friends by next Tuesday that they have stopped fighting and to forget about it.

4) P and E agree to ignore rumors about each other from other people.

Their mothers add:

5) J and C agree to arrange counseling for the boys.

A few agreements go beyond the ordinary. A friendship may be mended. In one neighbor situation, for instance, the two couples agreed to have a beer together one or two Saturdays a month. Other times the parties stumble on a truly new and neat solution. An unusual parent and child dispute about the 11-year-old son leaving the TV on all night because he always fell asleep watching late-night movies was resolved not with a set bedtime but this way:

1) T agrees to check out prices for a TV timer tomorrow, June

18. The timer will be set for 3 o'clock. U and T will share the cost.

2) T will take the phone off the hook and turn out the lights before he goes to his bedroom.

3) T agrees to be in at 10 on Fridays and Saturdays. U agrees to let T's friends stay till 11 on Fridays and Saturdays.

Writing it down

Putting down the agreement on paper has two benefits. First, a week after the mediation disputants may have sharply differing memories of what they each agreed to. The contract is uncomfortably formal for those who prefer to depend more on trust and friendliness. However, the written promises prevent misunderstandings. The contract stands as one safeguard against fresh explosions.

Second, the mediator has an excuse to insist that disputants review the nuts and bolts of each issue and commit themselves out loud. "I know you said you'd buy a lock. Can you give us a date?" Continually returning to the practical matters, the mediators pull attention away from arguing about unmediatable issues and remind people that this contract is real. They will have to live with those terms day in and day out.

We venture no answers on the warmly debated question of whether written agreements will hold up in court. The lawyers who have given us their opinions disagree. Therefore, we tell disputants who ask that we cannot predict how a judge will rule but that chances are the agreement will at least be taken into consideration. Other mediators avoid the question entirely by stating, "It's as binding as you make it."

If disputants are to maintain an agreement without recourse to the courts, the content must stand on its own. "The agreement should state clearly WHO is agreeing to WHAT, WHERE, WHEN, and HOW" (Beer, et al., 1982). The FSP *Mediator's Handbook* lists seven essential instructions to mediators writing up a contract:

Use clear, simple language
Be specific, set times
Be balanced
Be positive
Provide for the future
Dispose of charges or other formal proceedings
Review, all those present sign

Several of these points underline the non-legal nature of CDS mediations. The ordinary wording means that the recorded decisions are clear to any reader who attended the mediation. It probably strengthens the sense that the contract belongs to the people who are making the agreement. The notion of balance goes beyond the concept of restitution; many ingredients can be part of the measure of give and take.

Providing for the future means establishing some method for handling troubles next time. This most often results in agreements about who will call or come over. A go-between may be named. Some declare that they will "just ignore" future incidents. Others consider all problems solved, as with this man, who when asked how the six-year-old neighbor could retrieve balls which flew over his fence, insisted, "There will be no balls coming over the fence. She has agreed to control her kids."

Researcher Deborah Baskin (1984) observed that CDS mediators regarded this establishment of communication as their highest priority, on some occasions emphasizing this over the immediate concern of the parties for recovery of damages or other concrete changes. In this session, the mediator refused to accept the man's unrealistic picture of the future. She tried an end run: "If the ball goes over, do you want the boy to get it or his mother?" "No, not the boy!" he said emphatically. In a round-about way, agreement had been reached.

What does a written contract symbolize? Baskin (1984) speaks of three levels of agreement: familial, contractual, and adversarial. Adversarial conflict in U.S. society generally leads to sides, to battles, to winners. The parties often seek protection for themselves and punishment for the other side. Often an outsider is expected to referee the dispute and to decide the outcome. The conflict becomes a contest; the parties are not expected to be friendly. Contracts from some of the more bitter mediations reflect this hostility; every detail is nailed down. Note how precisely this successful agreement was worked out:

1) The A's and the M's agree not to block the driveway (own cars or friends' cars) for more than 5 minutes at a time.

2) The A's and the M's agree not to speak to each other directly or make faces, gestures, or touch each other for the duration of the A's residency and will communicate as described under 3.

3) If any party has a complaint they will write a note and leave it in the mailbox. Follow-up will be handled by Mr. A and Mrs. M.

Nothing is left hanging. Follow-up showed that the agreement held.

A written contract implies some formal distance between the parties also, but unlike an adversarial ruling, it is perceived as more reasoned and more balanced. It carries less emotional sting. A typical CDS agreement falls into this category. The parties have made a contract, with the weaker parties able to influence the terms. A party might claim he or she got the better deal, but will find it harder to claim victory.

The familial agreement is one where there is a family or friend relationship beyond the dispute. No matter if the issues at stake cause heated and prolonged argument, when a resolution is hammered out the parties expect the others to carry out their promises or else take up the fight again. Writing down the terms (unless nonchalantly jotting on a napkin during the dinner discussion) and especially *signing* that agreement signals a distance which most friends and family members are uncomfortable with. This concern surfaces from time to time in mediation, as with a woman in a common driveway dispute several years ago. They had been neighbors for 16 years, she said, and this was the first conflict. The mediator wrote: "We were able to come to an agreement, but when we were ready to put it down in a contract, M balked. She felt that it was unnecessary and inappropriate because of their long relationship. She would not be dissuaded, and eventually the parties left with a verbal understanding," but without a written statement. CDS has several such cases each year.

CDS-style mediation tries to move parties from the adversarial stance to a contractual one. The contract here is a sign of diminished hostility and of mutual responsibility. When parties attempt to go a step further, when the importance of a friendship or family relationship is re-established during the session, CDS's policy is to persuade the parties, if possible, to move back to the more formal contractual level of dispute resolution. Feelings for each other are unreliable barometers. Two years after the mediation between neighbors which ended in the "understanding," the woman called with the same complaints and expressed regrets that they had no written contract to refer back to. The next day or the next month often brings renewed fighting if there is no common reference to what was decided between elated participants during the emotional high at the end of a mediation session.

What does a good agreement do?

Even the best mediation sessions deal mostly with the surface of stormy waters. Written agreements help people change specific behavior. Hans agrees to take the garbage out every Wednesday morning. Hans does not agree to do it with a smile. If roommate Ron gets hot under the collar looking at overflowing wastebaskets, the friction between him and Hans will probably die down as long as Hans takes the trash out (even if he grumbles), and as long as Hans in turn sees that Ron is going to follow through on *his* promise to have Carole spend the night only twice a week. They have drawn face-saving truce lines. By eliminating the daily re-negotiation about who will take out the garbage and when Carole should visit, they avoid endless arguments over those faults and responsibilities (who should have cleaned the kitchen, who did last time, who missed his rent payment ...) which crop up like persistent weeds.

Meanwhile, the strong currents of values and attitudes flow on beneath the calmer surface. Mediation cannot determine if Ron has the right to have his girlfriend there whenever he wishes. Nor can mediation fix Ron's need to have everything in the house exactly in its place. And the new contract will not guarantee that the two men will like each other better.

Changes come slowly. If the wounds are not scraped open with daily irritations, mediators can hope that deeper healing will follow. When people take responsibility for changing their actions, relationships and personalities may change. The mediators will never know. Nor can they predict what will come of a discussion or an agreement. The best they can do is to help people stop rubbing salt in the wounds for a while.

Dispute settlement programs speak of dealing with "underlying causes." Usually they mean the interactions leading to the "last straw" event which has brought the dispute to public attention. In one such case, neighbors were making suggestions about problems with the children on the block, but the other woman did not seem interested in any of their proposals. Then she got up the nerve to say that she was sure her neighbors were all talking about her when they sat out on their front steps on warm evenings. The neighbors were taken aback and said it wasn't true. When this was aired and cleared up, the other problems which had brought her to file charges became insignificant; agreement was quickly reached. In this sense, mediation can pay attention to inner needs and make room for psychological gestures which may satisfy those feelings. An apology, an explanation, a touch of the hand—small actions which cannot fit into a formal agreement may ease the sense of injury, releasing disputants to settle more negotiable disagreements.

Nevertheless, most underlying psychological causes or social circumstances cannot be directly addressed in mediation. Vince is

not going to stop feeling lonely. The family on welfare is not going
to regain social standing. A tenement is not going to become a model
apartment building. Racist attitudes are not going to vanish. It is not
fair to the disputants to hold out promises of great changes in their
lives. Nor is it fair for mediators to blame themselves when the
disputants take most of their problems home again. The camel's
back is never broken by one straw but by three thousand and ninety.
In two hours the mediators can only take off some of the burden.
They cannot examine each straw.

Mediation is not counseling. It is not judgment. It is not justice.
The following chapters look at the boundaries of community dispute
settlement in more detail. For now, suffice it to remind ourselves
that mediation is a first aid procedure, not surgery. But sometimes
it serves as a bandage which keeps a situation clean enough to heal
itself without further need of expensive and painful remedies.

The Closing

It has been an intense two hours. The mediators thank
everyone for their time and review the progress the family has
made. Terry's mother slips a ten dollar bill into the donation
envelope. "I feel better after this," she says. They shake hands
and leave quickly.

The mediators put away the chairs and talk over what
happened. "They needed to stop twirling around in what they
wished would happen, and face the reality that Terry *is*
pregnant," says Kay.

"I thought the key was when the marriage issue was dealt
with directly. Terry wasn't going to say anything to them as
long as she suspected that not-so-hidden agenda," says James.

They turn their attention to evaluating their mediating.
James thinks he might have been too harsh with Mrs. Fabio
but Kay disagrees. "I was glad you stepped in there. She would
have had the whole discussion in shambles if she'd gone on
much longer."

"I think they got the best they could've hoped for tonight."
Kay opens her car door. "At least they have started talking
directly to each other."

In a few days, Mr. Fabio calls to cancel the second session.
They've met with Brian on their own. Everything is going fine,

he says. A month later, CDS is unable to reach the Fabios for follow-up. The mediators never hear how things worked out.

* * *

What Really Happens?

The stages of mediation process we have walked through were designed for resolving most interpersonal situations. (Although some types of intervention require further technical expertise in such areas as finance or law.) Inexperienced and emotional bargainers are moved step by step away from preoccupation with the past to planning for the future.

One picture of conflict, perhaps the first one that comes to our minds, is that of a struggle to meet opposing needs and goals. If there is no easy way to equally or equitably remedy the situation, then parties must accept compromise. The CDS mediation shies away from this notion of finite answers and resolutions through bargaining, preferring to structure the discussion more broadly as a problem-solving session. This approach assumes that mutually satisfactory solutions are possible.

CDS's view of conflict also incorporates the emotional dimension. The CDS mediation framework charts the disputants' psychological progression from a past-centered approach to a future-centered one. People begin with sharp goading or withdrawn politeness, and move to venting, to revising their picture of the dispute, to problem-solving, and finally to deciding. This sequence helps mediators understand what is happening and what intervention may work. "I have an awareness of what stage they are in even though they don't," says one mediator who enjoys watching group process. "I've learned that they have to go through the anger, through each stage, even though the way to solve the whole problem seems so obvious to me from the beginning," says another.

These stages are only one way to divide the mediation session into understandable sequence. The flow of events at the table can also be interpreted by looking at other dynamics. Such charts of the process describe how people pass through a series of intense emotions, how they alter their picture of reality, or how they move from alienation to a measure of trust. Some questions are better answered by these other maps of the mediation session. How do people move from one stage to the next? Where do mediations get stuck? What happens emotionally to the disputants? In particular, why does their attitude towards each other suddenly change?

Mediation as trust-building

At the CDS office, the staff person picks up the phone and for the third time that morning hears a well-worn line. "It's no use talking to him about fixing his fence. You don't understand. This man is sick." Disputants usually have as much trust as do enemy soldiers peering at each other through barbed wire. Someone offering to help make peace is greeted at best with skeptical relief and at worst with derisive hostility.

That most such disputants reach an agreement in two hours is remarkable, especially when you remember that the agreement relies entirely on the parties themselves for enforcement. This means that signing any contract is a risk; the disputants must have some measure of confidence that the other side will uphold its word. Yet about 75% of CDS mediations produce agreements (the percentage in programs with higher caseloads and mandatory mediation is even higher).

If a mediation is to work, the disputants must be willing to give it a try. This means coming to trust the mediators. Are they taking sides? Do they wince when someone swears loudly? Challenges usually come during the Uninterrupted Time. Interrupters want to see if they can gain control of the meeting. Quieter people wait to see if the mediator will fall into the other side's trap.

The disputants will say, "It's nice of you to come tonight, honey, but there is no chance on God's earth of you getting her to agree to anything," or, "We've been round and round through all this before." A few get up and threaten to leave. It is as if they want the mediators to say, "Don't give up, it's worth hanging in there."

At first the disputants notice that the mediators are actually listening to their story. These stories are well rehearsed. Friends, agencies, or the courts may have listened impatiently to their complaints. Now someone is paying attention. If the disputants get the sense that they will be respected and protected, the mediators have passed the test. When the disputants are then able to reach even a small point of understanding among themselves, those first tendrils of trust will probably take hold.

The floodgates open. With this commitment to the mediators and the mediation process, the disputants can then start trusting each other to change. They are ready to let the mediator help them strip away enough protective layers so that all can see the situation better. Their thoughts can turn to problem-solving instead of self-defense.

The Turning Point

This change of direction is a moving and mysterious moment. FSP calls it the Turning Point—that juncture when the tide changes: trust, which has been at low ebb, comes slowly creeping towards shore again. The moment cannot be planned or forced, but in session after session mediators report that in only a minute or two the whole mediation turns around. One mediator describes it this way:

> In every mediation I still think, "Oh this will never work," until half way through, the session reaches a peak. Emotions have been spent and people feel hopeless. At this point, a silence falls, time for absorbing and going beyond what has been said. I always hope the other mediator won't say anything. In our society we're not supposed to be silent; we have to fill the gap with music or talking. There is quiet, then suddenly it turns around. This seems to be a pattern.

The Turning Point often comes when one person takes a step towards vulnerability. This can mean revealing information that has been held back. It can happen when someone acknowledges the other party's point of view. Sometimes this comes as an apology. "I didn't know you thought I excluded you..., that your husband has been ill...." Sometimes the turning point comes when a note of confidence is expressed: "Hey, we can handle this."

While some disputants make such conciliatory remarks during Uninterrupted Time, until the disagreement is on the table the other party is usually disbelieving. (If you think I'm such a nice guy, how come you call the police on us?) When someone can be honestly angry and still say, "Look, I don't want you to have to worry about this either," then the listener is more likely to interpret the words as true feeling, not just as a sweet phrase to impress the mediators.

In one neighbor dispute, nasty words were flying:

> You yelled out at my sister, "Your mother wears Army boots." I heard you!

> Yeah? Who's the SOB who gave my mother the finger over at school last week? Nobody does that to my mother!

> LIAR! I did not.

Uninterrupted Time had to go for three rounds just to keep some order. Finally the mediator said, "Looks like nobody wants other people to call their mothers names." There were sudden nods from both the teens and the ten-year-olds. "What if you all just decided to cut it out?" They thought about it. The silence was like the pause before a pendulum changes direction. Then the oldest said, "Yeah, this is silly. You don't say anything about my mother, I won't say anything about yours. OK?"

By the end of the mediation, the boys were talking soccer, and the younger girls were playing together. Next door, their parents shouted at each other for another twenty minutes until another Turning Point, "What are we yelling about? Our kids know how to make up better than we do!" Somewhat sheepishly, the four adults came to an agreement.

When people leave without agreement, the Turning Point sometimes comes, but people are unable to commit themselves to a new path. The outburst of emotions and conflicting stories leads to preliminary discussion of solutions and then the moment of silence. But in these disputes, one or more of the participants cannot leap across the gap. They stand on the edge afraid to take the chance of trusting; they pause and turn back to their initial cemented positions. The solutions might be simple and obvious. Often the other party has been conciliatory, even kind. But if a person does not have that crucial belief in the other side's good intentions, the mediator and the other party are powerless.

One woman was an extreme example of this. The dispute was a typical barking dog problem. She was sure that the neighbors wanted her to get rid of her four beloved dogs. Three neighbors tried every tack they could think of—reassurance (the neighbors liked dogs, they only wanted the animals inside when they, the neighbors, were using their own yards), apology, listening, compromise. Nothing would convince her that their intentions were honest. For three hours she cried and shouted and accused. In the end, the neighbors gave up. There was no way they could prove their trustworthiness to a person who had learned to distrust so absolutely.

Trust is a vital ingredient of any successful mediation, and yet we have little idea of what trust looks like or how it can be nurtured. Where is the boundary between irrational distrust and wise caution? How can an outsider create an atmosphere where trust can grow? Dean Pruitt (1984) says that trust means believing that the other person is telling the truth and that the other side is ready to problem-solve in good faith. Tom Colosi of the American Arbitration Association (SPIDR regional conference, Philadelphia, 1982) suggests that the *predictability* of the other party's behavior is the key element, even when the behavior is predictably negative. One might add that this kind of trust is harder to establish when the remnant of the child's hopeful, magical belief that promises are promises ("But you *promised!*") is gone. Persuading people to take a chance that the other parties will uphold an agreement is difficult if the participants do not believe that the other people will behave with some rationality or, at the very least, with the logic of self-interest. What mediators do know is that a turtle cannot venture forward unless it sticks its head out to survey the world beyond its dark, protective shell.

Mediation as a jolt of reality

When discouraged disputants decide to gamble on this unknown process, they think that just maybe this person has the answer which will fix it. The mediator with the magic wand is tougher than disputants expect. As an agent of reality, mediators can see beyond the rationalizations and painful emotions which muddy the disputants' own perceptions of their situation. The parties, caught up in the world of their conflict, have edited their memories of what happened and wedged their positions between rows of sandbags.

The cold water shock of another view of reality may first hit when the CDS staff person setting up the session insists on examining that uncomfortable matter: consequences. The dominance of our court system and its emphasis on personal rights leads people to sue quickly, often without thinking about what the fallout of going to court may be. Yes, they may win. But will the neighbor really stop harassment after losing a court case?

Because CDS mediators have a strong stake in convincing people to mediate, they outline graphically (and at times one-sidedly) the benefits of looking at the real possibilities for the future instead of fighting about the unprovable and unchangeable past. Whether or not the parties are considering court action, the mediators try to lay out the personal consequences of an escalating conflict. What happens if this aggravation continues? Will your asthma get worse? Is there some other person you could work with? When people are part of an in-house dispute (within their own church for example), mediators may also ask about side effects, especially the impact their dispute is having on the whole group. Their projects may be suffering from the tensions. Is continuing disagreement worth the fallout? Although in truth the answer might be "yes," we have found that CDS mediators tend to outline the version of reality they are comfortable with; this is usually the viewpoint that leads to restoring peaceful relations rather than those which look towards establishing personal rights or upholding ideals.

During the session, the mediator is likely to confront both sides with pointed observations about their behavior or beliefs. During the first part of the mediation, each person is pushed to look at his or her own contribution to the problems. Before disputants can move on, disputants have to realize that the other side sees things differently—and not without reason.

If the Exchange begins to run in repetitive circles, the mediators use their outside view to push the discussion towards realistic solutions. "Her alcoholism may always be a problem—how can you cope?" Again, people are faced with consequences. "If she gets rid of her cats as you ask, how are your relations with her as a housemate affected?" When the parties are unyielding, the mediators can pull out what one CDS staff person describes as the most useful phrase in a mediator's entire bag of tricks: "Are you planning to move?" If the disputants say no, they intend to stay put (be it in their household, in their job, or in their neighborhood), the mediator does not have to point out the obvious. Going home with no agreement means going home with the problem again.

In a more positive sense, the mediators also remember the reality that every person at the table is, with rare exception, capable of changing his or her behavior. Mediators have an optimism which is usually more realistic than the disputants' gloomy outlook. Sooner or later people *do* find ways out of a difficult conflict. The mediator who holds that confidence can bring around the most intractable of disputants. Tough or idealistic, though, the confidence must be genuine; disputants will sense the faintest traces of uncertainty.

The "jolt of reality" view of mediation assumes that people will tend to make better decisions if their view of the situation broadens. Being "realistic" also means defining one's own self-interest. What is important? What do you want to happen and how can we make it happen? Caving into the other party's demands is no more realistic than laying out a series of non-negotiable solutions. CDS operates on the assumption that workable answers—real answers—come from looking at all the pieces that must fit into the puzzle—yours and theirs.

While the mediators try to put each of these pieces out on the table, in two hours they cannot assume they have reached an accurate understanding of the wider situation or the parties' views. The disputants' final decision may seem, therefore, to ignore facts and potential looming disasters. The pieces of their reality will have different weights. True, calling the police the next time is guaranteed to infuriate Ann's son-in-law. But she may prefer that to risking physical confrontation when she asks him to leave. The role of bringing the parties to face a truer picture is one of the most important functions of a mediator, even when the disputants see that picture in an unexpected light.

Redirecting energies and regaining power

The about-face in disputants' behavior can be astonishing. In one CDS mediation, two neighbor couples claimed they had not spoken for 18 years, and yet they were able to reach amicable settlement in one session. Several times a year, CDS witnesses such reconciliations between neighbors with long histories of antagonism. A look at what happens to energy and power in a mediation may help to explain such quick transformations.

People embroiled in disputes tie up tremendous energy in maintaining their conflict. Just staying on alert is tiring. Waking moments are occupied with thoughts of getting even, with complaining to all who will listen, with feelings of anger, guilt, sadness, jealousy—even hate. Many people also suffer physical pain from the stress. Disputants say they don't sleep well. They swallow tranquilizers and painkillers. The intensity of energy spent on the dispute has the same effect as holding a magnifying lens over a pile of dry leaves. Under the focused sunlight they begin to smolder, then burst into flame.

This intensity of focus distorts people's sense of perspective. Every word, every silence is interpreted as threatening. Every gesture is obscene, every action a personal affront. People wait each day for new incidents. In one CDS mediation, a man said he had not gone to the beach for four summers because the neighbor woman might throw garbage over his fence if he didn't keep watch.

As energy is sucked into the whirlpool of a dispute, those involved lose their sense of control. They are emotionally and intellectually cornered. There is little energy left for thinking about a mutually satisfactory way out.

The mediation session is designed to redirect people's energy away from fueling the fires of grievance and towards taking charge of the situation. Whether the Exchange is a time of raw emotion or of careful fencing, to be successful, the discussion must break out of the cycle of defense and offense and turn that fierce self-interest towards developing satisfactory solutions. If ordinary back and forth discussion does not break through, mediators can accomplish this by allowing the dog to chase its own tail, so to speak, in circular arguments until the disputants wear out and look for a more productive direction.

The persistent stretching of the disputants' viewpoint is tiring for everyone. Whether or not the parties show emotion, their feelings are also drawing on their reserves. People have been worn down with the stress of facing an onrush of emotions and new facts in a strange environment. This physical and mental tiredness may also contribute towards the disputants' willingness to stop fighting and to start thinking. The outflowing emotional energies have left a vacuum; defenses are lower.

The Turning Point is the moment when power returns. The disputants have reached the top of a long hill. One small movement like an apology or a concession holds out the possibility of bursting loose from this problem which binds them. For a moment they stop at the crest, and then they begin talking, gathering momentum quickly.

Other times the sense is more one of a wild mountain river. Sometimes ideas come pouring out, and concessions are made almost eagerly. The waters dammed up in perpetuating the conflict now spurt through the crack of hopefulness. Maybe a solution is possible! This euphoria is the beginning of learning to deal more confidently and constructively with the next conflict. The giddy feeling may give the disputants impetus to stick to that agreement when the cold reality of promises made hits them the next day.

Not all disputes produce such a Niagara Falls release of problem-solving energy, but it is interesting that disputes which have a long history seem more likely to experience this great rush of change which sweeps away many of the bad feelings.

We have looked at what happens in a mediation from the different perspectives of mediation format, building trust, future behavior, the voice of wider reality, and the redirection of disputants' power and energy. Mediators trained in other disciplines will find still other dimensions useful to explore: religious, psychological, legal, anthropological, social. Looking at each dispute through a variety of filters keeps the mediators' approach flexible. What do these disputants need to get themselves moving towards agreement? Whatever interpretations of the mediation process are most theoretically accurate or most helpful to the practicing mediator, more important than theory and most amazing is the simple fact we began with: usually it works!

Two: The Disputant

Who Comes to CDS?

"Prime mediation neighborhood." Driving through Upland's back streets to the Baptist church where mediations are held, one of the mediators points to cramped houses and common driveways with old trees spreading across boundary lines. "I'll bet anything those folks have a dispute going. It has all the signs." The yard of the ramshackle corner house is filled with tools and lumber. Next door, behind a new fence, the lawn and bushes are clipped, not a weed in sight.

Though the CDS program is open to all 555,000 Delaware County residents, most disputants live in these crowded, poorer neighborhoods which stretch along the city boundary and cluster around the factories which line the Delaware River. People who live in these neighborhoods where houses stand close together have few places to retreat from conflict. It is hard to avoid noise or parking problems. Areas where newcomers are changing the character of the neighborhood are also prime hatching grounds for disputes. Residents of wealthier communities can insulate themselves from this kind of friction.

Of the people using CDS, many are blue-collar and clerical workers, housewives, nurses, and people who own small businesses. Managers, teachers, and other white collar professionals come less frequently but are also represented. By our rough survey figures, the average income as reported by 27 families was about $26,600. (1980 Delaware County median family income was $23,105.) This was higher than we expected but still stands about $12,400 less than mediators' average family income of about $39,000. The survey respondents showed much higher income than the average for the townships most frequently served by CDS. (However, this figure is skewed in favor of those people more likely to return surveys and to report their income.)

Education levels likewise fall between the mediators and the poor: Whereas 80% of CDS mediators have completed a bachelor's degree, of our 42 responding disputants, 7 have less than 12 years of education, 18 have a high school diploma, 9 have some technical or college education beyond secondary school, 6 hold a bachelor's degree and 2 have earned master's degrees. These figures for income and education, while sketchy, support our outward observations and Baskin's research (correspondence with Wahrhaftig, 1980) which showed that CDS was not primarily a program for the poor and unemployed but one servicing lower income middle-class households.

Caught in conflict

Most disputants who reach CDS's doors are not people in unusual circumstances. Their problems are ones that most people have at one time or another: dogs, noise, rude children, property damage, name-calling. Nor are most of these people unusually disagreeable or stubborn. They are no more unfriendly or unreasonable than anyone else who feels entrapped in a conflict. Like the rest of us, they cope with friction and change—sometimes well, sometimes poorly.

When faced with a nasty conflict, people first try familiar ways to change it, whether that be punching someone, talking frankly, complaining, or leaving. Most choose to ignore growing tensions. "I just told my kids not to talk to them, to walk home on the other side of the street," a parent said recently, echoing the words of many who had sat before at the mediation table. Neighbors say with frustration, "I don't even say hello anymore." Often avoidance is an excellent tactic. The budding conflict fades away. Despite the presently popular encouragement to be open about feelings, to be honest, to state your needs, ignoring someone's rude or annoying behavior is often a sensible and workable answer.

Unfortunately, and unpredictably, some conflicts seem to thrive on lack of confrontation. Suddenly, something assumed to be an insignificant or temporary irritant turns out to be, in the mind of the other side, a major offense. Under attack, people begin to react with a series of socialized behaviors of defense and counterattack. A frosty stare is answered with a finger. The door slams. Stories spread. Someone hires a lawyer. Views polarize. Both sides plan their day around retaliation and the fear of it.

Direct confrontation now seems like a major, unpleasant task. Unwillingness or inability to break this spiral is often the prelude to mediation. The longer confrontation is put off... well, it may yet go away, but at what price waiting? Intervention from the outside becomes more necessary as the lines of battle become harder to cross.

Disputants, especially those who have lodged no complaint, are often caught unawares by this creeping chain of events. "I had no idea...," many begin their Uninterrupted Time. One woman said to the neighbor after they signed an agreement, "I thought you were a crazy man. All of a sudden there you were at my door saying you would sue me if I didn't move my car. It wasn't blocking yours and I didn't know *what* you were talking about."

Although disputants often see their conflict as one of irresolvable differences, usually those opposing stances are secondary to the emotional cloud which surrounds those positions. Anger and fear can undermine sincere attempts to resolve the problems. This is clearly illustrated during mediation; the issues in most disputes are quickly worked out when feelings begin to subside.

Few of us have formally learned effective ways to resolve conflict. Unskillful confrontations (poor timing, threats, or blaming, for example) add fuel to the fire. "I tried talking to them, but it didn't work. They wouldn't listen," said the man in the parking dispute above. From his perspective, he *had* tried to solve things in a neighborly way. He didn't realize that his direct approach was interpreted by his neighbors as hostility. In another mediation, one young woman did not understand how her explosions set off fresh rounds of troubles. She said she had every intention of following her half of the agreement to speak courteously: "We talk to them reasonably *if* they are reasonable. We treat our neighbors politely. But if they say something I don't like, I'll curse them out. I don't have to listen to those lies."

Why are people reluctant to mediate?

Most people are referred to CDS when, no longer able to handle the situation alone, they bring their troubles to public attention.

We are all disputants at one time or another, and yet few of us think of using third parties to help us when we reach an impasse. The last time you were part of an interpersonal conflict did someone act as mediator? Did the idea even occur to you? Probably not. The disputant who actually agrees to a mediation is unusual. No one knows how many people dismiss the idea before ever contacting

CDS. For the moment, we will look just at the decisions made by disputants who call the program.

Of those who telephone, many are ambivalent. Everyone seems to weigh the possibility carefully before saying yes. The second party (the one contacted at the request of the caller) is even more likely to reject the proposed meeting. In fact, in 53% of cases where both parties are contacted, one side refuses to attend. Another 28% are weeded out even earlier. For the most part, this means either that the case is judged inappropriate for mediation by CDS or that the caller decides not to proceed with mediation. CDS staff spends many hours convincing people to try it out. In the end, about 19% of referrals reach the table.

While there are significant social and political pressures which explain this low percentage, we will focus for the moment on the individual disputants. Why do they choose to come or to go elsewhere?

The immediate reasons people reject mediation soon become a familiar refrain to anyone answering the CDS phones:

Losing. The fear of being "done in" underlies many objections; disputants are afraid someone will force them to compromise or worse, give in. They may worry about losing self-control or wonder if the mediators will buy the lies of the other party.

Not wanting to meet. "We don't want to talk to those people." This reaction can stem from physical fear of sitting in the same room. People who have cultivated a cool, tough approach to the other party are afraid they will cry or become too angry. Other times feelings of disgust, even hatred, are too strong.

Feeling resigned. The voice of hopelessness, even in those who agree to come, is usually close to the surface. "They'll never mediate. Besides, it wouldn't do any good, anyway."

Preferring another way. Some people would rather try other options. Maybe the dispute is considered too important to forgo a court battle, or maybe they want an authority to settle the matter once and for all. Others prefer to let problems ride rather than rock the boat, particularly if the relationship to the other party is important.

Mediation is rejected by some who are uneasy using an unknown process. In court, disputants know, or at least think they know, what to expect. The rules are public. They have images about what happens in a courtroom. The outcome may be a gamble, but the number of possible results is limited. Litigants submit their problem and see what answer the system gives back. CDS disputants do not know how to prepare or what to watch out for—even when they are told ahead of time. For a person experiencing crisis, this unfamiliarity is too risky.

Wanting to win. These callers regard their conflict as a fight to be won, not as a problem to be solved. Sometimes they want to intimidate or punish the other party until they "behave." While these people also fall in the previous category of preferring another way, there is a drive for vengeance rather than a considered appraisal of options for resolution.

It's their problem. Disputants can be adamant that they have no personal responsibility in the situation. Their arguments take many forms: the other guy should pay; there's no problem; it's their fault, let them fix it; there's nothing to discuss. All of them translate into a contrived innocence which allows people to mentally wash their hands of the affair.

Because many parties decline to mediate, when a phone call comes in, persuasion is the program's immediate concern. When we ask mediation trainees, "What would be your greatest hesitation about requesting a third party for yourself?" they find that their "obvious" reason is usually not the one which most concerns the person sitting next to them. The person who sits at the CDS phone has the job of sorting out people's primary objections and then trying to allay those concerns enough that the person is willing to take a chance.

When do people choose mediation?

In the end, it is usually the growing feeling of "I can't live like this anymore" which brings a person to CDS. The idea of mediation seems more attractive precisely when it connects with the frustrated desire to get out of the mess. They just want things to stop.

People agree to come to the table for three main reasons:

1) They have few options left.

2) They want a chance to settle matters with the other party (or at least the opportunity to tell them off!).

3) They feel forced to come.

Limited options. Usually those who reach mediation have tried several tactics before they phone CDS. The police, the mayor, the principal, the district court—anyone who might have an answer has heard their complaints. When officials cannot help, disputants become put off and discouraged, particularly those who cannot afford lawyers or counselors, who cannot move away or transfer jobs. Many people spend hundreds of dollars even when they don't go to court. They put up fences and repair vandalism. Selling the house is not an uncommon solution. The easiest and hardest choice is to go next door and talk the matter out.

Just looking at the topic of a neighbor dispute, it is hard to predict which cases will come to mediation and which will be handled another way. The content of the dispute seems to be of minor relevance. One enraged woman appeared before the court after rejecting the judge's recommendation of mediation. When he refused to impose a fine on her neighbors, she appealed her dog dispute to the county court, even though her mild-mannered neighbors willingly and publicly agreed to all her demands and to every suggestion of the judge. Other people have brought serious problems such as runaway teenagers or physical assaults to mediation and have arrived at a resolution in one evening. Each person appears to have different levels of tolerance and stubbornness, as well as different ideas of what he or she wants to happen. Most people who call CDS indicate they have reached their limits of endurance: "I can't live like this any more," said one woman, who spoke for many. The difference is where, within social constraints, each individual draws that line.

Wanting to come. There are also people who actively decide to try out this new and unknown process before they have to do something more drastic. These disputants have reached some inner decision that they want to resolve the situation *and* feel good about themselves. They are the ones who say, "I wish we'd known about this earlier." "We just want to talk about it like adults." This can be a desire to act in a friendly way, to respond with reasonableness and maturity. They want to get along, to stop the nastiness. Often they are embarrassed to find themselves acting mean or getting upset at things they think shouldn't bother them so much. Disputants who are eager to try mediation often say they aren't the kind of people who call the police on neighbors. Some do not believe in taking neighbors to court.

Every once in a while, individuals who agree to mediate will say that because of their religious beliefs, they want to avoid responding to another party vindictively. One woman referred by the court secretary, for instance, cried with relief over the phone. She said she was a Christian and she had held off filing charges for months until the police and her husband told her she "had to." Since then she had felt so bad she couldn't sleep. Mediation was exactly what she wanted: a place to talk to this neighbor without worrying about physical attack.

Coercion, however subtle or imagined, is a crucial factor in most people's decision to mediate. Mediators regularly face participants who insist "the judge made us come." Children and teenagers, in particular, usually feel dragged into mediation sessions, despite the program's attempt to speak with each of them (not just parents) beforehand. CDS emphasizes voluntary participation as strongly as possible but cannot control the directives of the court who order complainants to try mediation. As we will discuss later, coercion is a major ethical issue for community mediation programs.

In CDS's experience, getting people to the table is often more difficult than mediating the dispute. Once they are in the room with the third party, the big decision has already been made, and they stand a good chance of reaching resolution. The challenge is convincing the majority who say "no" that mediation can short-circuit a lot of future trouble. To do that, mediation will have to be represented as a way to make talking to someone easier, since that is what most people think "good" families and neighbors should do in a dispute. As long as mediation programs are perceived as agencies or court-substitutes, we will continue to persuade mostly those few people who are predisposed to take disputes to outsiders and those who are desperately making one last attempt to get justice when all else has failed.

What do people fight about?

The shortest definition of a dispute is *trouble*. In our culture that means the parties conceive of themselves as on opposing sides, rather like players in a game. The other party's behavior or attitude is perceived as directed against oneself. People don't think of themselves as "disputants" (Cain and Kulcasar 1982); they are "having trouble with" someone. They may label the other party as sick, abnormal, or in need of control, but they do not categorize themselves. In other words, people in conflict generally conceive of a dispute as a state of affairs or a description of the *other* person, not as a statement about themselves.

The broader sense of dispute covers any believed violation of norms of living and working with others; CDS disputes can be reduced to the sentence "People ought to _____, and people shouldn't _____." The program loosely clumps under the word "dispute" those interpersonal problems which are limited to a series of incidents and a finite number of issues. We differentiate those which are conducive to mediation and those which are not but accept a large category of human conflicts under the dispute umbrella.

On a theoretical level, disputes mark the fault lines of society and are not viewed as primarily interpersonal events but as warning flags marking the points of strain in communities and societies. The tensions and concerns CDS is asked to mediate among neighbors in this county surface in session after session. In the Community chapter, we discuss what these disputes imply about our suburban culture, but for now we concentrate on the disputants and what they care about most.

Here are the five most common complaints CDS hears. (Note that many times one dispute involves more than one of these issues.)

Common Neighbor Complaints
(as recorded by CDS during intake and as stated in agreements)

	% of all cases where both parties were contacted
Harassment (including threats and namecalling)	35%
Property damage or theft	28%
Children under 13	29%
Fighting, scaring with knives or guns	18%
Noise	17%

In a study of early FSP mediations, Deborah Baskin (1984) also found that 57% of the mediations she observed involved "respect," an intangible issue which CDS workers may not bother to note in the files.

Property. Disputes reflect the lives people lead, the things which concern us the most. At the top of the list of tangibles in Delaware County is protection of property and the money it represents. Many things can set an unhappy neighbor off: untrimmed hedges, slashed tires, a blocked common driveway, or people cutting through the yard. At least three-fourths of complaints to CDS relate to property and its attendant issues of protection, independence, and privacy.

Independence. Home is one of the few places people can be autonomous and in control. Every month CDS hears a new variation on the theme, "I paid for it and I have the right to do whatever I want with it." If we paint our half of a twin house hot pink, if we choose to keep five dogs, if our friends come over for a rowdy picnic...and the neighbors don't like it—tough.

Privacy. "My home, my castle" is etched firmly in the minds of these homeowners who see their house as their greatest investment and their hard-earned refuge from the world. People want to live without the uninvited intrusion of neighbors. They believe they have a right to enjoy their home in peace.

Noise is, therefore, more than a distraction, it is an invasion of property and the privacy it supposedly guarantees. Trash and animal odors also drift across property lines. Cutting through yards is considered rude. A mediator may think the reactions are way out of proportion to the degree of actual disturbance. "I shouldn't have to wake up to her alarm at 5:00 a.m.!" one woman in a thin-walled duplex kept shouting at one session. The mediator felt sympathetic until she happened to ask the woman what time she had to get up. The answer was 5:10! It is that sense of being invaded, of one's rights being capriciously ignored, which infuriates.

Dogs. Nipping at the heels of many disputes is the neighbor's dog, a matter which, alas, deserves a chapter to itself. It makes noise but cannot be turned off, only muffled or muzzled. It threatens to bite children, according to wary non–dog lovers. Here is a mobile piece of beloved property which innocently invades the neighbor's territory. Each side is determined to protect its property from the other. "He threatened to kill my two dogs!" "Your dog does its business on *my* yard *every* morning."

Children. Unfortunately children are often seen in the same light: "I don't want anyone else disciplining my children." "Your kids make enough noise to deafen a rock band. I want them under control and away from my house." As for teenagers, "disrespect," noise, and hanging out—in fact just about everything teens do in public—come under fire from parents as well as neighbors. Somewhat to our surprise, when we tallied the statistics, children and teenagers were brought up more often than any other particular issue in CDS mediations. Younger children were a problem more often than their older siblings, presumably because they play outside in their own yards, therefore bothering neighbors more often than the teenagers who cluster in more public areas.

Status. Disputes over status and respect are also common. People complain of name-calling and insults. They feel snubbed when they are left out. Adults get angry when children don't speak politely. The property, noise, and privacy issues connect here, too. Trespassing is a sign of disrespect. Noise shows lack of consideration.

And since in this country privacy is a measure of social and economic standing, intrusions challenge the person's status.

Class. Sometimes respect is a cover-up for issues of class. The people next door are considered "trash" who are ruining the neighborhood. A van parked outside the family garage incenses many neighbors, especially when the business name and address is written on the side. They don't want the street to look too working class. One upward bound immigrant family actually told CDS that they would never mediate with the couple next door; she was only a secretary with no college degree, and they intended to harass her until she moved. On the other side, poorer disputants try to defend their own credentials: "We've lived here since we were married. If they don't like it they can move. This is a nice, respectable neighborhood, and we raised our kids to be respectful." One woman describes such a mediation session:

> *The children lied and the parents swore to it.... Some of the parents were motivated through spite to rectify the jealousies they themselves had for anyone living better than they do. I really had adults telling me that for the way I lived I was in the wrong neighborhood because these children are known as street kids—which means the parents close their eyes to the activities of their children.*

As suburban neighborhoods on the edge of Philadelphia change, different values reflected in different ways of living cause, or at least inflame, many CDS disputes. The most common points of disagreement are the expected: neat versus casual, quiet versus loud and lively, strict control versus loose discipline of children. These differences often split along generational as well as class lines.

What types of community disputes do not reach CDS?

Several kinds of family and neighbor conflict never reach CDS. These involve issues which society considers serious or which require long-term counseling or political action.

Interracial incidents. The program has not received the interracial or interethnic disputes FSP initially anticipated. This may indicate fewer interactions, fewer chances for friction, and fewer personal relationships at stake—and therefore less incentive to use mediation. Others point out that in racist incidents the neighborhood helps conceal the identity of the attackers, so there is no one to mediate with. Some believe the lack of interracial disputes is because CDS has not made extensive overtures to the black or Hispanic communities in the county. The Philadelphia Human Relations Commission reports the same phenomenon. Black disputes form a significant portion of their work, and they receive plenty of white disputes from all areas of the city. Yet in this large, multi-racial city, interracial and interethnic (cases where ethnicity is overtly stated as an issue) mediations are infrequent. (Howard, 1983: 77)

Landlord/tenant and consumer complaints. Disputes between landlords and tenants have low mediation rates. The power imbalance is too great here; the landlord has little incentive to attend, especially if the owner is an out-of-state corporation. CDS is almost never asked to mediate consumer complaints or other disputes with agencies and organizations.

Family violence, substance abuse. Domestic abuse, alcoholism, and drug abuse cases are regularly referred elsewhere. In these situations, it is CDS who decides that the subject is inappropriate, not the caller. From time to time the issue surfaces during a session but is treated as a matter beyond the scope of mediation, and again it is referred.

Money. Other disputes which seldom reach CDS are those which center on money. Property damage and theft, if they are considered serious, are taken to officials who have enforcement power. Only a few consumer complaints come in each year.

Assault. CDS does not have many cases of physical attacks—a noticeable difference from other community programs. As with situations involving money, it is not clear whether the disputants refuse to mediate such issues or whether the referral sources are making that decision.

Disputes as cultural patterns

If these conflicts sound familiar, it points out again that disputes are not chance personal problems which are somehow the fault of individual short-comings. Disputes grow in the soil of our culture, and like different species of plants, they inform the skilled observer about the nature of the local environment. In this instance, CDS's clientele reveal their communities' strong beliefs about ownership and image, whereas in the ghetto area of the nearby city of Wilmington, the court's dispute settlement program deals with issues linked to cooperating for survival (Baskin, 1984).

The set of values which governs the behavior and content of disputes between friends and neighbors can be seen in the following CDS case history of a dispute with interethnic overtones. This particular story is a simple one because the parties were strangers and the few issues were evident to everybody.

> *Dana and Annette did not know each other's names. Every afternoon, when Annette walked home from school past Dana and her friends, neither Dana nor Annette would step aside on the sidewalk to let the other by. Resentment grew, and each day they renewed their resolve not to budge. One morning, someone shoved, and a hair-pulling fight ensued. Annette's mother yanked them apart. That night, the other parents phoned, trying to be reasonable. Annette's mother responded, "I don't need to be lectured" and hung up. The next day her father escorted his daughter home from school to "protect" her. Spotting Dana and her friends across the street, he lost his temper, shaking a fist in her face and calling her names. What he didn't know was that Dana's family was watching from their porch and claimed later that they had heard the man's threats and ethnic slurs.*
>
> *There were no more efforts to be friendly; the police were called. They advised both parties not to speak to the other, so they didn't. "Assault," read the subsequent court charges. Dana's family wanted Annette's father restrained and punished.*

Why had such a small situation gotten out of hand? Each person escalated the problem by acting out a customary series of responses. The girls eyed each other's status on the sidewalk. They began insulting, then fighting about "insults." When the fight came as the next step, the mother played her role when she pulled them apart because, as she explained, "parents should stop it in case kids are getting hurt." Different stories—the viewpoints were quite distorted by this time—led to accusing and defending. The parents were scared by the escalation. They became suspicious and protective. Finally they burst the bounds of their tempers, hurling names, exaggerating the badness of the other side. Convinced that they were being mistreated and that there was nothing more they could do, they stopped talking and called the authorities. They no longer thought of *solving* the matter; punishing, in this case by filing charges, seemed the only way to set things right.

Key to that escalation were feelings about control of space and protection of children. Matters of respect and face kept things moving on a one-way street. Those feelings stoked the conflict daily and consequently also influenced the dynamics of the mediation session itself. Until everyone had blown off steam and established that their daughter was a "good kid," the mediation stayed in a holding pattern. The parties accused and counter-charged for a half hour, then came to agreement in fifteen minutes. The terms were simply that *both* girls would step aside for each other, and that rather than intervene, parents would telephone if another problem arose.

Often the tale of a dispute has the air of inevitable ritual, with each person responding in role. Actors in a wider frame, they do not see the stage under their feet. Their lines have been memorized years before. The mediation between teenaged Dana and Annette, because it does not add the complications of a friendship, is a neat illustration of this patterned action and reaction. Its very typicalness illustrates the effect of surrounding culture on our disputing behavior.

Friendly, neighborly: the mediation myth

Seemingly more controversial than *what* neighbors have a right to quarrel about is deciding *when* it is appropriate to abandon friendly relations for a publicly adversarial stance and *how* to take action. Should one complain to officials about a roommate who doesn't pay her share of the utilities? Is it fair to yell at a neighbor whose cat left paw prints on your freshly waxed car? (CDS has had two such cases.) Does name-calling justify retaliation? The answers hinge on people's beliefs about friendship and good neighboring.

CDS, like almost all other programs, categorizes the main kind of disputes it handles as those involving "ongoing relationships." In most mediations, however, neighbors are unlikely to have significant relationship beyond physical proximity. Not uncommonly, their only reason for contact has been the dispute. Of the last 20 neighbor cases the author mediated, for instance, only 4 groups had been friends previously. Disputants in 9 cases knew their neighbors by name and sometimes knew a little about their lives. Parents did not always know the other parents' names, though they were acquainted with each other's children. The children and teenagers, however, in all but one case, knew each other well. In 5 cases, the adult neighboring disputants did not even know each other's names.

The disputant questionnaires support this finding. Out of 33 respondents, 7 said they were casual friends, 12 claimed the other party was an acquaintance, 5 had never talked to them before the mediation. Indicating that there was no friendship but that the term "acquaintance" did not cover the relationship either, 4 people created their own category of "neighbor" to respond. Only one person had mediated a dispute with a good friend, the remaining 2 involved family members.

People may choose a few people in the neighborhood as friends, but rarely do they know all the families on their block. Usually, relations between disputing neighbors before the arguments began were at best a polite "Hello" and a pat for the dog. No wonder, therefore, that "leave me alone" is the primary attitude of most disputants.

If the offending neighbor is a slight acquaintance, chances are greater that the response will be based on the letter of the law rather than regard for the neighborly relationship. "I don't have anything against you. I just have to protect my property," said one man to his neighbors. In other cases, people seem mad at the world. The other party is a convenient target.

While neighbors have less hesitation than friends about fighting in public, the image of a "good neighbor" is still inhibiting. CDS research in one Delaware County neighborhood matches that of Merry and Silbey in Boston (1984): "Good" neighbors bend over backward to avoid taking issue with each other. "Talking things over" is the "best" way to handle trouble. When faced with the reality of a difficult neighbor, however, most of us prefer to grit our teeth and ignore rather than to complain directly. And so we wait until it seems silly to protest ("It hasn't bothered you for the last nine years, why are you mad all of a sudden?") or until the situation explodes.

Neighbors who are strangers can be quick to anger, but disputants who have been friends feel betrayed. When friends do finally decide to take action against each other, the resulting bitterness can resemble that of a divorce. Not surprisingly, in these situations one or both parties usually refuses to mediate.

Among those friends who do use CDS's service, the response to the situation is both angry and conciliatory. Feelings have been hurt and sometimes that is hard to forgive, yet friends also remember the better times. "I'd rather put up with the noise than break off our good relations," said one woman. Another explained during the mediation, "Things were OK before you married Gary. We didn't want to complain about him because you'd get upset, but...." One man wrote of his mediation with a friend, "I am still being taken advantage of but no longer feel it is worth fighting over."

For most of us, publicly complaining about relative strangers is more acceptable than airing troubles with family or friends. The remarks above reveal a strong moral feeling against taking such disputes to professionals. Friends and family feuds last many years before the will to put up with aggravation is worn down to the point where the dispute is brought to outsiders.

When the friendly, neighborly relation breaks down. Once people decide that talking to the neighbor is useless, the unwritten rules about good neighbors are no longer binding. People keep notes on each other. Protecting oneself and one's rights justifies actions which would be ordinarily out of the question. The game of "getting even" begins. It is interesting, considering the number of sophisticated retaliators who turn up in CDS files, that in studies of how people *believe* they should behave towards an offensive neighbor, this approach is never mentioned! In one case that has become a classic CDS example, a five-year-old shoved a three-year-old off a tricycle. The mother of the younger child hit the kindergartner. That enraged the other mother, who went over to the neighbor's porch and stole her potted plants. The first mother gathered up all the toys, frisbees, and balls from the five-year-old's house and locked them away. The next day she found her rosebushes uprooted. Eventually, they ended up in court with counter-charges: vandalism versus "stolen athletic equipment."

Both the loyal friend and the good neighbor are supposed to suffer wrongs and insults without responding. On the other hand, "not letting yourself get walked over" is a sign of strength. No one likes to feel weak or powerless, yet the polite way of dealing with conflict requires people to swallow the desire to fight back. If people are expected to ignore, or at most to discuss, an aggravating situation, getting back at the offender (even with a bit of undercover gossip) is understandably a satisfying way to feel that some justice has been done.

The Mediation Experience

They walk into the room apprehensive.

If one party arrives early, they usually talk to the mediators about those fears. Mediators will not listen to information about the situation, but it is hard to prevent anxious feelings from spilling out while everyone waits. Some say, brashly defensive, "They can say what they want, then we're going home. I haven't got much time to waste on this." They advise the mediators to be careful—no one can contain that other man's temper. "It's nice of you people to try, but we've been through everything, you have no idea. You just can't trust them." Though they themselves have come, they are sure that the other party—if they ever show—will never listen to reason. Are these disputants really feeling discouraged, or are they trying to win the mediators' sympathy?

Many people are openly wary. They won't look at the other side. Sometimes they stare coldly, with arms folded. Other people come in so quietly that it is hard to catch their names. It is hard to tell if they are afraid or shy. Maybe they are bracing themselves to get on with it.

Most people are understandably uneasy before a mediation, but a few people come in with full-blown fears. Occasionally someone asks for police protection and refuses to attend a mediation without it. In one case where the woman found the courage to come, the office warned mediators in a memo, "Cathy feels very threatened by the fact that the son...is a prize fighter and she is afraid that he will cause some trouble with her own son and husband."

Mediation requires hard work, both in plowing through emotional stress and in problem-solving. The office tries to prepare disputants for that ahead of time. They had particular trouble with this woman: "Kate stresses that the only thing she wants from a mediation is an agreement from the Howarths that they will never speak to her again. She says she has done nothing to them and is reluctant about mediation. I stressed repeatedly the necessity of working in the mediation and the necessity of wanting to make some changes. The only change she wants is the one listed above."

Once everyone has arrived, the tension builds. The Uninterrupted Time comes almost as a relief. During the usual mediation, disputants find themselves drawn inexorably through three phases. In the beginning they talk to the mediator; next they turn to contend directly with the other party. Only then do they move to the problem. As we described earlier, this can be an abrupt turning point. A good while later, just before agreement is reached, a backlash effect is not uncommon. Everything seems set until a disputant suddenly throws a zinging dart at the other side, some remark calculated to hurt. It is as if they are looking back and saying "Do I really want to give up this fight?" Usually this is a passing moment, however, and the agreement is finalized. Though the disputants say afterward that they were mostly aware of feeling stuck or of what the other side was saying, the mediator can see them guided like a toboggan down a track by the rails of the process.

The difficult person. CDS has, from time to time, encountered people who are incapable of participating in a mediation. They are often articulate and smart people, but they seem to crave the excitement of a good fight too much to actually end it. A few have been unable to trust anyone; they claw at everyone around them like a cornered cat. During a mediation they go from domineering to teary and confused.

Disputants' expectations of the other person can be unreasonable, but some cannot hear or understand anyone else's point of view. Wrote one mediator tiredly:

> *The Stevensons have very inflexible ideas about what constitutes "considerate" behavior, "excessive" noise, "good" neighbor conduct, etc. I question whether a pair of Trappist monks could live up to these standards, much less a healthy family of five kids aged nine to sixteen. No agreement was reached except that they all agreed never to speak to one another again.*

These "impossible people" are a small fraction of CDS disputants, but they preoccupy mediators. They are at once fascinating and frustrating. Such people are not a separate class from the rest of us, however. Rather they are caricatures of what disputing behavior looks like. Whereas most people go in and out of conflict, they have become stuck in the intense extremes of hostility. Addicted, like mercenaries are to war, they can no longer see the way out even when the mediators and the other disputants hold open the door.

The response of ordinary disputants to mediation is double-sided. They are glad to be there, glad to work things out. It can't often be said that they enjoy it. "After the first mediation, I didn't sleep for three days, the things he said upset me so much," said a woman following a hard but useful second mediation. "This time I knew I couldn't sit there and listen if he started up again. I told my husband I was going to leave the room and let him do the talking."

Others are less shaken by the session than they expect. "It was okay. I'd rather talk things out man to man but I knew I couldn't talk to them unless someone else was there. They wouldn't listen."

Watching the different people who come to the table, mediators learn much about mediating and much about themselves. "Why can't they see the obvious answers? How can they believe anyone would agree to *that*?" Disputants' unreasonable demands frustrate mediators. In truth, we all have trouble doing the "obvious" when we are embroiled in an emotional situation. Ron Kraybill of the Mennonite Conciliation Service tells audiences with serious amusement that some morning we will wake up as he did and realize that we are acting just like those "stupid" disputants over an incident.

Then too, occasionally a disputant leaves mediators with a sense of the generosity and courage which people can show even when they are feeling hurt or angry. In one mediation a young neighbor spent a half hour patiently, gently listening to the paranoic accusations of a disturbed woman, reassuring her. Then there was the young teen who told his mother that he worried that she was working too hard, and the woman sitting next to her grown daughter who said to her neighbors, "This is my daughter. I love her and I want her to be welcome in my house."

Moments of pettiness, moments of warmth and strength: "Disputants present us with a mirror," says Kraybill, "We can't separate our fates" (NCPCR conference, Athens, GA, 1983).

Satisfaction

Community mediation programs claim that disputants are usually satisfied with their experience. Of course, what they are satisfied with depends on their expectations. Did they mainly want the chance to tell the other side what they thought of them? Were they pushing for predetermined terms of agreement? Was their goal some assurance of better relations or to get out of court charges? Here are excerpts of staff and mediator comments in CDS case files which illustrate the range of expectations and the different degrees of "success" which can satisfy a party.

1) In a separation discussion, the wife had modest goals, and was satisfied with the results: "The wife felt the mediation process helped her and her husband to begin talking rationally about a very tough subject. The husband now understands how serious the problem is from her perspective."

2) "Sally said that the Jacksons were keeping their word, making every effort and not bothering their family at all. Respect is there where it wasn't before, she said. Mary Jackson said that it was good to get everything out, much better 'than having a lawyer say you can't say that.' She felt it was the best way to handle it."

3) This man wanted more than mediation could offer: Despite a favorable agreement where the other party agreed to pay medical costs and drop charges, "Mr. Little indicated that he was looking into other properties (much to Mrs. Little's dismay) and would like to move. He said he could not rid himself of the hatred of the Grays and these feelings were aroused each time he saw any member of the Gray family."

4) Another man who had planned to move wanted a mediation because he wanted a better way than the police, courts, or ignoring the problem. At the two-week follow-up he said he was overwhelmed by the lies at the mediation, thought his family had taken all the abuse, and did not want to make the first move at communication. Yet he admitted that all was quiet so far, and the neighbors were upholding their contract.

Despite differing reasons for being there, the mediation session seems to answer the expectations of many disputants. On CDS's questionnaire a number of disputants wrote anonymous comments about what they liked and disliked about the mediation:

> *It gives you a chance to express your feelings.*

> *It solved the problem.... The meeting relieved tensions between my husband and the neighbor's wife. In this sense the meeting was a success, but I will never feel friendly toward those people. The damage has already been done.*

> *[I liked that] we settled the matter out of court.*

> From a disgruntled woman whose mediation resulted in no agreement: *I thought it was a rather unpleasant and futile gesture. The mediators didn't explain enough about the process. There was repressed anger in the environment which was never resolved. If you want results, get a lawyer.*

> *I thought the mediation was very superficial. I believe that we might have come to an agreement if the other party had been truly willing to admit that she was not one hundred percent correct. I also feel that the other party has a personality verging on the pathological. I do not know if a personality that hasn't been properly socialized can be made to change her behavior through mediation.*

> *It gave us a chance to settle an argument. [I didn't like that] it doesn't prove who is right or wrong....*

> *It was objective, efficient, effective. The partial agreement wasn't fair,* he writes, *but blood from a stone set a precedent!*

> *[I liked] the whole procedure. They were kind, considerate, helpful, and understanding.*

> *Both parties were able to discuss their views in a rational manner with no outside interference.... I thought it was great.*

Some critics ask whether disputants' expectations are so shaped by talking to the mediation program staff that it takes little to satisfy them. While people do have sadly limited hopes, there is no evidence in any of the written responses to our survey or Sontag's 1979 questionnaire which indicates strong CDS influence. The quotes above are remarkable for their variety: each has singled out different facets of the mediation when talking about what they like or dislike. They agree with some parts of the CDS format and criticize others. The range of reactions to the quality of the settlement goes from outrage to delight.

Those same critics correctly suggest that satisfaction is not a measure of successful and fair resolution. Satisfaction seems to be an immediate reaction based on whether or not the parties left with a written agreement. Of 33 surveyed respondents, *all* of the people who said they were "not satisfied" or "upset" about the mediation had not come to agreement. They all described their feelings about the other side after the mediation as worse, same, or neutral. One would therefore expect the 15 people reporting that their agreements had held for at least several months to be satisfied, and they were. Not one was unsatisfied by the mediation. Of the 15, 6 reported feeling better about the other party. Interestingly, those whose agreements had collapsed shortly afterward uniformly said they were satisfied with the mediation.

One concludes that reaching some agreement, no matter how ephemeral, meets disputants' small hopes. Those expectations seem to be limited to the session itself, as if no one dares hold much hope for any future change. However, the high level of continuing hostility and reports of further incidents indicate that parties who do not sign a contract seem to be in for deeper trouble either because their dissatisfaction and bad feelings made resolution too difficult or because the failure of the meeting makes them still angrier.

Most likely the main satisfaction in every mediation is getting things over with. Emily Sontag's study early in the program's history (1979) found this feeling of satisfaction slightly above that of similar disputants in the lowest court level. Disputants going through either forum said, "I'm just glad it's over."

It is harder to tell whether participants are satisfied with the way the session was conducted. After a mediation, few disputants comment on the process itself. They have been concentrating on feelings and issues. They have little to compare the experience to. Nor does the agreement, unless it is unusually creative, excite them. Often, as the selected quotes above show, they speak approvingly of the idea of getting together to talk things over and praise the mediators for successfully bringing the other side to agreement.

More than being satisfied (that vague word) with the mediation process or outcome, disputants seem to leave with conflicting emotions: relief with a touch of disbelief being the most common. The other side actually dropped charges. We managed to talk without screaming at each other.

Uncertainty and disappointment show too:

I just hope this nonsense really stops after tonight.

Why couldn't we have done this on our own?

We just rehashed the same old stuff.
They'll never stick to it.

These are all actual quotes. One can speculate that other doubts are crossing their minds about what they have said and what they have promised.

Disputants may be happy that it is over and grateful to let matters rest. They may have somewhat more understanding of or even sympathy for the other side. Often they appear tired and subdued, perhaps as aware of their compromises and new vulnerability as of what they have gained. After expressing their thanks, they leave; usually the program does not hear from them again except during the follow-up phone call.

Mediation can make a striking difference in some situations. "I wish we'd known about you people earlier," said one relieved participant as she left. It is not an unusual remark. Several survey respondents agreed with the woman who wrote, "Mediation was the perfect answer. I don't think we could have resolved it any other way."

One local district justice likes to tell of the Fourth of July afternoon when he turned down a street where two feuding families lived. Realizing they would probably be home, he was considering taking another route, when one of the parties came running across the lawn. "Judge! Judge, wait a minute." Ready to hear the usual stream of complaints, the judge was astonished by what the man said next: "Remember that dispute settlement place you sent us to? Well, everything's been fine since." He then invited the judge to the backyard to join the two households in a barbecue.

A woman summed up the feelings for those who find true reconciliation during the mediation: "I haven't believed in miracles for a long time, but after tonight, I believe again."

Three: The Mediator

Lynn mothers three energetic children. Lydia works in the personnel department of an international agency. Al heads an HMO. Carol cares for the old people in her neighborhood. Brad is a carpenter. Betsey cooks for a Quaker study center. Mark is a community organizer. Jane is a retired court-based social worker. Bonnie is an organizational development consultant.

People with a bent for reconciliation work are found in many corners of a community. The school janitor perhaps, the short guy on the basketball team, the church secretary—we have all encountered these people and been grateful for their help. CDS has gathered these "natural" conciliators and other people who want to learn how to play that role effectively.

Although most groups have members who act as mediators, for some reason conciliation is still perceived as an unusual ability. "We are like a rare blood type," says one CDS mediator. While some people seem born with the knack, most mediators agree that many people can learn the basic skills of the trade. The aura of mediation remains, however. Tell someone you are a mediator and the most frequent reaction is, "Gee, *I* could never do anything like that."

Looking at the "rare" individuals who are drawn to mediating offers clues about what kind of people do well in this work and how our communities can find them. When we learn to recognize the mediators among us, maybe we will be better able to cultivate their skills. We will certainly discover many more natural mediators than we expected!

This chapter tells the CDS mediators' personal stories: what kind of people they are, what the mediation experience is like for them. We will let them speak for themselves.

Who Are the Mediators?

Just as few disputants purposefully seek out mediation services, until recently few people came into our training courses out of a long-held desire to mediate. They arrived at the door more by serendipity than design. "My friends dragged me in," says one with a smile. "I had to have a project for my club," another confesses. One woman thought she had signed up for a spiritual meditation workshop; today she is a skilled mediator!

In the last few years mediation and conflict resolution have become common topics in professional workshops and university courses. The media has picked up the idea. Lately, we find more trainees have clearer ideas about what they want to learn. During introductions in one FSP course, trainees gave their reasons for attending:

> *I am particularly interested in the nitty gritty of teacher/ administration conflicts.*

> *I'm a people-watcher. Settling conflict has been a life-long interest.*

> *As a social worker, I see many areas of application. It's an alternative to family court settlements which aren't happy....*

> *I'm interested in long-term, many-party environmental mediation, and I already use mediation informally in my law practice.*

Another person had been a disputant in a CDS case. Many were teachers and social workers looking for additional skills and possible job changes. Nearly everyone added that they wanted mediation skills for use in their personal lives too, especially those busy with parenting.

The number of people considering mediation as part of a profession is rising. Lawyers seek some alternative to unrelievedly adversarial work. Social service workers hear that mediation techniques can expand their range of skills. One other goal has risen rapidly on the list. Influenced by the increasing urgency of the anti-nuclear movement, many trainees are looking at local peacemaking as a realistic step they can take toward finding less destructive ways to address international conflict.

These are the outward attractions of learning to mediate. The similarities between mediators suggest that this kind of work meets some inner needs as well. Not infrequently, mediators feel that they have found their niche at last. They are the ones who always find themselves in the conciliatory role. Says one woman, "I know I've found the right place." Another talks about mediating between her brother and parents as early as she can remember. "I've always thought there must be a better way."

In an admittedly subjective analysis of mediator interviews (16 people) and questionnaires (27 full, 11 partial responses), we find that CDS mediators have certain common traits. They tend to value harmonious, strong relationships. Peace and nonviolence are issues they think about often in both religious and political terms. Helping others is a priority. Every single CDS mediator reports membership in a local organization other than CDS. They often serve on boards. No one reported taking a position of strong, public leadership on an issue, even though many worked hard as part of the group in advocacy and political causes. Whatever their work or volunteer status, most mediators are competent people who are part of their organization's dependable core. Listen to these themes surface in one staff person's interview:

> When I grew up at home it seemed like there wasn't a day of the week when my mother wasn't driving handicapped people and elderly people here and there, my dad got involved in the Scouts, I volunteered at the hospital.... I'm not a Quaker, but I believe in peace, especially through nonviolence. Violence just wasn't part of my world. Girls never used their fists. It is just part of my nature to talk to people and try to work things out peacefully.

Interestingly, several mediators commented on their distaste for organizing and administrative work. "I felt pulled onto the CDS board because I like mediation and want to see it continue," says one mediator, "but I don't like asking for money, or organizing all those things it takes to survive." Another woman comments, "I am not comfortable foisting my own opinions on others or being a salesperson."

Do these mediators have a particular bent towards solving people problems? Certainly they show marked preference for volunteering for work done in groups and for choosing careers in the professions which focus on human relations. Out of 37 CDS mediators, some of whom listed several occupations, there are 10 social workers, 9 homemakers, 5 mediation program staff, 4 counselors, 4 human relations and organizational development specialists.

This kind of volunteer service is not advocacy, education, or charity. It is clearly a new addition to the cluster of occupations and activities which center on helping individuals. CDS volunteers, whether or not they consider themselves natural mediators, are the people who want to set problems right. They like to facilitate meetings and to run small groups. They look for short projects with practical, visible outcomes. Mediators explaining their interest in joining CDS often reiterate these themes:

> *Group-process is an aspect of my work that I particularly enjoy in terms of dealing with people. I like it better than intense one-to-one counseling, and I don't do well in front of a crowd. Working with six to a dozen people—the dynamics fascinate me.*

> *Why do I continue? It's a productive, satisfying way to work at social problems on a small level and yet see concrete results.*

> *I like it better than case work because I don't have to worry about the relationship between me and the disputants. And it is more reality-based than some therapy which says "we can't deal with anything which isn't in this room."*

Two-thirds of CDS mediators are women. The traits we mentioned are often characteristic of what our society teaches girls. We learn to get along with other people, to smooth ruffled feathers, and to listen patiently. We are taught to keep our opinions to ourselves and to facilitate the leadership of others. Women have long been persistent in their desire for peaceable solutions. (Says one mediator, "We always say conflict is good but I have to admit my inclination is to jump in and try to bring harmony back.") Much of our world revolves around relationships. Many women were raised to be the ones who quietly restored the equilibrium when quarrels divided their family or community. Mediation is a new position for women to play out these roles. These private talents are now moving into a more public sphere.

Demographics

People are attracted to mediation for outward reasons such as career advancement or wanting to promote peace in the community, and for inner reasons of personal style and talents. Whatever the reason for learning to mediate, everyone is welcome to take the program's mediation training. Any person who completes the full course and apprenticeship may become a CDS mediator. The pool of 37 active volunteers in January 1985 looked like this:

CDS Mediator Characteristics, 1985

Age:

$$\begin{array}{rl}
\text{under 35} & - \quad 7 \text{ mediators} \\
35\text{--}49 & - \quad 15 \\
50\text{--}65 & - \quad 13 \\
\text{over 65} & - \quad 2
\end{array}$$

Race:

$$\begin{array}{rl}
\text{Black} & - \quad 2 \text{ mediators} \\
\text{Asian} & - \quad 0 \\
\text{Hispanic} & - \quad 0 \\
\text{White} & - \quad 36 \\
\text{Native American} & - \quad 1
\end{array}$$

Sex:

$$\begin{array}{rl}
\text{Women} & - \quad 27 \text{ mediators} \\
\text{Men} & - \quad 10
\end{array}$$

College:

$$\begin{array}{rl}
\text{Undergraduate Degree} & - \quad 25 \text{ mediators} \\
\text{Graduate Degree} & - \quad 12
\end{array}$$

Occupation: (The following categories had 3 or more mediators)

10	social worker	4	counselor/psychologist
10	homemaker	4	clerical
6	trainer/consultant	3	administrator/manager
6	FSP/CDS present &	3	business owner
	former staff	3	lawyer

Many people listed two occupations. The three retired mediators have been included under their former occupations. Spouses were mostly administrators, professors, K–12 teachers, or managers in sales or public relations.

Community: Twenty mediators live in or near the neighboring towns of Swarthmore and Media. The early mediators and program developers come from these communities. This region has a higher per capita income than most municipalities in Delaware County.

Family income: varies from under $10,000 to over $100,000, with the mean income roughly $39,000, about $16,000 higher than the county average. Half of these mediators earn less than $30,000, however. All of these lower income mediators are single, all but one are women. Mediators who appear to have high incomes tended not to respond to that survey question, so the median family income of CDS mediators is probably higher than our statistics show.

Religion (current affiliation or beliefs): We were startled to find that a large number, 17 (45%), consider themselves to be Quaker. (Publicity for CDS mediation training is advertised throughout the community, not mainly to Quakers.) No other denomination is represented by more than 3 mediators. There are a few Jews and several people who were raised Catholics. Otherwise, backgrounds were overwhelmingly white Protestant.

Class: The questionnaire asked "How would you describe your social class background?" with a blank space for people to fill in using their own words. Of those who responded, 11 CDS mediators describe themselves as middle class, 11 as upper middle class, perceptions which fit their other responses on education, career, income, community, and religion. Three said they had been raised in working-class homes.

All these figures reveal two important trends. One is the division between disputants and mediators, the other is the close-knit character of the CDS mediator group.

How different are CDS mediators and disputants? The demographics diverge in every category which reflects class, except race. Both groups are almost all white. Another similarity is the large age span. The youngest CDS mediator is in her early twenties. The oldest is eighty-five. Otherwise the statistics show a distinct difference between CDS clients and the group of volunteers. Mediators come from communities with higher income and higher education levels. Nearly all have a college degree (80%, compared to disputants' 19%).

The apparent similarities between mediators are significant. Though Delaware County covers an enormous range in income and in educational level, and though 9% of the population is black, the mediators who started CDS came from a distinct segment of that diverse population. Most of them were white women homemakers moving back into paid professional work. As in most organizations, they recruited volunteers through personal contacts. After eight years, newcomers still come primarily from the same white middle-class professional neighborhoods.

The homogeneity of CDS mediators made forming a program much easier. Goals and methods were set without disagreement. The ideas of empowerment and confidentiality, for instance, and the verbal, informal style of the mediation session were never questioned. People in the group knew each other socially and worked together with remarkably little friction.

What was a strength in creating a new organization became

restrictive during the following stages of expansion. The gap between disputants and mediators proved harder to close than CDS hoped. Those few from the county's poorer communities who did take the training have remained on the sidelines. Why haven't people from neighborhoods most served by CDS warmed to the idea of becoming mediators? One can make a few guesses. The active mediators developed a program and a mediation style that was natural for them. The mediation format, for instance, is highly verbal, and program goals grow out of a liberal worldview. As a result, those who come from different backgrounds may find CDS norms uncomfortable. A good number of mediators are attracted by the training, only later deciding to volunteer for CDS. Ministers in poorer communities who were trying to find members to attend our training reported that there was not much interest in self-improvement courses or anything reminiscent of school. Many work irregular shifts or hold two jobs and cannot attend such a course regularly. Lastly, like attracts like; people generally prefer to spend their spare time with friends.

The distance between mediators and disputants is a norm, not a rule, and the tight circle of mediators is widened from time to time by someone who is different. Nevertheless, as we shall see throughout this book, class divisions pervade the nature of CDS, its successes and its failures.

Qualifications

The rapid professionalization of the dispute resolution field will necessarily further split the mediators from the mediated. Volunteer community programs which require would-be trainees to have graduate degrees severely restrict the kind of people who can work in the program. Rather than limit the pool of mediators, CDS chooses to handle disputes where no specialized knowledge in matters such as investments, environment, or human behavior is necessary. Yet even that open policy has not succeeded in attracting a more varied group of mediators.

Once training and apprenticeship are complete, neither education level nor occupation appear to predict mediator ability. Indeed, Charles Bethel, a Washington, D.C., mediation trainer, notes ruefully that for lawyers, social workers, and counselors, learning to mediate is often a matter of "un-training"; those who have no ingrained professional habits can be at an advantage. Part of CDS's mission is spreading mediation skills (not just the service) throughout its communities. Seeking volunteers with professional qualifications negates that goal, especially since such academic credentials seem to be unrelated to the quality of intervention. Disputants, in CDS's experience, are indifferent. Any questions about mediators' qualifications are rare. They are more interested in results.

Will professional, state, or federal certification requirements prohibit volunteers like those at CDS from acting as mediators? In community dispute resolution (not divorce, labor, environmental, or other specialized areas), mandatory higher education seems as much a way to draw circles around potential profits as a way to protect the public. Defining expertise as a mysterious art limited to those with long training is a typical step in demarcating new professional fields and comes at a time when younger social workers and lawyers are worried about earning a living. As in other professions, a monopoly of skill is still undergirded by an ethical commitment to service ideals over profit (Wilensky and Lebeaux, 1958: 258), but service means doing *unto*, not doing *with*.

Loose requirements for mediators mean less control over mistakes. Irresponsible actions are harder to monitor or prevent. Of particular worry, for example, is the intermediary's desire to "balance" and "reconcile" family or interracial disputes, when one party has a decided power advantage over the other. As one advocate for women's rights points out, the professional and the lay mediator are equally likely to bring misinformation and prejudice with them into the session. This argues for certified training which ensures background and experience in certain areas before trainees can call themselves "mediators." Again, we find degree requirements irrelevant. While many of the fears raised by mediation's opponents are based on a greatly exaggerated picture of the powerful decision-making mediator (a concern more accurately focused on court-appointed mediators), even voluntary community programs like CDS need to assure the public of their competence.

To protest the probable exclusion of community mediators as state legislators increasingly heed the call for certification is perhaps at this point like trying to catch a balloon already loose in the wind. A public-sector mediation program in Pennsylvania recently lost their most gifted and experienced mediator because she did not have sufficient formal education to pass necessary civil service exams to be employed as staff. The evidence is that many kinds of people can learn to mediate well. We will only deprive ourselves if we decide that the basic human act of reconciliation is an expensive and esoteric skill safely practiced exclusively by an educated few.

CDS training

The call to find mediators from many sections of a community is by no means an argument against thorough preparation for that work. Bill Lincoln, a well-known trainer of mediators, says unequivocally, "Mediation is *not* doing what comes naturally" (SPIDR 1983 conference address). While we might qualify that statement somewhat, certainly even the most natural mediator learns a great deal from training.

Today, any new program has access to the training and experience of others. In 1976, however, Neighborhood Justice Centers and public community mediation programs in the Middle Atlantic region could be numbered on one hand. CDS's new staff members were all experienced trainers in related fields. Although everyone was learning through trial and error, they insisted that volunteers receive full training before presiding at a mediation table. That training requirement has remained firm policy. CDS mediators spend twenty hours in FSP's experiential training course. Over the years, this preparation has become more skill-intensive but still includes a look at intangibles such as respect for disputants, mediator limits, and issues of bias and ethical conduct. Much of their time is spent roleplaying disputants and mediators. The change over the twenty hours is fun to watch. The framework and approach are quickly absorbed by most trainees, and they improve rapidly.

By the end, the participants have determined whether or not this is work they want to do. They are nervous about facing "real" disputants. An apprenticeship follows training to make those first dives into real-life mediation easier. This means observing or co-mediating with an experienced mediator until the person seems capable of handling most situations. After several months of preparation and anticipation, the trainee has finally become a mediator.

Training professionalizes and channels a person's behavior. Techniques are self-consciously learned and critiqued. The trainee becomes more aware of what he or she is doing. Self-confidence may be somewhat shaken at the beginning, however. "This is a lot harder than I thought!" is not an unusual reaction after the first roleplay. The job of the trainer is to rebuild that confidence on a sturdy base of knowledge and practice. The resulting blend of ease and firmness signals competence and professionalism to disputants.

It is hard to give high quality training to mediators without adding that flavor of so-called "professional" behavior. Mediation falls into the slot of social service, and we all have notions about how social workers and counselors behave. Both the disputants and the mediators have deeply etched images of what competence looks like: a calm, gravely assured manner perhaps, or body language which leans forward and takes up space. Linguists have identified "helper" speaking patterns, the voice a teacher, a nurse, or an official will use ("Now how are we doing today?" "This way please."); mediators, too, may slip into this bright, impersonal mode.

Training emphasizes another hallmark of the professional: the responsibility to improve. The twenty-hour course is only a beginning. Mediators gather several times a year for specialized workshops on topics they have requested. Social occasions are filled with shop-talk. CDS volunteers eagerly travel to conferences and workshops. Lately, several have joined professional societies. This trend shows CDS moving away from the original idea of transferring mediation skills to many groups throughout the community.

The process of training and subsequently working as mediation teams has produced remarkable unity among CDS mediators. We have mentioned before the easy acceptance of the mediation format and program objectives. The one volunteer who learned to mediate in another program is the only person who regularly challenges the way things are done. That the dovetailed effect of the training and program operation produces such uniformity probably reflects several factors. First, CDS goals fit together logically and have held up through the test of repeated experiences. The mediators' similarity in background and character is a second factor. Third, training further weeds out, rightly or wrongly, people with different styles and beliefs. Lastly, the mediation course molds trainees into our conception of competent mediators. Training is an instrument for initiation and for preparation; although it means CDS loses a measure of creativity and variety, that experience is necessarily a cornerstone of any effective community mediation program.

Satisfactions

Once volunteers begin mediating, they almost never leave CDS's ranks. At an international conference, a new mediator asked a room full of veteran community mediation directors how they kept their volunteers. Although busy urban programs reported turnover, smaller programs agreed that volunteer enthusiasm for mediating just didn't seem to wear thin.

One reason people stay is that volunteering for CDS requires no regular commitment of time. The office calls about a specific date. The mediator can say yes or no. This appeals to the volunteer who is already juggling family, job, and a multitude of activities. It can be squeezed in during free time or dropped during busier times of the year. Unlike most volunteer tasks, CDS mediation doesn't turn into an obligation.

More importantly, mediation satisfies. Some strong words summarize the main reasons CDS volunteers stay on the roster year after year:

Euphoria
Challenge
Helping
Mission
Personal benefit

Euphoria. The sense of what we call the "mediator's high" is at the heart of this satisfaction. People mediate because they hope to change people's lives in some small way. Each mediator's concern is slightly different. The exhilaration of a successful mediation, however, is a feeling which stands apart from those objectives. Listen to what mediators say about the times when things work out well:

I feel elated. It's a marvelous feeling, gratifying. It feels like you've changed the world just because you made a dent.

Mediation is the first time they see other people's problems and point of view. Afterward, I have a temporary personal high. When it is a real coming together, people are euphoric.

I feel ecstatic after every single mediation. I'm like that lady who said to her neighbor at the end, "Couldn't we do this every week?" When you have one where people really do try and get out of themselves and into the other person's shoes a little bit, you're onto something of religious and personal significance.

They have done something difficult which requires intelligence, empathy, cooperation, and sometimes guts. In a short time they have moved discouraged disputants into a new dimension which can have long-term, positive repercussions in their lives. The disputants themselves, as we have seen, are often incredulous and pleased. Sharing that feeling and knowing that one's own skill has helped bring that about makes mediations which end in reconciliation special.

Several weeks ago, an old woman and a young mother hugged and kissed each other, crying, at the end of a mediation. They had barely known each other before the session. I don't get as excited by a successful agreement as

I used to, but their relief was so great, like the big boulders they'd been bent over carrying had just rolled away. On my way home, I found myself getting teary just thinking about it."

In my first mediation the neighbors had gone ten, fifteen years without speaking. They ended with a handshake and smiles. One invited the other out for a cup of coffee. I felt glad and thankful, joyful to have been privileged to be part of the process and witness it.

For some mediators, the charge of energy comes during the height of the session when the fur is flying. "I love the screaming, I really do," says one mediator who has never been heard raising her own voice. "It's like riding a galloping horse into the wind," says animal-lover Eileen Stief. "You have to hang in there and keep all your wits about you to keep everything on track." Once mediators get used to the sound and fury, they report that their original discomfort with anger has vanished. They even come to enjoy it.

Challenge. The challenge is not just lasting out the great emotional release but in keeping the raft under control as it barrels through the rapids and guiding it to a safe end:

I like the orchestration of it, from the gentle nudge to the direct push.

All these feelings, thoughts, and events whirling around, says Betsey Leonard, circling her fingers to illustrate. *It is like cooking leftovers. All those ingredients that are hard to combine you have to put together in the right order, the right way, so that people like it and so they get nourishment from it.*

Entering a helper relationship is always somewhat chancy. Mediators may fail. They may be verbally or physically attacked. The satisfactions of helping must be great enough to compensate for giving time and taking risk. (Titmuss, 1971) Mediators motivated by a sense of challenge ask for the difficult cases and spend hours plotting ways to break through the impasse. For them, satisfaction comes from pitting their own wits against seemingly irresolvable situations. Risk brings excitement.

Helping. Many people are excited by mediation because it is an unusual way to help people. What's more, the mediator can see immediate changes. "I enjoy mediating because you can see results quickly and watch people come together. I like to help people solve their problems. The magic of it." Another agrees, "I like to deal in tangibles." She speaks for many in CDS who enjoy working with disputants to find practical solutions. Those with more global hopes believe that their work goes beyond creating agreements to helping the person and the community change the way they handle conflicts.

Because for CDS helping is a one way street—we help them, they do not help us—it is perhaps more difficult to maintain the vision of mediation as something anyone in the community can learn to do. Again, the difference in mediator and disputant demographics is important here. In modern society, welfare is given to the stranger. It assumes a degree of distance between helped and helper. (Wilensky & Lebeaux, 1958) We enjoy the intellectual challenge of mediating, the sense of adventure. Less awarely, do we like the feelings of control and superiority which helping others stimulates? One mediator talks about how she confronted those attitudes in an early mediation:

> *I have a prejudice against disputants who come from different backgrounds..., underlying feelings of superiority. You soon learn! In one mediation (I felt pretty humble after that one) these two women—I was scornful of their speech. I know better, but there again.... Then the other mediator said with warmth and love how much she respected them and gave them well-earned praise. It opened my eyes.... You think you've reached a point where you are fair, that you are able to have a proper perspective. It was the most impressive thing that ever happened to me in a mediation.*

And so the helper, too, was unexpectedly challenged by mediation. Perhaps that afternoon she learned more than the two women did. That is one of the unplanned benefits of helping others.

Sense of mission. Nearly every CDS volunteer takes pleasure in helping others, but for some mediators this becomes a well-articulated sense of mission. One person who works with women prefers mediating women's disputes. She often takes advantage of the situation to point disputants toward ways they can take charge of their lives. Several mediators are dedicated to helping people to release anger. Some use mediation to educate parents about better ways to relate to their children. Their beliefs spotlight the most significant division in CDS mediator ranks, one discussed at length in the next chapters: defining the purpose and limits of their task.

The sense of mission commonly begins with a religious conception of what mediation is and how disputants can grow spiritually from their experience. "Mediation is peacemaking at a basic level. I believe every person to have a potential for good. There *is* some basic unity between people, and it is definitely worth going for it." One of the CDS founders comments, "Some of our volunteers came through church presentations. There is a strain of wanting to live out your Christianity. Not in a proselytizing way; it was unsaid, but I think it was there."

One man has made the religious perspective the core of his mediations:

> *For me it is an attempt to make religion work in everyday life, not just a social or intellectual activity. Human beings have real difficulty putting religious truths into practice. It's an uphill battle. I don't see a whole lot of ways groups can express love and harmony in a socially acceptable way. An ideal mediation is a like a [Quaker] Meeting for Worship called to resolve particular issues. There have been times when the people didn't even know about Quakers that it was a gathered meeting; there was a Christ presence.* [Note: "gathered meeting" is a Quaker expression which means an occasion where the group collectively experiences the Holy Spirit.]
>
> *I actively seek to help bring about a world where people seek Truth together, act out of Love, work to have enough for everyone, and seek for Christ together. This is a beginning of practicing getting closer.*
>
> *The last mediation I did was to me a failed mediation because 1) there was no basis or groundwork laid for harmonious living and 2) one person took from the other. The body English was stiff and rigid with set faces. It was resolved, but they weren't happy. The judge was delighted. It was better than where they were before. But they didn't get to the point of forgiveness.*

The other mediator at this session was uncomfortable with this man's sense of mission. "He kept us an extra hour and talked about 'the itch for rough justice' and the 'nature of human relationships.' I probably would have let them go with a less satisfactory agreement and taken their decisions at face value. I don't like imposing our own idea of what good neighbors should be. But then I tend to stick to issues and problems." Before the second session, the two mediators talked it over but came to no resolution. Their purposes in mediating were too different.

Personal benefit. At the close of this chapter, we look at what mediators have learned. Besides developing skills, however, there are more immediate satisfactions. Taking a small part in the lives of people we might otherwise never meet is fun. In addition, some enjoy mediation's element of the unexpected. You never know beforehand what the people will be like or what will happen. Each session is predictable—to a point. The rest is often a surprise.

The Mediation Experience

Expectations

How do mediators approach an upcoming session? Hopes, expectations, fears—they all influence how the mediator will act during a mediation. The interview responses revealed expectations which varied from unabashedly starry-eyed to resigned "realism."

> *I'm idealistic. I go into each mediation with the idea that there* is *some solution.... I come in looking at what I hope for these people: "What is the optimal outcome?" I'm always having the hope that things will end happily-ever-after* (Laughs).

> *I try not to expect anything except what the office has written so I don't waste so much time. Sometimes the "problem person" isn't.* She adds emphatically, *I hope for but do not expect agreement.*

> *I expect them to negotiate in good faith and honesty. I think that they can accomplish something.*

It was amusing to note that mediators who had a rosy view of mediation and of the capability of disputants reported many successful mediations. Did their views actually influence the disputants or merely reflect a tendency to see agreement before it was there? There is actually evidence for both. Co-mediators wryly note that idealistic mediators erase less positive aspects from their memories but they also report that those high expectations helped coax disputants to work things through.

Expectations change with experience. Everyone remembers their first mediation. Often what happened was not what they had expected! Two reactions stand out. First is the discovery that those trainee fears were partly justified; no rehearsal can completely prepare a mediator for the improvisational theater of a mediation session:

> *The father was an air force officer with six daughters. The oldest was eighteen and had run away. He wouldn't have any of it, he was running a tight ship. He wouldn't come in*

the door. I was flabbergasted. It wasn't like anything I'd been trained for. We did persuade him to sit down, and we worked out that the girl could come home for her things. The mother was completely cowed. It was just the other mediator's bag; she was able to keep him there till the end.

I was not prepared to deal with a large circle of twenty-five angry, vindictive people. They stood up and shook fists and pointed fingers. They screamed so loud we couldn't understand what they were saying. The parents were prompting and manipulating their children. The three mediators had been strategically placed to flank the warring parties. I found myself a rather thin wall between several fiercely shouting people.

The second revelation is watching the process really work. Disputants in a roleplay can only approximate emotional reconciliation, and trainees find it hard to believe that "real" people's feelings will change so dramatically.

I was lucky. It had been a long-standing feud. They went out together afterward to talk some more. It was amazing.

As mediators come to base expectations on what has happened in many sessions, whether they see their response as successful or inadequate will influence their enthusiasm and determine the actions they take at the table.

Failures and fears

Failure: every helper struggles with it. Mediators feel they have let disputants down when they cannot bring people through the process. "I feel if only I'd been better.... I always agonize awhile." Usually any mediation which does not produce an agreement is regarded as a failure. The program teaches volunteers that contracts are not always desirable or possible outcomes, but the feeling of personal failure is strong.

After facilitating several sessions where disputants go home without a contract, mediators may adjust their definition of failure. A half-hearted agreement is sometimes better than none. If the mediators can observe some positive change of attitude, that may be the measure of time well spent. "Negative agreements get me down. At least I hope that they agree to communicate." The people with a sense of mission feel this failure keenly.

The hardest thing is giving up on people, says one woman, ticking off the names of four infamous women who were disputants:

When I see that some resolution could be reached, but somebody just can't—either the pathetic characters who seem to have no resources or the ones who are so blocked that there is nothing you can do. All that energy and those possibilities and they can't be turned around from making things worse for themselves.

Intellectually, we tell ourselves that the results of a mediation session are unknowable, that sometimes an agreement is unwise, maybe unreachable, that a good mediator knows when to quit. Not surprisingly, in reality such sessions leave volunteers discouraged. Those with fragile self-confidence shy away from "difficult" mediations or request a "strong" mediator to work with them.

Mediators who have developed a high level of confidence may give the session scant thought beforehand, but for some the fears linger: "I have become accustomed to that 'Oh my God' feeling that I am walking into an unknown situation with an unknown person," says a long-time mediator. The disputants are strangers. Angry ones. Will somebody toss out a wild card? Can I handle an outburst? Will one party turn out to be there just for show?

I'm petrified that I'm going to say something wrong and botch the whole session. What if they get violent?

My concern is always will I have trouble removing them from the legal frame: Who is in the right? Who has the law on their side? I worry that the men there might get out of control physically—have a fist fight—or get tempted to. I don't worry about women.

The last case I did, I approached with a lot of dread. It seemed like a situation far gone. [After talking to the people by phone] I was afraid there were hidden agendas, too many unknowns. I don't want my own time wasted.

I'm afraid of losing control, something might blow up, get violent, you can't retrieve anything, can't keep them talking. Never had it happen, but I keep wondering.

These worries center on 1) violence and controlling the session and 2) making mistakes or being no help. During the session these fears may fall away. One mediator says she finds the beginning of the mediation difficult. "I don't feel effective until I personally connect with the people and figure out their perspective or language." Others agree that the unknown is harder to face than the actual people. Fears can be overemphasized here, however, and even the most anxious mediators look forward to each mediation.

As mediators gain practice, fears dissipate. Pragmatic and optimistic expectations temper each other. Mediators are less inclined to scale down their confidence in the disputants than to adjust their concepts of what mediation can do.

At the table

What do people experience when they are in the midst of mediating? In our interviews we asked people to describe what they think about and do before, during, and after the session. A mediation session is a three-ring circus. So much is happening at once. The descriptions gave a small glimpse into each mediator's way of thinking. Which arena of the circus receives the most attention? This perspective ties in directly with when and how a mediator choses to intervene. Here are some of the responses.

Eileen Stief:

I've never been scared. In the beginning there was a sort of excitement. Now, I'm just sure it's going to be interesting. I prefer not to imagine what might happen. I'd rather hear from the people themselves.

I have a split attention. Part is listening to the person who is talking and the other pays attention to what's happening with the other people around the table. I don't consciously look for things to do in the mediation. I get in and go with it. I'm looking for common points of interest and possible agreement, but I don't think in terms of solution till much further in. At first, I try to get a sense of them and their situation. And I'm trying to get them to talk to each other. During some sessions I do a lot of analyzing, especially if there are difficult people involved. It isn't a set procedure; it's an immediate response to need. I tend to be the one who remembers the picayune or procedural pieces and what parts are left to cover.

Afterward, I analyze it to death! What chance does the agreement have? With co-mediators I look at the balance of how we worked together. There's the element of gossip, too: "Couldn't you have died when she…!" The other thing is what we could have done differently.

Anne Richan:

Before a mediation, I read the records and preview the Opening Statement. That and the Uninterrupted Time are the easiest part. Listening and affirming people are not hard for me. I get nervous about where it'll go after that—the transition to problem-solving and having that be productive. When people are yelling, I am comfortable stepping in when they aren't operating within the structure. During Building the Agreement, I freeze: "God, what do I do now?" When I try something and it doesn't work I think "We're stuck and I'm supposed to be helping these people." It's better with another mediator there, someone to caucus with.

The latter part of the mediation is excitement and satisfaction. I don't have that much investment in a signed agreement. If I feel people come out further ahead than when they started, I can have the same kind of feeling.

Hugh Dickinson:

I always wonder about the clients. All I know are the names on a sheet and the rough outline of a situation. Will one dominate and the other sit back? Will someone be aggressive and talkative?

I get anxious about loss of control, particularly if they keep dragging in the past over and over. Sometimes I don't know whether to break in and nudge them towards the future or to let them play it out. I like the sense that the co-mediator and I are in league with each other, in sync. I respect the process and the belief that people should work things out freely. But there is a certain compulsion in me to keep things moving along. It's hard to let things run and not enforce structure too rigidly. I am always aware of each stage, whether they are venting about the past or talking over the future.

Being "on" means having to listen very intently and being careful about my entries into the discussion. After they leave, letting down my guard is a relief.

Pam Medina:

I go in with the attitude that the mediation can work. I used to make judgments beforehand, to be more aware of the person complaining because there was more information about that person's side.

During a session I really hear both sides. Other than keeping people quiet and structuring the issues I haven't had to use power, but I am in control. I think "I wouldn't have done that" or "Solve it this way." But I've been able to shut up and not give advice. I respect others. Anger used to frighten me, but I've learned that it is part of the process. In *all my mediations people have never gotten too angry to control. They stop themselves.*

   After: In closing I get them to take credit. I tell them "This worked because you were willing." I think, "I've survived this. I helped people find a direction."

The most interesting part of interviewing mediators was finding out how differently each person approached the work. Despite outward similarities in CDS mediator style and philosophy, everyone looked at the mountain from another vantage point. Where Hugh Dickinson watched the process of moving from past to future, Pam Medina saw people working through their anger, Eileen Stief watched for signs of common interest on which to build agreement, and Anne Richan worried about finding solutions. A mediator's particular focus colored each answer to the interview questions. It follows that CDS needs to be careful when a mediator reports a good or successful or disastrous session, as each person defines those words quite differently. When we look at personal benefit, that last motive mediators mention for continuing their work, these personal differences again determine what has been important for each individual.

What do mediators learn?

A 1980 CDS study found that most mediators reported having mediated outside CDS at least once. Some had intervened many times on the job. Nearly every parent reported using mediation skills on the front line at home. Only one remarked ruefully that she had been unsuccessful. "My kids can smell 'Mom's mediation stuff' a mile away." Even those who hadn't mediated much outside the program were pleased with the changes in their own approach to conflict.

Mediation has helped shape my philosophy, style, and beliefs. It helped me formulate ideas about how to handle interpersonal relationships. Mothers can often take over and dictate right and wrong in an argument. Now I sit them down and say, "What do you need? You talk it over." When people have problems I advise them to sit down and talk. I have become more forthright...and confident.

An older mother agrees that mediating has changed her behavior in the family: *I listen all the way to the bottom to find the ferment sending bubbles up through the whole mixture. I always tell my daughter and husband, "I'm going to shut up and listen till you're all done."*

I would have quit my co-op in a huff last year if I hadn't learned to confront people in non-destructive ways.

I learned to pick out those essential pieces I can do something about and leave the rest alone.

The woman turned to the other party and said, "Now that we've resolved this, don't think we're going to be friends. I still don't want to talk to you." I thought, "You can't be neighbors and not be friends! I want them to be friends." Then I caught myself and thought, "Wait a minute, that wasn't what they came for." Now I can step back and let people solve their own problems.

The experience has made me less volatile. I can look at a situation more impartially. I can tell people in my family that they are wrong without rousing resentment. As she speaks, the woman smiles and adds, *Also, I have started using strong language. I used to* hate *those words. Now, I get the greatest satisfaction from it!* She throws up her hands and laughs.

Professor Sally Engle Merry frequently remarks that community mediation seems to empower mostly the mediators. This is unquestionably true for CDS volunteers. The task is one which pushes and pulls people to change, sometimes in unexpected ways. Those changes are not just the development of new skills but the reshaping of attitudes. The woman who found herself looking down on disputants who didn't speak good English, for instance, and the mediator who realized that some neighbors didn't *want* to solve it her way both said their outlook had changed after those incidents. Even though most CDS volunteers mediate only a handful of times every year, person after person testifies to the difference it has made in their lives. As Ron Kraybill of the Mennonite Conciliation Service says: "Mediation will turn you around and not let you go."

Four: Outsider in the Middle

The intermediary role is an ancient one. Secrecy and respect surround the intervenor with an aura of wisdom and importance. This mythic character contrasts somewhat amusingly with the crisp and direct style of today's professional mediators and the "just folks" image put forward by community programs like CDS. Myths are not easily erased, however, and therefore our look at the mediator role during the session begins with the "outsider in the middle," its ramifications and variations. The perspective of the person who finds him or herself acting in that role follows, centering on the power available to the person in the position of mediator. Why are mediators allowed to intervene? What will disputants expect and permit?

The Outsider

When mediators step into a dispute, they evoke two powerful and seemingly contradictory images: that of *outsider* and that of the *middleman*. Since "image" is the key idea here, instead of explanations, we start with a list of pictures and emotional associations.

Outsider:

strange	safe
barbaric	unattached
innocent	foreign
unemotional	unbiased
unconnected	different
ignorant	knowledgeable

When do you ask a stranger into your house? Who is allowed into the back bedrooms—those private places where most freinds do not enter? Usually, it will only be a stranger with some credential: a doctor, perhaps, or an electrician. The mediator, too, comes into private rooms a stranger, a stranger with unfamiliar credentials but with the promise that some trouble might be fixed, even healed, a barrier removed. The door is opened eagerly by a few, warily by most.

Not all mediators enter a dispute as strangers, but even the most familiar mediator must stand a distance apart; otherwise she or he no longer serves as a facilitator, but becomes an active decision-maker. The distance required for the disputants to believe the mediator both safe and impartial is not always the same; some mediators must be more outside than others.

One step outside

In most daily conflict situations the mediator is only one step removed from the difficulty, as when a father helps two daughters negotiate use of a car, or a store manager calms down a defensive clerk arguing with an angry customer. Although we are not discussing informal intervention in this book, this stepping in from the outside after spotting trouble is a service that family, friends, and co-workers frequently offer each other. We accept the help not because it is necessarily skillful, but because we trust and understand the mediator enough to feel safe.

Two steps outside

When CDS first started, it planned to begin small offshoot programs serving different neighborhoods. The staff envisioned such projects using mediators who would be two steps removed from a dispute. These people would possibly know the disputants and certainly be familiar with the neighborhood, but they would not be connected with the particular conflict. This model is common among traditional village cultures where arguments are settled by an elder in the community who has the formal sanction of the group to push disputants toward emotional release and resolution. Ethnic and religious communities in the United States often retain this characteristic until assimilation or antagonism splinters their tight-knit structure. (Auerbach, 1983; Yaffe, 1972) Several programs, most notably the San Francisco Community Boards, have successfully organized dispute settlement services with mediators who belong to the same neighborhood as the disputants.

In suburban Philadelphia this model has proved unrealistic for several reasons. First, mediators cannot represent the consensus of a community because the mixed population unites on very few issues. Take the "good neighbor" ideal, the most persistent common value mentioned by mediators and disputants, and ask what "good" means. Some will tell you "minding your own business," while others will say "being friends, helping each other out." Second, in suburban communities with such varied backgrounds and outlooks, mediators are unlikely to push their own values, and when they do, the disputants are more annoyed than shamed! Wide differences in social status make the issue of values even more strained. Third, middle-class mediators have a difficult time recruiting working-class colleagues and equal difficulty bringing in disputes from wealthier neighborhoods. Therefore, matching disputants with mediators from down the block is unusual; in half of Delaware County the disputants are missing, in the other half there are few available mediators.

Our mediators are uneasy about formally facilitating in sessions with people they know, even when the disputants claim not to care. The personal connection, no matter how casual, adds another dimension. Mediators report feeling self-conscious about the possibility of bias or perceived imbalance. When they intervene in disputes among their friends or in the workplace, their own reputation is at stake. Our training sessions have also made mediators cautious about standing too close to a dispute, lest their impartiality or credentials as outsiders be questioned.

Three steps outside

The next degree of outsideness is the mediator who comes from a similar background but is a stranger to that community. A teacher with children of his own who mediates between a parent and teacher in another district, for instance, might understand both the outward circumstances and the inward values of the disputants. This combination saves us the discomfort of admitting a need for help to our immediate community but gives the security of a sympathetic peer. A stranger who is one-of-us; what a powerful combination of familiarity and impartiality!

Mediators find that when they follow up a case by phone or meet disputants later on the street, the response is on occasion embarrassed, abrupt. The mediator reminds them of a time best forgotten, of a time when they had to ask an outsider for help. Crisis counselors report similar reactions from some clients in public. In this suburban society, the dividing line between outside help and taking care of one's own problems is sharp. Although seeking help from outsiders is increasingly accepted, for many people, bringing private matters to a stranger remains tinged with an assumption of personal failure. In emotional mediations, the stance of strangers seems to help the disputants feel safe and the mediators more certain of their role.

Four steps outside

Most CDS mediations are even one step further outside. We have noted that the mediators and disputants come not just from different communities but from different social and economic backgrounds. How this class division affects the number of disputants willing to contact the CDS office or changes the outcome of a mediation we cannot document. Surely the self-confident "I can solve this myself" realization is diminished when the disputants find themselves once more being helped by an agency run for them by middle-class volunteers. One woman from Darby spoke frankly to a CDS staffperson one day. She said she would much rather go to a local store-front agency in Darby where the staff talked like she did and she knew they understood than go to the county seat where agency people were cool and everyone dressed up. She felt looked down upon.

Five steps outside

Larger disputes may be handled by another degree of outsider: the specialist mediator from another region. The old joke about an expert being someone more than 100 miles from home is a telling comment on the power of the outsider. Of course that person may not know anything more than the person next door. But as an outsider, the expert brings, at a minimum, a different point of view. By travelling a long distance, an expert shows clients that their concern is important. And it means that she or he will vanish again and no one has to worry about gossip nor about hurting the consultant's feelings when advice is ignored! Labor negotiations are the most familiar example of a situation where mediators are imported.

The concept of the outsider, then, is a continuum. At the familiar end, the mediators can represent the moral and social concerns of the disputant's community. They know the nuances of accepted behavior and values. Mediators are more likely to grasp the situation quickly and know its realistic solutions. They may have a second-nature knowledge of what mediation approaches will work. The danger here is emotional involvement in the dispute which can cloud a mediator's judgment and inhibit the disputants. At the stranger end of the spectrum, the mediator's stake in the terms of agreement and affinity for one party's position lessens. The security of privacy for the disputants is greater, and they are more likely to believe the mediators to be impartial.

Coming in as an outsider, the mediator is fresh prey. Here is a new person for the embattled sides to win over! During Uninterrupted Time, people pour out their stories hoping that the stranger with authority will side with them. "I know my kid's no angel, but you are a parent, you know that kids'll be kids." "Can't you see how I feel working with that kind of rudeness every day?" They are quick to notice a mediator's approval or disagreement. The mediator who shows it soon loses the disputants' confidence. The outsider has taken a position inside the circle. In a similar position is the mediator who wants to be liked as one-of-the-gang. This person will want to sympathize, to nod understandingly, to speak of his or her own similar experiences. The mediator is then in the awkward position of an outsider trying to become an insider. The mediator becomes neither, losing control of the mediation as soon as the role of outsider is abdicated.

CDS believes that effective mediators come into a session free from strong emotional investment in the conflict issues. They come clothed in neutrality, competence, and authority which disputants, in CDS's experience, rarely challenge. They are free, too, from responsibility for decisions made at the table; once the parties leave, the mediators will be strangers again. Any mediator who chooses to become an insider with disputants forfeits these crucial strengths. The advantage of the outsider is one of disputants' perception, not of official power.

Coming and going. Such one-time or limited interaction is a key to the success of an outsider. Disputants know this mediator will not become involved in their lives. Like travellers on the train who spill out their family troubles, they know that they can risk intimacy with this random person who will debark at the next station and disappear down the platform stairs back into anonymity.

The Middle

Mediators are never complete outsiders, of course. No human being is completely strange to another. Most mediators have known firsthand the problems which come to the mediation table: family strain, betrayal by a friend, arguments over money, loud and unresponsive neighbors, or the bitter end of a love relationship. We are all bonded to each other by these common experiences.

These connections are important to many disputants. They want to know whether the mediators have teenagers too, for instance, or whether they have ever lived in a row house. Since one assumes disputants respond better to mediators who seem to empathize with them, the mediator's other image as "person-in-the-middle" is a vital counterbalance to the cooler detachment associated with outsiders.

The word mediator derives from the Latin verb *mediare* which means "to be in the middle." Probably this concept has always been central to the role of peacemaker. A mediator who wades confidently into the center of an emotional and confusing session provides the stable point for the negotiations. Messages and feelings go through the mediator's clearinghouse or at the least are tempered by that central presence. They hold the reins of the process. From that middle vantage point a mediator can presumably see each side's position with less distortion than the negotiators themselves can.

The range of roles a middle person takes on is suggested by the following array of *middle* and *between* images. Note how much easier it is to picture the middle roles in terms of objects rather than in terms of the emotional associations which characterized the outsider role. This matches the practical, active position of the person in the middle. Here it is not so much who you are—or appear to be—but what you *do.*

In the middle:

fulcrum of a see-saw	data processor
telephone wire	the norm
hub of a wheel	half-way point
switchboard	electric adaptor
referee	buffer
matchmaker	fence/wall
straw target bull's eye	wedge
volleyball net	dodge-ball survivor
peephole	interpreter
filter	mail carrier
shuttle	

Some of these roles are used often: mediators act as filters, for instance, when they screen out nasty remarks, or as referees during a shouting match. Other roles are pushed by the disputants: they may want the mediator to act as a shuttle so they can avoid an emotional scene, or perhaps they will use the mediator as a target for frustrations.

An impartial person in the center also acts as a barrier. This calms the disputants' fears of being verbally or physically attacked. It also seems, in CDS's experience, to prevent volatile people from resorting to physical violence. Usually when a session begins, the disputants look anywhere but at each other. They tell everything to the mediator as if they only grudgingly admit the other's presence. For those who dislike confrontation, it is easier to say, "That woman has lied to me twice about this," than to look her in the eye and call her a liar.

Like the policeman directing rush hour traffic through an intersection, mediators can, by standing firmly in the middle, control the direction of the session so that people channel their energies more productively than in previous encounters without a third party. The mediator conveys ideas, deflects abusive remarks, and works to open up the thinking of all sides. Everything is funneled through that central hub until enough trust is established for direct discussion.

The middle is instinctively given the position of authority. As we saw, this expectation of control is one of the keys to a mediator's power and, conversely, is one of the roadblocks to reaching effective agreements. Ideally the mediator enters a dispute from the outside by gaining the parties' confidence, then moves to hold the central position of power until the disputants are able to take over direction of their problem-solving discussion. The mediator moves into the background here. After monitoring the final details of agreement, she or he relinquishes all power by leaving the center and becoming an unconnected outsider once again.

Mediator Power

One of the puzzles of the mediator role is why the temporary position of outsider-in-the-middle holds such power. At first glance, there is so much community mediators cannot do. They can't force someone to reveal information or to tell the truth. They cannot even make either party attend the session, much less comply with the agreement afterward. Where are the robes and the rules, the discipline and enforcement? Without the hallmarks of authority, the mediator appears weak.

Who can blame disputants who are skeptical about submitting to seemingly ineffectual mediation? When disputing parties believe that they can work things out themselves, a third party seems an unnecessary intrusion. If they cannot talk without yelling at each other, then they search for someone strong enough to keep the other party in line. A voluntary mediation program does not look promising.

Regardless of initial appearances, mediators do wield power. They are able to affect people's actions and decisions. The majority of disputants follow the mediators' directions with little protest. This mediator power derives from both real and perceived authority. In other words, the ability to mediate depends partly on knowing how to conduct a session and partly on the respect disputants hold for the position of mediator.

Real authority. As the person-in-the-middle, the mediator has several strengths. These rest on the structure of the mediation session and somewhat on individual skill and personality. Control of process is the keystone of these aspects of "real" authority:

control of process	some control of
ability to persuade	emotional levels
ability to coerce	expertise in the subject
mediation experience	under dispute

Perceived authority. Real authority comes from the third party's actions; perceived authority accompanies the outsider-mediator through the door. It is based on several specific qualities:

the role (expert, outsider, authority)	appearance of impartiality
	who you are (what sex,
confidence	age, race, profession)

Mediators may use or resist the disputants' deference to these perceived characteristics. Nonetheless, when we face disputants we are players in a larger game of perceptions and values in which we cannot make the rules.

Controlling the process

First and foremost, mediators control the process. Every other power in the "real authority" list is used to maintain or further it. This control means the ability to set the agenda and to change it arbitrarily. The mediators direct events at the table: the pace, the methods, the number and timing of caucuses. As a last resort, they can terminate the session, a fact which can be a useful reminder during a difficult mediation. Control means defining and enforcing rules. It means requiring people to speak or insisting on silence.

Volatile disputants are often caught off balance because those rules are unfamiliar to most of them. When an argumentative disputant was asked for the fourth time to wait for his turn, he protested, "I thought this was supposed to be give and take." The mediator responded that this was true *after* Uninterrupted Time.

The man nodded obediently and said nothing more until the Exchange. She knew the rules and he didn't.

Mediators know what will happen, they have seen other situations work out before. The neutral ground belongs to them. "They've been through the process and they know that it works even though the people who are in it at the moment can't *imagine* that they're going to come out with anything," says one mediator.

Controlling the process is distinct from telling the parties what they should negotiate. CDS insists that the content of the dispute rests *solely* with the participants. They alone decide to reveal information, to compromise, to determine issues, to leave or to come to agreement.

Skill and knowledge

Trainees often remark that mediation is a much more powerful skill than they expected—and more difficult! Any mediation session can follow a dozen branching paths; mediators must continually choose between one approach and another. Will a separate meeting with Jon break momentum? Do I press Mr. Gallagher for more information to "unstick" this problem? The mediator who chooses with a sure touch appears less tentative, more confident, and more in control.

As anyone who often sits through committee meetings knows, the person facilitating strongly affects both the mood and the outcome of a discussion. Setting an appropriate tone can be critical. A quiet, reassuring approach can help anxious and emotional disputants; for high voltage disputes an unshakably level voice can cut through effectively; others respond well to tough, fast-paced facilitation. Besides creating an appropriate atmosphere, the experienced mediator has a range of options which lead a discussion in one direction or another, thereby determining which issues receive attention and which get tabled. One such tactic might be picturing the "ideal" future, another could be asking each side to summarize the other's position. When disputants observe that these suggestions actually help, they are likely to allow mediators more leeway (power) to direct the session.

A mediator's expertise and access to information enhance facilitation skill and self-confidence and, therefore, power. Not only do the mediators know more about mediation, they also know more about community conflicts. Actions which surprise and infuriate neighbors are usually old stories to CDS. Mediators have seen several successful solutions to problems with common driveways, or division of household responsibilities, or local vandalism. They know what happens to disputes in court. The parties also know that mediators may have more information about the other side. Showing such knowledge is one way to establish credibility—that bedrock of power—with disputants.

Expertise undergirds the mediator's ability to persuade. The feeling of being trapped in a bad situation appears to open participants to new ideas from outside. Mediators' persuasion can rest on agent-of-reality logic and information: "If you don't drop charges, the other party may not agree to this contract at all. How eager are you to recoup damages?" Persuasion relies too on the power to bring out or suppress emotional responses. One CDS mediator has such empathy that her warmth unfreezes the iciest of disputants. Another uses anger to good effect: "Look, if you are going to carry on like this, we might as well go home." Morality, too, has power for the persuader (that is if mutual morality can be found!), as when a mediator appeals to a party's sense of fairness or to their stated desire to act in a "Christian" manner.

Confidence

A sense of assurance that disputants can work things out—one mediator calls it "blind faith"—is one of the most valuable contributions a mediator makes to the session. The third party's view from outside spots the ray of light through the tunnel. After all, they have driven the road before. That confidence in the mediation process and people's ability to get through it is a powerful impetus for disputants who have been looking at an impenetrable mountain of boulders for too long. CDS volunteers almost always need to offer reassurances. "I know this is difficult, but you already have several places of agreement here. I think some of these other things can be worked out."

Invariably, in interviews and workshops the question comes, "What if people get violent?" Here is where the power of confident expectation is most critical. Many cases have a background of fights, threats, guns and knives. Yet CDS in nine years has had no incidents of physical violence during a mediation session. While every mediator must prepare to handle such an occurrence (other programs have reported violent incidents), the main deterrent seems to be the atmosphere of the negotiations. A tone is set from the beginning which does not explicitly forbid such behavior; it simply assumes that people will act with propriety, that anger will be expressed in words—not acted out. Disputants take their cues from the demeanor of the mediator. A dramatic example of this occurred when CDS mediated a gang dispute. The police warned CDS not to meet with these dangerous young men unless an armed officer was present. The mediators declined that advice and met privately with the teenagers and their parents. "They were docile as lambs," said the mediators afterward. The respectful atmosphere had prevented the habitual violent confrontations.

Perceived authority

The appearance of impartiality is essential to maintaining the confidence of the disputants. The disputants' antennae are acutely attuned to the mediator's perceived fairness. Since our discussion of the outsider-in-the-middle has laid out the different ideas of what constitutes sufficient separation from the dispute, here we simply note the word *appearance*. True neutrality is probably never possible. A mediator can feel strongly biased, yet still behave impartially, that is without openly taking sides.

The image of authority. It is hard to underestimate the importance of the mediator's *role*. When we talk about mediators as outsiders or as persons-in-the-middle we are speaking of roles, not individuals. The role of authority figure is also a source of power separate from personality and skill. It influences the way disputants respond and, as we see in the next chapter, also shapes the way mediators act. This is one reason why very different CDS mediators bring disputants to satisfactory resolutions. Another indication of the importance of role is that the parties do not address the mediators by name; they are anonymous authorities.

Often disputants picture the situation as a private courtroom. Mediators are invested with the power of a judge. Disputants, like all of us, have grown up with judges as models of public dispute settlement and with lawyers and defendants as models for the aggrieved behavior. Many come to mediation primed to enact this drama. Evidence is piled on the table. Parties interrupt each other in eagerness to set the mediators straight. Without accepted and public images of mediators, the disputants equate mediators with a known authority role. It is unusual to find a disputant who accepts the mediator as an ordinary person who happens to know how to facilitate in conflict situations.

Whether or not mediators enjoy that ascribed authority, they do benefit from the disputants' belief in their power. The respect or even fear accorded to someone in an authority position helps mediators set the boundaries of acceptable behavior during a mediation.

Another kind of perceived authority stems not from what you

know or what you can do, but from who you are or, more accurately, who you appear to be. Probably age is at least initially the most critical factor. Age means life experience, and the disputants generally respect older mediators; they seem to give weight to their requests and suggestions. Likewise, teenagers seem to respond better to young mediators. Race, sex, class, and whether or not the mediator is a parent may make a more subtle difference, but CDS has found no evidence for any of these characteristics particularly determining outcome. From time to time someone will request a certain kind of mediator. Presumably having a third party of similar background promotes feelings of trust and the hope that someone like them will sympathize with their point of view. In any case, disputants by and large do not appear to care who the mediators are. The outsider's anonymity is more important than empathy.

How Much Control?

The mediator and the negotiating parties play back and forth in many combinations: directing, demanding, persuading, acquiescing, and insisting. Two opposing questions about mediator responsibility arise. 1) How can I maintain enough control to help these people reach agreement, or at least to make sure that no one is hurt? 2) How can the disputants take the lead in resolving this situation?

Controlling but not controlling, influencing but not influencing. Insisting but making no decisions. We claim to be leaders in resolving tough community conflicts but we will not force a compromise. Mediators supposedly direct the dispute resolution process yet insist that power lies with the people involved. Isn't there a basic contradiction, or at least, a host of obstacles, in giving disputants wide rein if you want to get somewhere?

The CDS concept of dispute settlement holds the mediators responsible for using their skill and authority to build the confidence and capability of the disputants. But what happens in a tense session where reaching agreement is urgent? In mediations where mediator and disputants disagree sharply on what is fair or rational? The mediator has to deal with the people who are unable to listen, the ones who can't explain their own thoughts and feelings, much less play with possible solutions. The interaction of mediator and disputant power is necessarily less neat than CDS would like.

Consider the CDS mediation over a man who had threatened his neighbors with a gun. From his first sentence during Uninterrupted Time, he had maintained his right to shoot anyone who invaded his property. The mediators, barred from acting as lawyers, could not discuss the legality of this view, so they tried several ways to get this man to comprehend the neighborhood's understandable disquiet. Finally, they forced the man to agree to allow his neighbors to walk on his grass. Contrary to all CDS policy, the mediators had taken charge of the *content* of the contract. He agreed reluctantly and signed. No further incidents were ever reported after that mediation. Did the mediators overstep their bounds?

Openness, a strong value for most CDS mediators, is another area where using pressure is a sensitive matter. The mediator wanted fifteen-year-old Steve to tell his parents what living arrangements he would like. Steve would not talk. How can Steve learn to negotiate if he can't explain what he wants? But perhaps Steve was silent because he couldn't explain to his mother why he wanted to leave home—perhaps because her new husband hated him?

Use of techniques and influence must be considered in context. Encouraging trust, for instance, is generally believed to be helpful in a mediation. Usually mediators approve when someone displays genuine emotion. Participants are led to talk about the future and to leave past grievances behind. But in some circumstances those moves may put a disputant at risk. A simple question like "Steve, how could living at home be happier for you?" can be empowering if Steve can think of specifics, but if Steve insists he wants to leave home, that same question might be easily translated as "We adults think living at home would be better for you."

Normally, the mediator does not walk as thin a tightrope as this discussion might indicate. Disputants are remarkably tough-skinned and resilient; if the mediator makes a false move, the parties often keep talking as if nothing happened. When they are ready to try something new, the mediator's remarks will register. One mediator, for instance, said to a particularly unreasonable disputant, "But it's *her* house, she has the right to do what she wants in her own house." The man did not acknowledge that she was talking until a few minutes later when she began to discuss something he was ready to concede.

When we look at these examples of tension between maintaining mediator control and empowering the disputant to eventually take that control, three perspectives are useful. First, the basic division between the mediator's responsibility for *process* and the negotiating parties' responsibility for the content and *outcome* of the session is still useful. Our mediators report this helps them draw a clear line between appropriate and inappropriate intervention. "I remind myself during a session that...this is not my problem. I have no responsibility for what they say, think, feel, or do. They don't have to come out with an agreement," explains one man.

Second, the mediator is not trying to take away power from a strong party so much as to shore up the disadvantaged one in order for more equal negotiations to take place. The mediators use their own power to educate, to break open and hold space for the less powerful to speak and to be heard. They ride herd on dominant parties—insisting on a pace and a courtesy which allows the other parties room to negotiate on more equal terms. The goal is to increase participants' skills and understanding, not to pare one side down to fit the other's size.

The third perspective lies in viewing power as an ability to focus conflict, to choose, to act, to persuade others to act. It is *not* a finite quantity parceled out between each party and the mediators. Enabling others does not mean giving up your own portion of strength or abdicating leadership. Some of the power mediators exert—by using the ability to be objective, for example—cannot be given or taken away even if the mediator wishes to be less influential. When a disputant suddenly sees the situation in a clearer light, the mediator's objectivity has spread, not transferred!

Mediator responsibility

Disputes can have major consequences. During one session an employee was fired by his friend, the manager. Several hours after a mediation over a neighborhood dog dispute, one woman left her husband. We cannot take responsibility for drastic action which grows out of long-term dissatisfactions, but we sometimes are in a position to push something over the cliff or to help people take a step toward solid ground.

We ask disputants to make themselves vulnerable. Frankness seems to be important in reaching even the most unfriendly of agreements. We hope their commitment to the agreed contract is not only rational but emotional. To usefully plan for the future, they have to reveal part of themselves to people who have angered and hurt them in the past. What can be done must be done judiciously and thoughtfully.

We know what a mediator's limits are; we know our strengths. How can we make sure that we discipline ourselves to work within those boundaries? CDS uses no official code of mediator ethics, and in North America, programs are just beginning to develop such written codes of appropriate behavior. FSP training delineates a number of ethical guidelines. When a new situation arises, mediators habitually consult each other, with much weight given to CDS staff opinion.

Handling power responsibly, even with guidelines, is nevertheless a matter of quick situational decisions. What should the CDS mediator have said when a mother promised that if her teenage daughter (who was present at the mediation) caused any more trouble, she would beat her out on the front lawn so the neighbor could see that she was being disciplined? How should mediators handle allegations of abuse or alcoholism made during private caucus? When are mediators responsible for considering the interests of an unrepresented party?

As outsiders, we remind ourselves to go gently; we do not have to live with the consequences of what happens at the table, but the disputants do. As persons-in-the-middle, we push ourselves to facilitate with skill and sometimes with toughness. The people at the table deserve our best efforts. The responsibility is a brief one, yet for two hours it is all-encompassing. The intensity of that concentration of mediator authority, skill, and knowledge combines with the disputants' desire to settle; the results affirm that through the intercession of an outsider in the middle something powerful has happened.

Five: Shaping the Mediator Role

Many currents have helped shape the individual CDS volunteer's approach to the third party role. What models contribute to our working images of that mediator role? In what ways do mediators' backgrounds influence their style and their purpose?

First, let's digress a moment to an imaginary scene....

Role Models: Limits and Uses

Wednesday Night at the Movies. On the TV, the defendant's attorney is humiliating a lying witness with fast and tricky questions. The other lawyer jumps up. "Objection! Your honor, he's badgering the witness." The judge looks blandly over his glasses. "Overruled." The questioning begins again. "Now it's important that we get all the facts straight here."

From the couch, Mark lets out a yelp. "Mom, Janey's kicking me again!"

"Jane, you go work upstairs. Next time, it's no TV for either of you. For a whole week."

"Mark's just sore because he and Jeff got into another fight before school and Mrs. Tanaka yelled at them and they both got detention."

"LIAR!"

"Can't you two just talk like decent human beings instead of pinching and tattling and I don't know what?" Dad tried to sound reasonable. "Look, why don't we discuss this right now? If you kids could set up a homework schedule...."

* * *

In a given day we watch many ways of intervening in conflicts. Today, Mark has observed third parties 1) intimidate, 2) advocate, 3) protect, 4) invoke law, 5) determine facts, 6) separate disputants, 7) scold, 8) punish, 9) attempt to persuade disputants to talk, and 10) give advice.

Every mediator brings pieces of these images to the mediation table. Training helps sort through the appropriateness of different ways to approach dispute settlement, but in the thick of a tense or unexpected situation, it is easy for the mediator to fall back on the more ingrained models of a parent, or judge, or counselor.

Direct models are hard to come by. In North America it is difficult to witness a mediator at work. Labor, consumer, and international negotiations occur behind closed doors. There is no custom of settling personal disputes through formal mediation. Furthermore, talking things out, while sensible, is regrettably lacking in drama. What TV show would pass up the fireworks of a trial for a few hot minutes of Uninterrupted Time during which no "bad guy" emerges but everyone agrees to work things through? Without an ingrained sense of their role, mediators must still rely heavily on their own common sense (that product of personal experiences) and their accumulated images of other kinds of dispute settlement.

Other third party roles offer a mixed bag of lessons for the mediator. In each type of intervention we find techniques and attitudes of time-tested value. Other parts must be cut away because they violate key principles such as impartiality or because they reach beyond the permissible scope of mediation.

The following section summarizes some of the pitfalls and advantages of imitating these third party models. We base our thoughts on the stereotyped images, not the individual characteristics of a real counselor or parent or boss, because it is this mental file of generalized roles which forms a common base for people raised in this society.

Advocate

But Mrs. Simmons, said Henry, a mediator in one of our training roleplays, *boys need play time and a chance to make friends, don't you think? Joe has a right to decide how to spend his free time.* Joe burst in. *See Grandmom, I told you that you were being unfair.*

Henry has just stepped into a swamp. He saw the underdog in the mediation, young Joe, knuckling under to his Grandmother's demands without protest. If Joe didn't get some free time to himself, troubles would certainly continue. Besides, the boy was fifteen and old enough to make his own decisions. But when Henry decided to support Joe, he ended up arguing Joe's case *for* him, based on his own values—hardly the act of a neutral facilitator. If Henry is very lucky, Mrs. Simmons might respond "You're probably right. I just get nervous about his friends." But more likely, she will hold her own. "Well, if you know so much about raising kids, you do it. In my house, I make the rules."

The three dangers of advocacy are, first, alienating the other side and losing one's impartial standing; second, unwittingly bringing one's own values and priorities into someone else's situation; and third, showing an impatient "here, let me do it" attitude which discourages weaker parties from bargaining for themselves.

On the other hand, as professor and mediator James Laue's writings remind us, mediators are responsible for equalizing negotiating power as much as possible. Henry might have been able to make the same point to Mrs. Simmons this way: "Let's look at what you both think is a realistic amount of free time for Joe to have each week, time which he could spend more or less as he pleases. Joe, you first. What would be okay with you?" Joe now can serve the ball in the next round. He is asked to think and talk for himself.

Many of CDS's original mediators volunteered in a local youth advocacy program, but staffperson Eileen Stief was strict from the outset: "Pigeon and duck, you can't be both at once." In a touchy situation where just clarifying one person's position to the other can be misconstrued as taking sides, the mediator has the sensitive task of helping every person negotiate effectively without appearing to favor only one party's rights or suggestions.

On a wider scale, CDS members disagree about whether mediators should be allowed to promote certain groups or ideas. These are the volunteers who carry a self-conscious sense of mission whom we mentioned earlier: feminists interested in strengthening women's relationships with each other and Christians who want disputants to experience divine reconciliation. Others want to promote better parenting, or believe that most disputants should go to counseling. When a mediator is strongly committed to such goals, it is hard to resist overt attempts to reform disputants. Often, the best answer has been for mediators to avoid cases which tempt them to cross that line.

Advocates also provide a positive model. Surely, mediators want to adopt the advocate's attention to what is fair and the skill in shoring up the negotiating position of weaker disputants. The mediators' sense of mission can serve them in good stead, as long as they keep the best interests of all parties in mind.

Lawyer

You know she does have a right to park in her own driveway.

Would you characterize your relations to Tom before this incident as satisfactory?

The trial lawyer's art is verbal and directive, at times intimidating. Parties are molded into adversaries fighting to win a contest. Lawyers are trained to zero in on issues which fall into definable categories where specific actions can be judged. Facts are uncovered to find fault. If there is bargaining or problem-solving, the attorney speaks for the client. (Remember, we are talking about general media images here!)

Mediators, on the other hand, regard disputes as complex circumstances with mutual fault and indeterminate facts. People are expected to think for themselves, to cooperate in finding agreement. Cross-examining may help determine the facts of a case, but in a mediation, pinpointing what happened is usually a one-way alley running the wrong direction. The aim is not to reconstruct or to blame but to reorient disputants towards what future changes they want. And in cross-examining, guess who gets to do all the hard work? Yes, the mediator, of course. The disputants only have to respond. To take on the cloak of lawyer is to shoulder the responsibility to set matters right.

Disputants strain to draw mediators into expounding the law. They ask about anything from dog ordinances to civil rights. Although community mediators may want background information about relevant laws and ordinances, finding out the law is solely the disputants' responsibility. The community mediator is *not* a lawyer and must never give legal advice. To do so contradicts the intent to provide a mechanism for resolution outside the courts. And, without membership in the Bar it is illegal.

On the positive side, lawyering rubs shoulders with advocacy. Devotion to the ideal of justice is important, especially since disputants often enter a mediation wondering if they will be forced into an unfair agreement. Lawyers also cope easily with anger, intimidation, tears, and fears. Like priests and counselors, little fazes them; they have heard worse.

Judge

A judge can decide what the court believes is the truth. He or she can declare an action to be right or wrong. Disputants who are out to prove their case want to pull mediators into this role. However, any judgment by a mediator is, by definition, unfounded; mediators do not have the training, the evidence, or the authority to make anything more than an educated guess. Any mediator who puts on the judge's cloak of majesty and air of final wisdom is making false promises to the disputants. They may believe they are receiving due legal process. The mediators' opinions may be accepted as the one correct answer or even as the law.

Mediators must pick their way through conflicting evidence and loud accusations without pausing long to weigh the merits of anybody's story. If refraining from open judgment is difficult, quieting one's voice of internal judgment requires greater vigilance. These thoughts sneak out indirectly through advice: "Maybe you could call Gail's mother instead of disciplining her directly," and through value statements: "He can hire and fire anytime he likes if he owns the business."

In other respects judges are good models for mediators. They are trained to listen attentively to all sides. They are committed to giving each person a fair hearing. A TV judge is often portrayed as unflappable, invoking the rules of procedure to overcome momentary disruptions. A sense of order and due process gives a courtroom session a dignity and importance beyond the individual person of the judge; likewise mediators learn to use the process as a ritual which has power beyond their own personalities.

Finally, a judge represents the judgment of a community, a role which places disputes in the context of their effect on other uninvolved people or more broadly on "society." Mediators also stand for the values of a community, specifically the desire to see people get along and learn to solve their own problems cooperatively.

Parent

"But Daddy, Edith hit me first!"

Parenting probably requires more dispute settlement skill than any other job on earth. Parents quickly learn to see the wider situation, not just the immediate quarrel: Edith may have hit, but Garrett broke her bike yesterday, and both of them have had a hard time with studies lately. Even on days when parents intervene roughly, unwisely, or unfairly, their children appeal to them out of faith that their parents care what happens to them.

For good mediators, like parents, what happens to the disputants matters. They want to see the tears dried. They want to help straighten things out. They reach out to understand and to empathize. However, the mediators cannot afford to pick up other elements of the parents' role: deciding what is going to happen, distributing blame and punishment. Mediators also cannot risk those threats and hurtful remarks which parents may make when pushed beyond their patience. Most difficult of all, CDS tries not to teach any values except those thought to help the success of the session and the maintenance of the agreement (the value of talking things out, for instance). The habits of preaching and teaching die hard; most CDS mediators slip into that mode from time to time. This happens because, as we have said, some mediators believe this to be their function, and partly because we are only semi-conscious of the many values we hold and espouse.

Boss

You can bring a horse to the trough, but you can't make it drink, goes the saying. How often unsuccessful mediations feel like this! The solution is right there, and the disputants will not budge. Trainees often fall into the trap of maneuvering roleplay disputants into "logical" solutions. Determined to draw up that contract, they sweat and push until they have something on paper. When they are done, they have constructed a reasonable agreement for their mock disputants—with no idea if it will last.

Sitting outside a dispute can quickly change to sitting above it like a judge on the bench or a boss behind the big desk. The boss moves in and tells people what they are going to do. "Obviously, Mr. Frisch will have to pay the damages. Now what will you offer in return?" Stereotype bosses also use their position in the system to compel action. "You realize I'm going to have to tell the Board that you have not tried to reach any agreement."

In real mediations, these tactics may shove people towards true agreement. Often disputants expect to be shoved. That CDS asks mediators to hold back from forcing disputants into contracts is more a matter of commitment to empowerment than a rejection of aggressiveness as unworkable.

On the other hand, the firmness of the boss role can be essential when the mediation session needs a tight rein. Disputants are forced to tackle the issues and find *practical* solutions. The boss-style mediator confronts without qualms the foot-draggers and name-callers, the interrupters and the "innocents." A boss energizes a problem-solving session with the conviction that a situation can be, must be ironed out. He or she will not settle for anything less than full effort.

Counselor/Social Worker

The counselor's ability to understand why people are acting as they do, especially under the stress of conflict, is an essential third party skill. The mediators may need to know whether or not a disputant is hiding something. How hard should they press the person to talk? It may help to know if the problems mainly stem from one disputant's personal troubles or to know whether a disputant can be expected to stick to an agreement. A counselor has learned to analyze who in the group holds the power, where the process is blocked, how to introduce problem-solving. Much of mediators' and counselors' work is second-guessing the disputants.

Counselors and social workers generally share CDS mediators' objectives and attitudes. They want to help people cope with their lives better. They value the art of listening well. The purpose is to help people initiate change in their lives. With such closely overlapping goals and skills, it is not surprising that even experienced mediators have trouble explaining where mediation crosses into counseling territory.

After a session, the mediators usually analyze the people the way a counselor diagnoses a client: She needs to feel respected, he obviously doesn't trust his in-laws.... Such talk is fun and interesting, but usually irrelevant. The mediators do not have enough information or training to accurately assess motives or character.

Even when the analysis is on target, mediation is limited to changing specific behavior. Mediators cannot revise beliefs and attitudes. Some disputants come to mediation because they specifically do *not* want counseling. CDS mediators are asked to honor the limits people set for what they are willing to undergo.

Disputants often claim the other party is "sick," a remark to take lightly. If CDS took this remark seriously, it would facilitate few mediations! In fact, a disputant may be troubled or sick by most people's standards yet be quite capable of coming to and abiding by an agreement. Occasionally, people who are unable to negotiate at all appear in a session. Usually every agency in town has seen them. With the exception of such disputants (and you soon know if you have one!), the issue of the participants' mental health seems best left completely out of a session.

Besides the temptation to delve into personalities, the mediator using a counseling or social work model has to be cautious of the desire to make everything better. These people have come for help. We address a few pieces of their need and send them home with larger problems untouched. The limited and often temporary nature of dispute settlement intervention is hard for many mediators. And many of us have people who stay in our thoughts long afterward: the confused ones, the brave ones, the ones whose lives seem dark and narrow. We want to help more, but as mediators we can't.

Friend

The go-between friend is someone who can be trusted with a delicate and private mission, someone to whom the disputant can speak frankly. "Tell Bob I didn't mean it. It was just a mistake." "Bob, I don't think you need to worry. Marie says...."

The friendly emissary often has a strong wish to straighten matters out between two other friends. The words and emotions of each party are softened and carefully remolded in the telling. This person often knows well the situation and its history. Disputants may compromise to keep the friendship not of the adversary but of the intermediary. As such, the go-between has a good chance of bringing about some resolution.

Mediators need a go-between's tact and empathy, especially when convincing disputants to try out a mediation session. Some explosive community disputes are handled better by go-betweens than CDS-type mediators. In one case a whole street had caused an uproar for several years. The man at the center of the difficulties could not understand his neighbors' point of view enough to stop screaming and start negotiating; mediation was impossible. CDS facilitated neighborhood meetings and private meetings with the man instead. As they went from house to house they reworded and interpreted.

This sort of shuttle diplomacy avoids the sparks of direct encounter. As with other third party roles we have discussed, the go-between carries the burden of finding a way out. CDS's goal of giving people practice in working through interpersonal conflict explains the program's usual reluctance to act as messengers unless it promises to lead eventually to direct confrontation.

Here in the USA where friends are quickly made, people warm to a friendly mediator and do not seem suspicious. If the mediator takes on more pieces of the friendship role, however, the disputants turn away. Sharing personal stories, for instance, crosses the line into familiarity. "Yes, I know what you mean. Our cat used to bother our neighbors too." The mediator is asking the disputants to be interested in him or her as a friend would be. "Oh, really? Did they harass you about it?" The disputant, however, is concerned with his or her immediate problem, not with the opinions and feelings of the mediator. The friendly offering of sympathy or touching someone may also alienate one or all of the disputants. Confidences are shared with a mediator as nameless outsider, not as friend. The image of impartiality is ultimately more important for a mediator than perceived friendliness.

Putting the pieces together

Personal style develops from the interaction of third party images, training, experience, and personality. No matter how the individual CDS mediator has combined these ingredients, however, the similarities in approach far outshine the differences. In any program, mediators learn to combine problem-solving with insistence on disputant responsibility; tough control with empathy. Mediators everywhere consistently use a series of concrete skills: summarizing, confronting, agreement writing, and analyzing power balances, to name a few. Nevertheless, CDS has a distinct mediation style. We turn next to those wider influences which account for those particular characteristics.

Other Influences On The CDS Mediator Role

Expectations

People who call CDS are looking for a service that will work. Their hopes for the outcome determine the kind of third party they want. Here are some of the aspects of a mediator's role which are most important to disputants:

Power. If they make any request at all, it is usually for a "strong" mediator. They want the other party kept in bounds and they want someone to fix the problem. This comes out during preliminary interviews. "No one can shut her up. She lies, even in front of the judge she lied. Please assign your best people to this," is a common plea. People who inquire about the possibility of mediation want to know whether or not CDS can "make the other party behave." They may set conditions: "We're only coming if you make them keep their animals off of my property." People who are feeling victimized are afraid of sitting in the same room with the other person. These disputants want a mediator who has power.

There is one fear of mediator strength which should be noted: disputants wonder if the mediators will push them around. They are afraid of being forced to sign some agreement against their will.

102 / PEACEMAKING IN YOUR NEIGHBORHOOD

Disputants hope for a mediator with muscle who will keep the other side in bounds and a courteous, sympathetic mediator who will understand their own position!

Impartial listening. Disputants answering the questionnaire who commented on the mediators were mostly interested in CDS's impartiality. They wanted equal attention, and they wanted the mediators to believe their story.

> You don't show more interest in one party than the other.
>
> You make people feel at ease.
>
> I didn't like it when the neighbor lied and convinced you people they were telling it as it was.
>
> You have a thankless job, but its good you're there to listen.
>
> [I liked that the mediators] were non-biased.

Facilitation. Some liked the mediators' role as facilitator and listener because it gave them a controlled opportunity to resolve the problem.

> An objective party could hear both sides of the story and encourage us to listen to each other as well. Helped lessen power plays, abusive language.
>
> Each party was allowed to express our [sic] viewpoint…, to vent feelings and focus on specific issues.

Protection and control. Safety concerns were even more important to this woman:

> The parties…were bent on venting hostilities at us. I think the two mediators did a very good job in channeling these hostilities in a more reasonable frame. [I didn't like the fact that] there wasn't any protection. What would the mediators do if the mediation got out of control and…became violent?

The appreciation of mediators' unbiased and courteous attention reinforces the CDS mediators' vision of their work. However, the hidden and outspoken demands for strength, protection, and control create confusion for many CDS mediators.

Mediators' conceptions of power and process

While agreeing that a mediator must be in control, CDS mediators tend to approach the question of third party power from a different angle. *Power* is a word they use uneasily. Far from being an asset, it is pictured as undue force, force which may potentially override the disputants' ability and responsibility to hammer out an agreement themselves.

> *The crucial element in the mediation process is that the mediators have no power to dictate the outcome or enforce the agreement, so that the participants' energy goes into dealing with the issues rather than vying for the mediators' approval.* (1984 CDS program description)

> [What power do you as mediator have?] *I never thought of my mediating in those terms. It gives me a bad feeling; I resist the word. I can't associate power with such a situation. Power is not associated with helping people.*

Because disputants consistently push mediators into the role of powerful authority, CDS's Opening Statement has changed over the years to state explicitly that mediators are not judges nor decision-makers. "What comes out of this mediation is up to you," disputants are told. "We are here to *help* you reach a workable solution yourselves."

But isn't this a good thing? Didn't CDS, like most dispute settlement programs, deliberately design the mediation to give the disputants as much power as possible in settling their own affairs? Taking the back seat conveys confidence in the disputants.

We are back to the false notion of power as innately manipulative and finite. This reasoning explains why CDS mediators so often hesitate to take command, why they are leery of employing "power" when a session is getting out of hand.

What kind of ideology and experience reinforces this CDS mediator philosophy? The background of the program and its mediators suggests three influences: the anti-authority mood of the 1970s, CDS's Quaker roots, and program leadership by women.

Distrust of authority and institutions

We wrote earlier of FSP's three project guidelines of *empowerment, alternatives,* and *nonviolence.* It is telling that the program has not selected more outwardly directive words like *leadership, education, action,* or *change,* which could equally describe FSP's approach. This choice of passive words marks the times of their origin; for many, the later 70s and early 80s were years of internal searching for personal fulfillment, not of wielding outward power. Paul Lacey (1982) describes the middle-class white professional culture, to which most Quakers and CDS mediators belong:

> [In their alternative lifestyles, they] *struggle with demands of equality and individuality within a community.... They are suspicious of appeals to authority to settle any question; truth, they believe, is a very personal thing. They do not want the institutions to which they belong to dictate beliefs to them, for that is to close off the search for truth which is so essential to our spiritual growth.... Power itself, in any form, is the great evil. (1982: 6-7)*

Later he adds another telling paragraph:

> *Virtually everyone in a Quaker institution wants to be outside the sphere of responsibility, but well inside the sphere of influence.... We want to champion Community in opposition to the institution; we want to stand for Equality in opposition to authority. We want to be the ones to speak Truth to that convenient abstraction, Power. (1982: 21)*

Lacey has unerringly picked out the code words which form FSP philosophy. The same catch phrases still surface in CDS mediation rhetoric which allies itself with *community*, with the right of the poor and powerless and the individual person to determine his or her personal truth, and against the powers of institutions and authorities. In this spirit, CDS was developed to attack problems of justice on a local and interpersonal level by helping disputants to change their individual ways. Participants would discover their own abilities, define their own answers. Process, for some mediators, became more important than the specific outcome of a session.

It has only been recently, during the mid-80s, that CDS has followed the general trend towards accepting institutions and the need for power and leadership. Pressuring disputants before or during mediation is now more acceptable; relations with the court are closer; the program is more willing to present itself as a social service agency.

CDS mediators are still rooted in the earlier ethic. It was that approach which drew many of them, and volunteers with other attitudes are not coming in. Therefore, during mediation they are, in the 70s tradition, cautious about trampling on the "lifestyle" of others. Believing that disputants know their own situation best, mediators shy away from making value judgments or identifying the "truth." FSP trainers teach new mediators to edit out their prejudices and their "shoulds" as much as possible. What Deborah Baskin (1984) calls the impossible vision of a culture-free vacuum becomes for many mediators the ideal stance: no influence, no opinions, no judgment.

The Quaker influence

From the beginning, CDS's religious base was kept in the background. When the program was under FSP's auspices, most disputants seemed unaware of the Quaker sponsorship. Today's program, now independent of the Friends, has no religious affiliations. Mediations and meetings are still held in churches and meetinghouses. While this probably lends more of a religious air to the mediation session than CDS admits, the mediation is run as a secular forum.

In spite of this neutral appearance, CDS was, and is, a program rooted in the religious community, and this legacy has been significant in determining the policies and the style of the program. Over a third of the approximately forty active CDS mediators consider themselves Friends. Charles Walker of FSP points out that Quaker affiliation has left a distinct imprint on CDS. The following pages (introduction and outline) are adapted from his 1984 unpublished article.

Conciliation and civil disobedience are two strands of Quaker tradition. Neither the mediator nor the advocate can claim to represent the true Quaker spirit. During the days of the civil rights and anti-war movements, looking for a middle ground was, for a while, to invite suspicion or outright namecalling. Confrontation, once relegated to radicals, became a commonplace and accepted political method. As revolutionary ardor has cooled, and movements slowed down, the conflict resolver has emerged again as an honorable role.

Quaker culture and religious orientation have both underlined the task of reconciliation. A predilection for this quiet job arises from a number of characteristics:

1) Belief that conflicts are not a simple right or wrong. If all views are heard a consensus rather than a victory may emerge.

2) Emphasis on reconciliation rather than defeat. Victory is suspect mostly because it means defeat of another, which brings attendant perils.

3) Special concern for "enemies" and adversaries; a desire to hear their claims and criticisms.

4) Sympathy with victims. Disputants are often victimized by the

other party, even by the very burden of the conflict. Following a tradition of siding with the downtrodden, of being their advocates and helpers, Quakers hope to liberate people to be truly themselves, to be creative and not just reactive, to be more than victims without turning into victimizers.

5) A historical peacemaking tradition, and a reputation for intermediary work. Mediation combines the peace and justice traditions in a communitarian context. From this perspective, community mediation is a natural direction.

6) A low-key style appropriate for mediators. Friends prefer understatement and avoid ridicule or sarcasm or insult. Humor is gentle rather than abrasive.

7) An insistence on the personal and the experiential, distrust of the ideological—our own ideologies unacknowledged or concealed—and distrust of creeds.

8) A sophisticated system of "communal discernment," making decisions as a group, training in facilitating and consensus procedures. (This is discussed more fully in the consensus section of the Mediation Model chapter.)

9) Approaching reconciliation as a mission arising from religious discipleship. The frequent connections CDS mediators draw between local and international peacemaking are a product of this sense of purpose. (Walker, 1984)

Friends Suburban Project sits squarely in the center of these Quaker traditions. The East Coast Quakers are self-consciously and proudly anti-authoritarian. They believe that individuals must be given freedom to find their own way without advice and interference. They have no official creed. In place of doctrines of belief, Quakers rely on a high respect for careful procedure to keep individualism within bounds. The consensual process allows many points of view to be considered. It encourages warmth and tolerance. People are less likely to split into factions with set demands. The clerk of a business meeting is not supposed to impose his or her will on the group; on the contrary, holding back one's opinions is considered proper. But she or he *is* expected to guide discussion neutrally so that each person can be heard.

If this approach sounds like our description of CDS's mediation sessions, it is no coincidence. (And we will look at other areas of overlap later.) But there is a catch. Quaker "non-authority" only works when the group understands the process. Meetings quickly disintegrate when someone breaks the unwritten rules against polarizing tactics. This happens when people begin lining up sides or hiding information, when they continually interrupt or make non-negotiable demands. In the US democratic tradition, such strategies are employed as a matter of course. In public decision-making, the Quaker practices of communal responsibility, joint problem-solving, and flexible positions are all somewhat strange notions to most disputants.

To many mediators, however, these cooperative attitudes are central. Even the ones who do not belong to the Society of Friends say that they were attracted to the program because of the emphasis on consensus and group process. They are uncomfortable with the dual role they play of magistrate and Quaker-style facilitator:

> *It's bizarre because on the one hand you're trying to put the solution or the power to a solution in the hands of these people, and on the other hand you're having to play an authoritarian role to get them to shut up and cooperate.*

> *I feel that I'm a facilitator and a vehicle. But I've found that disputants come in feeling weaker, they look up to us, their eye contact is with us. I straighten up and convey a little authority at the beginning so I don't lose them.*

Like Quakers discussing their Meetings for Business, the mediators approach the process with a touch of reverence. Again and again, they claim that their job is to get out of the way of the process. They marvel at the magic way it dissolves hostility.

> *The people anticipate that you are going to do something. There is total bafflement, they don't know what they're there for. Then they get pulled into the process, involved.... It amazes me that it actually happens in a fairly predictable pattern each time.*

> *I was beginning to get tired of encounter groups. When I shook the ashes what seemed left of value was group process. Most people think of content and forget process. The old human relations was mostly venting and expressing, but no linear structure that would lead to something productive by the end of the experience. Mediation combines a framework of phases, and sticks to that discipline, while at the same time allowing people the freedom to express themselves and let out their feelings.*

It's a natural process. It has a lot of common sense to it.

You have to be in a mediation and see it come together to sense how it really works.

The process itself is impressive. It's the process more than the mediator that makes a difference.

Some even inject a note of salvation: *I see mediation process as...non-hierarchical and empowering...with mediators acting as non-authoritarian leaders who provide structure for change that will, ultimately, save this planet.*

Many mediators, then, see the power of the mediation process as removed from their own capabilities. This sense of an experience which ultimately lies beyond deliberate human efforts is a natural interpretation for Quakers, who believe that the guidance of the Holy Spirit during a Meeting transcends a person's intellect and defies self-conscious control. You can prepare for the experience, you can learn to follow its signals, but the process has a direction and momentum of its own.

Women's experience and the mediator role

CDS was founded by women. Two-thirds of its mediators are women. Without getting into the chicken and egg question of whether mediation attracted women or whether women structured the CDS mediator role to suit themselves, we can see many connections in the way CDS mediators approach their task.

Situational and relational morality. The influence of women's thinking on the mediator's role is illuminated by Carol Gilligan's research on the way women approach moral issues. (Gilligan, 1982) She finds that women often make ethical judgments on the basis of relationships, which means they are made in context. Women are concerned with the effect of a decision on the people involved. Will someone be hurt or exploited? How far should someone be responsible? On the other hand, Gilligan says, men have a bent towards defining universal principles and rules which govern behavior and especially control aggressiveness. This orientation underlies the legal resolution of disputes: the truth is extracted as accurately as possible, and judgments are made on the basis of predetermined laws and priorities. Likewise, rules are invoked in human relations to keep aggressive behavior from disrupting such settings as families, meetings, neighborhoods, and courtrooms.

CDS's concern with the particular situation (as opposed to the abstract issues of justice raised) and for the future relations of the parties are distinctly related to Gilligan's description of how women make moral decisions. The question to disputants is not "Were you doing something wrong?" but "How can you get along better?" Instead of collecting facts to make an accurate judgment, the mediators try generating ideas and concessions to resolve a problem. One woman explains:

> *The facts are so full of holes. Anyway, the idea that if you produce the true facts you will then get a fair solution—it's an illusion. You have to get people to divorce all those abstractions of justice, right and wrong, and punishment from what is going to work for them. I want them to figure out a practical solution to what they need.*

This orientation towards situational, practical morality persists even though the majority of disputants (men and women) come to the table ready for a battle about facts, eager for a judgment based on law and fairness. For months they have honed their arguments, preparing themselves to win in a man's moral world. The mediators describe their task as weaning people away from this one way of resolving disputes and teaching them a personal, future-oriented approach.

Helper and peacemaker. CDS mediators often picture themselves in traditionally female terms as the helper and the peacemaker. Readers will find many mediator quotes in this book which illustrate that desire to facilitate the growth of others. Contrast that service image with this CDS mediator's description of a predominately male, court-based program where he received his training:

> *We sat there with power, at least people thought we had it. We did anything we thought we could get away with. We would tell them they were on Prosecutor's Probation, which doesn't exist,* [Author's note: That program has long since discouraged this practice.] *or that if in six months we found they weren't complying we'd have them brought in. We'd come in there in suit and tie—we played the part. And it's interesting, in follow-ups, you know it really worked, those agreements still held despite being thrust down on the disputants.*

CDS mediators, men and women alike, are more committed to empowerment and something they vaguely label "process." They tend to speak of peacemaking, the satisfaction of dealing with visible, resolvable problems. The men often enter the mediation training because they are revolting against adversarial methods they have encountered at work. It is good to watch these ideas becoming "human" rather than "feminine." The mediator from the court-based program, now a dedicated volunteer with CDS, goes on to explain how his approach has changed:

> Hiding that I'm an attorney is hard. A couple of times, mediators mentioned it. The whole mediation took on a different tone. They get away from working it out themselves. Now they have someone to ask questions.

Lack of confidence. Another way the CDS's mediator role has been molded by the suburban white woman's experience is less positive. Some of the Quakerly belief in the sanctity of the process and the dislike of claiming power we observed above sounds suspiciously like a lack of self-confidence. A large number of CDS's best mediators speak disparagingly of their own competence. They defer quickly to a co-mediator who supposedly has the answers and the skills they lack. While insecurity strikes everyone from time to time, women in particular seem to sink into this kind of powerlessness.

As director, consultant, and trainer, Eileen Stief frequently talks to women from several programs who feel uncertain about their abilities:

> Why did CDS end up with so many mediators who are timid and insecure? We see people we know are very capable pussyfooting around. E just let A push that disputant into an agreement because she didn't think she was as good a mediator as he was. She knows perfectly well that she was right. But she didn't speak up till afterward. I think I assume a self-confidence in strong mediators that isn't always there.

She goes on to describe the larger consequences of this lack of confidence:

> There are three pieces of fallout. One is the dependence on two mediators. I prefer mediating with another person, but I'm not afraid to do it alone. Another is that investment in empowering people is equated with not being assertive and strong when it's needed. So mediators sit back and let people muddle through. A third is this lack of belief in your own skill. Like when G didn't take command of that father who was treating his son so coldly in the mediation because she thought the disputant was a psychologist.

Another group of women mediators show greater confidence in their mediating skills. Possibly they feel secure because they picture their task as a natural one. As women, they have often played the reconciling role at home and at work. The ones who are nervous about their capabilities seem timid about acting in a *public* role of authority; they see themselves entering alien territory where they might make critical mistakes. They assume that disputants or the other mediator probably know more than they do.

If this hypothesis is true, confidence may be based not on objective assessment of one's own skills but on the mediator's image of her role: is she entering the foreign "male" world of public problems and public power or is she bringing disputes back into a familiar sphere of interpersonal reconciliation?

No wonder community mediators at CDS are puzzled when asked what power they have in a session. Many have chosen mediation because it is a helping role designed to be unauthoritarian and unthreatening. They don't *want* power. In this role, they will not have to declare strong opinions, or push for reforms. No one asks them to take a public role; the task is private and anonymous. When disputants reach agreement, the mediator carefully takes no public credit (except with other mediators!). Satisfaction is supposed to come from leading others to positive action.

Six: The Mediation Model

Values and Assumptions

The CDS mediation model grows out of a rich soil of philosophical assumptions, assumptions about people and conflict and change. While these ideas have been surfacing throughout this book, they deserve direct attention. We set them out to sketch a rough map of the underground rivers which nourish what we see in the landscape above. Looking frankly at these beliefs can help us understand why CDS mediation has taken its characteristic form and to evaluate how that format helps and limits the mediator's task of resolving disputes.

The most noticeable assumptions are ideas about how people grow and change. In her analysis of CDS, Deborah Baskin sees these beliefs arising from social service's therapeutic model (Baskin, 1984). We have adapted her list of values to fit our observations of CDS. Most CDS mediators will qualify some of these points, but generally they base their work on the belief that people:

1) Are willing and able to change their behavior.

2) Should be responsible for running their own lives.

3) Prefer to be friendly, warm, honest, open, cooperative.

That in interpersonal relationships:

4) Conflict is made worse by poor communication and cannot be resolved without improving that communication.

5) Understanding each other usually leads to better relations.

6) Many people want, or at least can learn, to live peaceably.

7) Persistent conflict can be resolved by confronting, by talking things out.

8) Disputants are the experts on their own problems. With help they

can make better decisions for themselves than others can make for them.

9) People are more willing to negotiate when they are treated with respect and when they do not lose face.

10) When people work hard to reach agreement, they will be more committed to respect the contract.

These beliefs vary from mediator to mediator, of course. Inarguably, CDS attitudes fall into the "therapist" approach to conflict resolution described separately by Baskin (1984) and by Merry (1984) in their comparison of mediation styles in different programs. Success is defined by the degree of reconciliation, not by the speed of reaching an accord. Healing individual disputes is considered a step towards resolving larger social conflicts. The mediator is a helper. This contrasts with what Merry calls the "bargaining" model which assumes that disputes arise from societal conflicts over resources and power, and that a contract is therefore a compromise between irreconcilably opposing interests.

These liberal social service values are the mortar which holds together the CDS mediation model. Uninterrupted Time, for example, is designed to help people to better understand each other. The Exchange provides an opportunity for emotional outbursts; the mediator often gives crying or shouting disputants a long leash, again because the mediator and CDS believe that venting can move people towards greater reconciliation. During the problem-solving phase, the mediator is taught to emphasize the parties' ability to determine the outcome.

Many of these beliefs are overtly stated by mediators during sessions. The CDS mediation model presents a self-conscious ideology, and whether or not they believe in it, neither mediators nor disputants can easily sidestep its strong push.

Any firmly defined philosophy is open to criticism, especially when, as we have done, its tenets are simplistically listed like line items in a computer program. These values, however, have much to offer mediators. Respect for the disputants' capabilities allows them considerable latitude in defining their own disputes and in deciding what they want to do about them. The belief that parties have to go through the process themselves helps mediators refrain from proffering advice and judgments.

CDS's self-image

The trappings of a CDS mediation session say much about its

self-image and its philosophy (although as we see in the final chapter, the old warning about telling the book from its cover is a useful caution—that image can at times fool both CDS and its disputants). The location of the mediation session is an important clue. By and large, CDS uses social rooms in local churches. This sends several messages to the disputants and the community. Meeting in the neighborhood shows the program's willingness to accommodate participants' needs. It also underscores the program's independence from the court and adds a faint religious air. (If any party prefers not to mediate in a church, CDS arranges for a room in a public building.)

The second thing disputants see is the dress and manner of the mediators. They usually wear street clothes, not business dress. Their language is casual and friendly. With each other they use first names. When they seat people and give the Opening Statement, there is no sense of keeping people tightly controlled and separated. No mediator sits in a distinctly head position, and throughout the session mediators confer and casually alternate leads. This informality, it should be noted, is *not* the opposite of seriousness. CDS mediators are serious about the intensity disputants feel and the significance of what each has to say. The intended message for the disputants is: we know what we are doing, your situation doesn't scare or upset us, something will be accomplished here.

CDS's choice of terms is also revealing. Most mediators discourage such court associated words as *hearing, caucus, complainant,* and *respondent,* as well as words denoting legal categories: *assault, harassment,* or *trespass* for example. The program wants to move people away from behaving as if they were in a courtroom and towards letting go in a less rule-bound discussion. The disputants do not need to pay much attention to the mediation structure and in fact may be unaware of it.

No release forms are required beforehand. The contract is plain, with only spaces for addresses and names at the top, signatures at the bottom. Although disputants may draw up a legal agreement if they wish, in practice no legalistic language is used.

One small item sums up CDS's portrayal of itself: scrap paper. The mediators always put a pile in the center of the table should the disputants want to take notes, especially during Uninterrupted Time. Sometimes they sketch diagrams of property lines, or their children occupy themselves drawing pictures. The scrap paper is thrifty (some would say cheap), informal, practical. It is there if people want to use it, reminding them that *they* are the ones who are working at this session. CDS would hope that disputants use those same words to describe the session: economical, informal, optional, practical.

Format and Policies

In the community mediation trade, nothing seems to excite as much lunch table disagreement as discussion of mediation format and policy: Two mediators or one? Face-to-face meetings or lengthy caucuses? Thirty minutes or three hours? Each proponent advocates not just a method but a philosophy and a set of goals underlying that preference.

In Chapter One we walked through the divisions in the basic CDS mediation session:

Opening Statement
Uninterrupted Time
The Exchange
Building the Agreement
Writing the Agreement
Closing Statement.

This format has changed little since the first days of CDS when Eileen Stief, Betsey Leonard, and Emily Sontag put together a combination of the American Arbitration Association negotiation model and their own ideas. Real mediations are not as neat as this anatomy, yet the framework is still accurate enough that mediators trained by FSP consistently use it to structure and to evaluate the session.

CDS made more choices in forming its mediation model than one might expect from seeing the simple session outline. Notice in the following description how many of these characteristics flow from the assumptions we discussed previously.

–Disputants' participation is largely voluntary.

–Sessions last about two hours. Occasionally a second session is held.

–The mediation is conducted in a private neutral place.

–Mediators are volunteers. Mediation training is the only requirement.

–The tone is "laid back," informal and friendly, often starting on a first-name basis. Mediators strive for a warm, positive atmosphere with displays of toughness when needed.

–Unless there is trouble, mediators allow discussion and emotions to flow rather than maintaining strictly defined structure.

–CDS places high value on emotional release. Mediators are asked *not* to coax feelings out, however.

–Psychological analysis and counseling are considered inappropriate.

–Mediators focus on controlling the process (as opposed to content). They summarize and direct more often than they dig for detailed information or engineer solutions.

–CDS encourages maximum negotiation face-to-face at the table using separate meetings when deemed useful (not as a fixed part of the schedule).

–All present are equally involved—each person in each party is asked to speak. Everyone signs the agreement.

–Mediators explore different facets of the dispute—not just that event which brought disputants to the table.

–CDS insists on *written* agreements.

Logistics

The seating arrangement is not prescribed. Sometimes it is formal: parties sit facing each other on two sides with mediators seated at either end. Variations depend on the shape of the table, the nature of the dispute, and the preference of the mediators. Mediators sit where they can see everyone and each other. Parties are asked to sit where they can talk directly to the other side. Unless physical threat is possible, the mediators make no particular effort to keep people separated. Interestingly enough, although mediators argue for one way or another, the program has not noticed connections between different seating patterns and corresponding results.

The average CDS session takes about two hours. This gives sufficient time to uncover all the important issues as well as to allow feelings to emerge. Longer sessions wear participants out. "What if people are still in the middle of the negotiations?" we are often asked, especially by programs with open-ended timing. Having a deadline, "We need to wrap up by 9:30," is a useful incentive to center on building the agreement. Most people are tired after two intense hours. If needed, a second meeting is scheduled so that people are fresh. Sessions shorter than an hour are those involving only one or two issues which also carry little emotional baggage.

Some programs consider two-hour sessions inefficient, but

venting emotions takes time. It isn't neat and controlled. Sometimes when the parties have concentrated on solving the problem to the exclusion of emotional realities, the trust or understanding which shores up difficult agreements is missing. "We'll try it but I know we'll end up in court. Nothing will satisfy him, ever," said one man after one such short session. Their agreement had covered each concern, but neither side gave it much chance of working.

For a court mediation program handling dozens of cases, efficiency means getting a contract in writing—quick. For a community program receiving fewer cases, tight scheduling is not a problem. Efficiency means taking care of long years of disagreements and hurt feelings in one or two sessions. If the difficulties are resolved, if the people stop calling the police and the judges, if they are better able to handle the next problem they encounter, isn't this effective use of time—theirs and ours?

Counseling

If there is danger in the longer, more emotional style of CDS's mediation sessions, it is when mediators sail near the therapist's waters. How much emotion belongs in a mediation? CDS's answer is that it is the *purpose*, not the *amount*, of that release which is the measure of appropriateness. Is it helping people get somewhere? To understand each other better? Is the tension level going up as a result? CDS mediators generally consider the release of emotion to be beneficial, but they are told neither to encourage nor to discourage people's outbursts unless someone's behavior is counterproductive or abusive. CDS generally permits mediators to decide how much venting is useful and what level of explosion the disputants *and* the mediators can tolerate.

"Some mediators' interpretation of leaving space for expressing feelings goes too far," says one CDS staffperson. "The mediator shouldn't hold still for a torrent of namecalling. We have to model some degree of respect and civilized proceedings. After all, I don't expect people to spit on the table or stick chewing gum under it or pull a knife. They should be free to be angry and to cry. They should say what they need to say. But we shouldn't tolerate verbal knives. I suspect that a lot of attack and abuse is permitted in the name of ventilation."

Many people who come to CDS are unwilling to consider counseling. CDS wants to respect disputants' wishes; they have asked for help in resolving a particular dispute, not for emotional release or for therapeutic diagnosis of their problems. For this same reason, early CDS trainings advised mediators and staff to be careful about referring people to other services during a mediation or on the phone, unless someone specifically asked for such information (which they often did). The two current staff members have social-work and court-office backgrounds, respectively. They actively suggest resources to disputants.

Mediators: one, two,... many

A staunch advocate of solo mediating might say this heading should read "One Too Many." For some this is a heated subject, however, and no matter for puns. In many programs, mediators work in pairs only during apprenticeship and thereafter facilitate sessions alone. Two mediators confuse already tense disputants, these programs say, because people don't know which way to look. The sessions run more smoothly if one person is organizing and directing discussion. Coordinating with others is one more interaction to distract the mediator's attention. Teamwork, especially with someone you don't know well, is not always easy. Pairs may sit back and assume the other person will handle a difficult outburst or will remember what a rambling speaker said. Things slip through. The edge of attention is sharper when you have only yourself to rely on.

A particularly skilled CDS mediator explains how mediating with a partner complicates the session:

> *I always need to be aware of my level of activity. You have to watch for signals, watch that you aren't dominating or not holding up your end.* [There may be] *differences in what you see as the right way to go. Communicating with the co-mediator is another problem.*

Although mediators are free to caucus apart from the parties, few do so. Most often, they are afraid of leaving the parties alone, or they are reluctant to criticize the co-mediator.

Mediating alone is more efficient for programs too. There are fewer schedules to juggle, and for those that reimburse mediators, fewer stipends and travel expenses. The program can operate with a smaller number of mediators.

At the other end of this debate are the community panels pioneered by such groups as the San Francisco Community Boards. These boards are usually a mixture of the community's racial and ethnic groups. Some programs restrict membership to lawyers and social workers. In most panels, tasks are divided among mediators so that one or two people do most of the facilitating. Depending on the program, the rest of the panel takes notes, questions disputants after their presentations, writes out the agreement, or confers with the lead mediator.

CDS has used mediator pairs from the beginning and never seriously considered anything else. While acknowledging the advantages of single mediators mentioned above—as our mediators have noted on the few occasions when they worked alone—the program prefers coupling mediators for many reasons.

First, it answers the mediators' needs. The founders of CDS were accustomed to working in teams. They found that mediators learn from each other (especially important when the program was new and many things were being ironed out by experiment). They rescue each other from mistakes, from feeling stuck or panicked or biased. New volunteers hesitate to mediate alone; pairing provides apprenticeship. Even for experienced mediators, it is an excellent vehicle for evaluating your own mediating and for learning from others. Perhaps too, skilled teamwork models productive cooperation for disputants.

The same mediator who described the drawbacks of co-mediating goes on to say that she still prefers the team:

> The first reason is it is more fun in pairs. There is someone to talk things over with afterward. Also, there are some things, like writing out the agreement, that I don't like to do. I'm just as happy if the other person does those jobs.

This policy of pairing seems comfortable for disputants also. In separate meetings, no one is left alone wondering what the mediator is saying to the other party. Disputants have more chance of feeling easy with at least one of the mediators. Furthermore, mediators can be chosen to reflect disputant differences in age or sex or race. Careful selection also allows staff to find two volunteers with complementary strengths. Pairs provide a safety valve for maintaining impartiality by noticing a partner's biases, and when appropriate, taking over the lead.

Most mediators like the opportunity to divide tasks. One person may take notes and think about potential areas of agreement while the other referees discussion, for example. In hot situations, two heads are still better than one, as long as mediators are trained teamworkers who support each other's decisions and confer honestly.

Like panel programs, CDS also prefers pairs for ideological reasons. It undercuts the mediator-sitting-in-judgment image held by many disputants. CDS mediators usually sit apart from each other—at either end of the table or else one on each side with the parties. Without a focal point of authority, the disputants find themselves presenting grievances directly to the other party.

Nevertheless, CDS is not rigid about the pair rule: from time to time someone mediates alone; more frequent is the use of three mediators in large disputes or when a trainee is observing. A CDS mediator who mediates alone in her job assisting employees with grievances comments: "When it is just two people, I'd rather do it by myself, but when I have more it is really tough. I'd prefer someone else there, especially if I am used to working with that person. It keeps people from trying to play favorites."

Good teamwork is a hard-won achievement but brings substantial pay-offs when it works well.

The facts: How much should mediators know?

Facts are like ventriloquist dummies, Aldous Huxley is reputed to have said. They say different things in the laps of fools and of wise men.

Ahhh, the facts! Workable decisions cannot be made without them and yet pursuing the "truth" can lead mediations down an endless road to nowhere. The major issue for structuring a mediation model is how much the mediator needs to know before and during the session.

Preparing to mediate. CDS mediators disagree about how much information a mediator needs before entering a session. Some want to approach the meeting with a clean slate. The background information on the case from the CDS office, they say, builds up preconceptions which get in the way of listening to the parties. CDS staff know the disputants all too well by the time they brief the mediators. They know dozens of details on one or both sides. They may sympathize with one person. Faced with laundry lists of opposing information, some mediators request a simple summary of major issues, names, trouble spots.

Experienced mediators are often easy with mediating "cold":

> Unless it is a complicated dispute that needs homework, I just get the bones of it and get the names straight.
>
> I prefer not to imagine what might happen ahead of time. What goes down on the referral sheet is often very different from what comes out at the table. I like to hear it from the people themselves.

When the office warns that one party will be difficult, some mediators are intimidated or on guard from the beginning. Besides undermining a volunteer's confidence, the information may be misleading. Some potential trouble-makers turn out to be understanding and conciliatory. Meek and agreeable on the phone, some disputants surprise everyone with a shower of obscene words.

This discrepancy between telephone and session behavior is not unusual. Issues, too, may also change from the time people called to the time they reach the table. Eileen Stief refers trainees to her favorite example of how different a story can sound:

> During a CDS preliminary interview, Agnes was raging about her neighbor's ten-year-old who had threatened her child with a knife. This was not brought out during the mediation. Concerned, one mediator took Agnes aside. It turned out that the "knife" had been a plastic letter opener and that no one thought it significant anymore.

On the other hand, many CDS mediators believe forewarned is forearmed. They feel more comfortable facing feuding strangers when they have as much background knowledge as possible. Information from the office is critical to choosing what tack they take in organizing the session and directing discussion.

Another reason comes from a long-time mediator, who likes to prepare herself for a session by imagining what these people might have in common. She envisions how things could be better for them. Although other mediators disagree with this projecting of common ideals and possible solutions before even meeting the people, this mediator is uncommonly successful at getting people to look at the positive and move ahead to amicable agreement.

During the session. Once at the table, the issue of information gathering becomes one of selection. Where is the line between facts that are interesting and those that are necessary?

The temptation for most of us is to puzzle out what "really" happened, or what "really" motivates people. Like detectives, we may want to ferret out clues and secret information from the players. This natural curiosity can drain the mediation just as surely as do the disputants' quicksand arguments over the truth.

Setting the record straight is a primary agenda item for most disputants. Rumors and misunderstandings have gone unchecked for weeks, even years. What can mediators do when, as is usually the case, each party has a clear and contradictory memory of the same situation? Pity the bewildered mediators in one CDS common driveway dispute: the first household claimed the drive was long and narrow, the second maintained it was quite wide and short! How can the mediator ever know for sure the disputant is telling the real story? On-going disputes are frequently too complicated, the pile of relevant "facts" too stretched, for the mediator to ever be sure of what happened. These matters are for the courts and arbitrators.

The uses of information-gathering. For the first hour of mediation the parties most often wrangle over the past. When the Exchange is stuck in such a "Yes, you did!" "No, I didn't!" pattern, mediators report impatience. They want to talk about feelings, problems, and terms. Nevertheless, fact-finding has a place. It helps mediators and disputants to understand the issues and later to check the workability of suggested agreements. It also serves as a vehicle to keep people talking.

Sometimes the mediators address inconsistency in facts as one agent-of-reality way to loosen positions, as when in Chapter One the mediators confronted Terry's parents with the contradiction between keeping their daughter away from her baby's father and hinting about marriage. Without care, such confrontations on facts may echo of the courtroom, backing disputants into uncomfortable corners. "How can that driveway be two cars wide if you say you have to back out for each other?" Mediators observed in CDS manage to sound less accusatory by remarking that they were "confused" by what the disputants had said.

In the laps of wise mediators, bringing out facts can put emphasis on measurable reality—that part of a situation which lends itself to specific points of agreement. "Is there a third desk for special projects?" "What time do you arrive home from work?" Neutral questions inject a calm note into the proceedings. People know what to do with simple questions. For this reason, high emotion or guarded reticence can both be channeled into problem-solving by limited, deliberate fact-collecting. Information-gathering is also a means of showing and sharing power: authorities are allowed to ask questions. A well-timed request for information can effectively bring the session back into the mediators' hands.

Subjectivity and suggestions. When mediators gather facts for other purposes they are likely to find themselves delivering judgments or making proposals. While CDS mediators generally refrain from overt judgments, giving suggestions is foggier territory. CDS mediators, despite program ideology to the contrary, nearly always make suggestions about the content of an agreement. Usually, it works.

The disputants agree. The problem of incomplete background can foil mediators, though, as someone notes:

> Often when I've made suggestions, both parties have quickly vetoed it because of further information I didn't have. Because CDS doesn't ordinarily visit people in their homes, I can't really hear how much noise a stereo makes through the wall or know that the obvious solution I see is unacceptable to the neighbor on the other side of the property.

More importantly, suppose the mediator does have a good idea of what occurred. What does a mediator do with those facts, especially those which determine a fault? Suppose Jane says in private session, "Sure I threw a rock at his window, and he deserved it, too. But I'll never admit to it because I'll never pay for it." It is difficult to use information which disputants are determined to hide unless the mediators construct the agreement themselves.

Another difficulty is that truth is malleable. Facts are the beams which hold up the disputants' position. They are carefully sanded, sorted, and arranged. In a culture which puts great faith in "hard and cold fact," it is hard to remind ourselves that what we are hearing always comes through subjective filters.

The facts even have a mysterious way of growing more coherent as trust builds, as in one mediation where the disputants finally realized that all their arguments had started with something a third neighbor woman had said. She had been playing them off against each other by telling opposing stories in each ear! The "truth" began to take a different shape.

If the mediators have faith that most people, once a base of trust has been established, are capable of resolving their own problems, it follows that, as when Agnes no longer needed to mention the knife, the disputants will usually bring out whatever information is pertinent to their own concerns. When key information must be forced out, it may be time to consider another forum for resolving the dispute.

Law and formal authority

Another concern for a developing program is the degree to which the mediation imitates a legal approach. We have already discussed CDS's reasons for avoiding legal terminology, fact-finding, and sitting in judgment. A parallel rule restricts participation in the mediation to the parties themselves. Lawyers are excluded from all CDS mediations.

Again, the rationale is the same: the program does not want to confuse mediation sessions with the legal forum. CDS's philosophy holds that people should talk to each other directly. Talking through lawyers reminds people of their mutual animosity. Discussion becomes restricted to legal issues. People count minutes; they are paying dearly for each one. In mediation, any participant has the opportunity to check an agreement with a lawyer before signing. CDS rarely mentions this, however, and only a few people have ever requested it.

Despite the attempt to maintain independence, any mediation format is inevitably influenced by the disputants' and the mediators' ideas (accurate or not) about the legal system. Legal definitions of what is right and permissible shape the issues people outline at the table. Agreements are often based on the model offered by laws and local ordinances. The bargaining happens on the courthouse doorstep; disputants know that failure to agree can mean moving indoors.

Separate meetings

The CDS mediation format does not automatically include caucuses. The private conference is nevertheless one of the CDS mediators' most valued tools. During a called break, each mediator takes aside one party (rather than, as in some other programs, asking one side at a time to step out). A separate meeting is used to calm an uproar or conversely to get discussion moving. They can be a time to explore positions and proposals with each person privately. Kay, you may recall, spent time doing this alone with pregnant Terry while James spoke with her parents. Those meetings were critical in moving the family through their impasse. Children and teenager disputes in particular benefit from these separate meetings. They seem to reach agreements only away from the protective eyes of their parents.

Sometimes the momentum is such that the mediators decide to forge ahead at the table without a break. Often that decision is based on the belief that talking it out face-to-face is important. "I don't use separate meetings as often as I should because I'm so glad they've finally gotten together to talk things over," confesses one mediator. Some feel that more secrecy will endanger the thin bonds of trust which the mediator is trying to strengthen. During post-mediation evaluation, though, mediators' most frequent criticism of themselves is that they did not take advantage of the separate meeting option.

In many other programs, disputants spend less time around the table. According to mediators and trainers who use regular caucuses, the primary benefit of separate meetings is that people open up to the mediators in private and make offers or explanations which would never be mentioned in front of the others. During this initial meeting, mediators will probe for more facts and feelings, then usually ask the person what their bottom line is or what they want to see happen. Subsequent caucuses and joint sessions may then be used to shave away the differences in the two bottom lines until compromise is reached.

Consensus or compromise?

While sharing the British feeling that compromise can be a sensible and honorable decision (we don't want to compromise the term!), the difference between compromise through bargaining and consensus through problem-solving is fundamental. In a compromise, the mediator encourages each negotiator to temper his or her wishes in the interest of settlement. The solution lies along a line between the parties' starting positions.

This compromise procedure sounds reasonable, especially in divide-the-pie circumstances. In more complicated conflicts, meeting halfway can be unreasonable, as this incident during a training roleplay showed: The Pratts were elderly, they needed quick access to their car in medical emergencies, and they could not carry groceries in when they parked on the street. They refused the neighbor's request to park in the common drive, insisting the drive must always be clear. The mediator pressed them; surely they wouldn't mind as long as someone was home to move the cars? Could guests at least park there? Stalemate: the Pratts said no. Meeting halfway assumes that both parties have starting positions which are equally (un)reasonable. Negotiations scholar Dean Pruitt (1983: 173) comments that compromises arise from lazy problem-solving involving a half-hearted attempt to satisfy both parties' interests. The mediator had a number of issues to play with in this neighbor scenario, but by limiting his efforts to pushing for compromise on each point, he lost the chance to create a give and take agreement which could have balanced the open driveway with, perhaps, a promise from the Pratts that they would stop calling the police.

Consensus implies a *situation* rather than *sides*. The wider circumstances are considered. Rather than "How can we bring the demands of each party closer together?" the mediators ask, "How can this situation be improved?" Finding answers to this second question may take more think time, but it may save a lot of persuasion time later if the mediator drafts a compromise and then has to persuade the parties to buy it. Such problem-solving is good practice in breaking away from thinking in dualities: Is this good or bad? Should he leave or stay? Ought she pay a higher percentage or lower? Are they responsible for this mess or is he?

One advantage of a consensus procedure is that problems can be defined several ways. This helps release the parties from set answers. Ideally, the substitution of the word "situation" for "problem" allows people to outline the dispute as it appears to them. They can take a wide focus or a narrow one. They can look at root causes or restrict discussion to immediate solutions. The issues can be seen from different perspectives: as emotional hurts, as distributing limited resources, as matters of principle—whatever has meaning to the people involved.

Consensus, the process of coming to a new solution acceptable to all participants, also leaves more room for fresh ideas. Remember the agreement between mother and son about the television? When they came to mediation, they were deadlocked on the subject of bedtime. The mother did not like him falling asleep over the TV and having it on all night. The son wanted to watch an 11 o'clock show from bed every evening. For months they had argued about what time the son should turn off the TV and go to sleep: 10 p.m. or midnight? When the mediator centered discussion on the issue, not the solutions (i.e. the TV blaring all night, not the boy's bedtime hour) the idea of a timer was broached. Suddenly the either/or choice was irrelevant. A new approach solved their problems simply, without haggling over time. Usually compromise is just one of several solutions, and sometimes it is the most satisfactory. But CDS has tried to help disputants approach terms of an agreement with as much imagination as possible.

Because Quakers sponsored the development of this CDS program, many mediators were already well-versed in facilitating difficult consensual decisions (although the religious process is somewhat different from secular consensus). They believed that people who lose to a majority can drag their heels or build up internal resentment; a consensus, though time-consuming, is more likely to be carried out by all involved. In Quaker business meetings, people are expected to tackle issues as a group problem instead of as a battle between two sides. The CDS mediation model was consciously adapted from this experience.

In terms of empowerment, consensus gives less powerful negotiators more say in the outcome because there is more room to redefine the problem and hence its potential solutions. And they can veto any measure. The goals of CDS for its community project fit this outlook easily. CDS prefers that disputants leave with no contract rather than grudgingly sign an agreement. The strength of commitment to that agreement is the only way to enforce it. Without true consent, the contract will have a shaky future at best.

Consensus-based mediating is not as dominant as our CDS ideology would have us believe. Although people are not asked to bargain, they often don't have many ideas or solutions when they are given freer rein. Often the disputants arrive at neither a new solution nor a compromise. Rather the terms are, from each party's view, what they have been doing all along. In other words the agreement reconfirms people's own best image of themselves. This feeling often lies behind this kind of contract: "Mr. Yanich agrees to use polite language to Ms. Bowers." Mr. Yanich may have insisted throughout the mediation that he never spoke rudely her. The agreement slips around the issue of whether he did or didn't. In the interest of appeasing an angry neighbor, Mr. Yanich is willing to "agree" not to do what he already—in his eyes—doesn't.

Evaluating and changing the format

The CDS mediation format has grown from FSP's analysis augmented by mediators' experiences. During CDS's formative years there weren't many programs in existence, which meant that policy and format were pieced together with little access to the observations or thinking of other groups. No one systematically asked disputants for their opinions. As a result, some issues received careful attention, such as the subject of training and others, like mediating in pairs, were never debated. The structural simplicity of the process did not require a layout of complex rules. Without the necessity of developing thorough written guidelines, CDS mediation practice and philosophy continues to center on mediator lore and informal discussions: this is what has worked, this is how we do it, and sometimes more rigidly, this is how it should be done. Although the CDS board has control of all mediation policy, for the most part FSP's training and its *Mediator Handbook* have molded official policy by default.

Outcomes

Any evaluation of a mediation model must pay close attention to the actual outcomes of the process. For now we will restrict our discussion to the results experienced by individual disputants. These can be measured in many ways. The content of agreements can be examined in terms of fairness. We can ask whether disputants get what they want and how well the agreements hold up. We also need to look at what agreements do not cover: protection and vindication, for instance. Is there evidence of flexibility and creativity in the solutions people devise? CDS disputants meet in the shadow of the courts; whether or not they have filed charges, the possibility of legal action is usually in the back of their minds. Therefore the mediation outcomes are necessarily compared to probable outcomes during adjudication. What are the advantages of each process in terms of what the disputants take away? Finally, we examine the topic of empowerment, the ultimate outcome CDS claims to seek.

Does mediation bring about just resolutions?

"Mom, she is LYING!" shouted one fourth grader during a mediation, pointing her finger at the neighbor woman. "Make her stop." The girl burst into indignant tears. When adults are ensnared in a dispute themselves, the child's indignation comes back: "That's not fair! He ought to pay for this." "It's the principle of the thing," a disputant will argue. That principle of elementary justice is a rope with two strands: vindication and fairness.

Vindication

Vindication has two faces. The first one we recognize as part of justice: Wrong is labeled wrong. Innocence is declared. Damages are repaid. The other face is the urge for revenge.

Will someone ever even the scales? Mediation is limited in its ability to satisfy that desire. Fault is only determined if one party chooses to admit it. Restitution happens only when the party at fault agrees to repay. CDS mediators cannot punish anyone or even give a reprimand.

In our eagerness to convince people that mediation is a better way, we forget that even an amicable contract does not necessarily erase the desire for vindication and that such feelings are an understandable response to mistreatment. As one woman who reached a detailed and courteous agreement with her neighbor but still refused to drop charges of assault said, "I have to have the satisfaction of having the judge point his finger at her and saying 'guilty!' I don't even care if he lets her go with no fine."

If mediators cannot guarantee restitution or exonerate the innocent, they can still discuss those issues. The matter of revenge, however, can rip apart any well-intentioned mediation.

There are some times when clients have to get even. I say

to them, "Listen, you can spell it principle or principal, which
do you want?" But they often say "I don't care, it's worth it."
They think this is Right, this is the way it should be.

Most callers who desire vindication of principles or of their actions
weed themselves out during preliminary conversations with CDS
staff. Those that come anyway go home unsatisfied. Disputants'
hidden or blatant desires for a pound of flesh usually destroy any
chance of settlement. During one session, the respondents had
agreed to everything the complainant wanted. In fact she
acknowledged that they had already made all the changes she'd
asked for. Everyone was very nice. Yet no progress. It was forty-five
minutes into the mediation and still no wording of the agreement
was acceptable. The mediators broke to speak with each party. The
woman dropped her pretense of polite cooperation and announced
that she had requested mediation to impress the judge, but she
would never never never agree to anything. Her disabled son was
out waiting in the car, she said, and she couldn't leave him any
longer. She walked out with visible pleasure. How much can
mediators do when faced with such determination to find revenge?

CDS points out to callers that mediation is a cheaper and more
reliable way to get what they want. "The most you can lose is two
hours," they often say. But for some people, spending $500 to reclaim
$200 in damages is a small price for the satisfaction—just once—of
seeing "the system" give them due justice.

The kind of satisfaction mediation gives is strikingly different from
the "I was right! I won!" people seek in the courtroom. Disputants
look relieved, they shake hands, sometimes they hug each other.
In Chapter One we quoted a very short contract where two families
agreed never to speak with each other. They hurried through the
session, refusing to deal with a long history of hostility. By the end
of that mediation they were tripping over themselves in their
eagerness to talk. "You keep to your side, we'll keep to ours, if
that's the way you want it, it's fine with me." "Enough of all this.
We used to be good friends, didn't we?" "We've both lived here
more than thirty years, our kids grew up together." "Remember, we
even took a vacation in the Adirondacks together." No one
commented on the irony as they chatted around the table.

Fairness

If mediation is personally satisfying, it is not because a disputant
has been proved right but because the relationship is brought back

within the bounds of fair play. That brings us back to the issue of fairness, the second strand of the rope.

Fair play seems to translate itself into several concerns during a mediation. First is the issue of the mediator permitting "lies" to go unchallenged. Many survey respondents, like the fourth-grade girl, were unhappy about this part of their mediations. "I thought it was a waste of time when the neighbor lied and convinced you people they were telling it as it was," wrote one. Unless mediation itself becomes a mock court, there seems to be no answer to that complaint except the courtroom. The second perception of fairness, whether in the court process (Tyler, 1984) or in mediation, is heavily based on the ability to tell one's full story and to be listened to by the authorities. The mediation process is ideal for frustrated parties who want all the information out on the table for consideration.

CDS's survey of reported satisfaction indicates that actual terms of agreement seem less important to disputants than the act of reaching agreement at all (see Chapter Two). When people were asked what they liked about the mediation, most responded that they appreciated the mediators' attentiveness and courtesy, and that they were glad to talk to the other side. No one said they liked mediation because the terms of agreement worked out were good. Either people have a very low expectation of what a fair solution is, or else the mediation process does not shove them into contracts they don't want: of 24 parties who reached agreement or partial agreement, 21 said their agreements were fair. One other said the agreement was not fair but was much better than expected.

The balance of the agreement in neighbor disputes depends on the good will and imagination of the disputants. Nevertheless, whether disputants are stubborn or persuasive, conciliatory or pushy, the back and forth is unlikely to end precisely on even terms. For a person in a weak position, admittedly, the bargain can be a humiliating one, as teenage runaways returning home under parental conditions can testify. As far as one can judge from simply reading through CDS files, very few of the contracts seem unfairly lopsided; often there is evidence that the mediators have tried hard to record some positive promise of action on both sides. Cases with overwhelming differences in power, in CDS's experience, rarely end up in voluntary community mediation. Either the disadvantaged party seeks the protection of due process, or the powerful party (a landlord, for instance, or a school principal) doesn't bother coming to the table because it can dictate terms without discussion. This means our community mediators almost never face the issue of signing a patently unfair agreement. The mediation falls apart or the parties don't come in the first place.

Mediators do consciously and unconsciously guide the nature of the agreement, as suggested by our earlier discussions of 1) the similarities between agreements and 2) the unifying effects of background, selection, and training. The mediators' ideas about just solutions may not be the disputants', but they often sneak into the agreements anyway. A mediator may press housemates for an even split of rent, for instance, but they may consider ability to pay, amount of free time, or other factors more important. Academic research on what constitutes a fair solution reveals a host of variables; principles such as equality, need, self-interest, and merit are invoked in different situations by the same person. Convictions about what someone deserves may conflict with what is possible. What benefits one, harms another. Because mediation tries to move away from the dictates of law, the concept of justice becomes all the more elusive.

Seemingly fair agreements may break down. Some people are too angry to want to be fair; some want to look for a still better deal. People continue to break the terms of the agreement in order to protect themselves (usually while complaining that the other party's word is only worth that scrap of paper it's written on). Fairness is in people's heads, and no one can judge the weight a person gives to such intangibles.

Probably an agreement is more likely to hold when people think it is the best they can get, whether it is just or not. The person on the giving end decides that the trade-off of restoring peace or keeping a job is worth the sacrifice. Weariness, bother, humiliation, pride, dependence, magnanimity—dozens of reasons surface to push them towards agreements which do not give them what they could get or what they perhaps deserve to get. A weary staff person wrote this note in the file of a dispute involving unusually difficult people:

> M called CDS saying she was so upset that she didn't sleep all last night because of the lying in the mediation. She mentioned specifically talk about her mother and motorcycles. I asked her if she talked about these things at the mediation but she hadn't. I asked her about the agreement and signing it, and she said the only reason she did was to get out of there.

Follow-ups within two weeks and again a half year later reported cool feelings but no problems. Even with her dissatisfaction, she didn't crank up the dispute again. The price of her definition of fairness was too high.

How much should mediators become the guardians of fairness when the disputants have given up? How fair should a decision be? There can be substantial differences between contracts attempting to be morally just, those stipulating a balanced give-and-take, and ones laying out a reasonable compromise. Whatever the standard of fairness, the issue of fairness is weighed against the probability of the agreement holding up to the satisfaction of the parties.

In the last analysis, mediators can help move towards a solution all perceive as just, but they cannot promise fair results. The agreement may be lopsided. One party may be lying. Someone may be unable to articulate or fight for what they want. Ignorance of the law may result in an agreement which courts would declare unjust.

Having looked at the matters of vindication and fairness, we return to the question: Does mediation promote just agreements? Some ingredients are certainly there: People have a chance to be heard by their adversaries, there can be restitution for damages, and the opportunity to reject unacceptable terms. Agreements arrange reasonable distribution of tasks and rewards.

We can safely say that mediation offers the *possibility* of a just agreement, and that may be all one can say for any kind of dispute settlement, including litigation. If disputants are relatively matched in power or truly committed to a workable solution, the agreement may be as close to a fair and beneficial outcome as anyone could hope for.

What gets settled?

Does mediation settle things? CDS does not have access to the follow-up information needed to determine this. Certainly, the majority of people contacted by phone report that things are "Okay" or have died down. Research on the Neighborhood Justice Centers, and on the programs in Dorchester, MA and in Brooklyn, NY (Cook et al, 1980; Felstiner & Williams, 1980; Davis et al, 1980) suggests that the rate of breakdown is similar to the percentage of recidivism in adjudicated neighbor disputes.

A few people do bring fresh complaints to the district justices when their agreements break down. Of the 34 parties who filled out the questionnaire, 7 have returned to court. Three of these cases had reached agreement in mediation, with the parties describing the contract as fair and the mediation as satisfactory! ("The mediators were great, too bad I can't say the same of the neighbors," wrote one.) In these cases, the problem was litigated some months later when troubles started up again. Since the disputants who returned to court and those who were still angry with their neighbors sent back their survey responses before anyone else, 7 out of 34 (20%) is probably an exaggerated percentage of recidivism. We have no accurate district court statistics on which parties filed fresh suits. Judges using CDS report that mediation nearly always marks the last of a party's repeated court complaints.

How different are outcomes for people who bring home court judgments from those who have mediation agreements? There are similarities. They have something concrete in hand, whether it is a judge's order or a CDS contract. Like court rulings, CDS contract terms are routine and tend to underscore the existing values of the larger community.

What they lack in creativity, CDS mediation contracts make up in flexibility. Courts rule on narrowly prescribed issues. CDS disputants do have a wider choice in what to discuss and in the details of what they decide. Agreements do show that people negotiate around the particulars of their situation. If a person has an odd work schedule, for instance, or a knack for pruning, this is taken into account. They are able to make decisions about things which bother them which the law does not cover, and CDS agreements show that the disputants often chose to deal with these matters as seriously as the legal ones: "Adele agrees to call Pat if the children are playing ball in her yard again." "Hank agrees to a 9:45 lights out on school nights."

Sontag's FSP research (1980) indicated another main area of difference. People who had experienced mediation reported greater understanding of the other party (44%, compared with 18%) and a dramatic drop in feelings of hostility towards the other party. Many (38%) CDS disputants reported feeling less hostile, in contrast to 18% of those who had gone through court; 62% and 45%, respectively, had not changed; and 37% of the litigants reported feeling more hostile. Not one of the CDS disputants, even those who had unsatisfactory sessions, said their feelings of hostility had risen. CDS rode in confidence on these findings for many years. Unfortunately, our more recent survey found that 26% (9 disputants) felt worse about the other party since the mediation. Of these, 7 people had reached no agreement. Another 17% felt better about the other party, a figure equivalent to Sontag's findings for parties who had gone to court. In both cases, samples were small; hence any results are suggestive, not definitive.

Outcomes between court and mediation cases also depend on the function of those institutions. Merry (1979) contends that people don't expect the court to *settle* things, they expect the court to punish, to be a sanction, to be a card in their deck. Filing suit can give weaker parties more leverage to insist on change (McEwen and Maiman, 1984). Mediation agreements work towards stopping the aggravations and help repattern interactions. Disputants who want vindication, leverage, or enforced punishment are not satisfied by mediation. Likewise, the court outcome often does not answer the desires of some complainants who just want peace. The cases which come to mediation have sometimes been in court before; the disputants report retaliation and bad feelings. They are upset to find that the court punished but did not settle the problem. The judge dealt with the facts and reprimanded them for their negative feelings but did not help them get through that hostility to find a new basis for existing together with less friction.

Conciliation does not always happen in CDS mediations, but certainly it occurs more often than is possible with a court decision. A shaky mediation agreement at least brings a cease fire; if the lull can help the vindictive emotions subside, the insults and incidents which stoke the fires may also stop. Problems which have been avoided during mediation have a way of resolving themselves quietly if good relations are allowed to build. Once the battle is over, people make concessions which two weeks before would have been unthinkable.

One CDS volunteer sums up the issue of outcomes from her perspective:

> Just from my follow-up phone calls for CDS I know that a lot of disputes continue. It doesn't surprise me that there is still bitterness and anger. That happens in a family too.... I am glad to see them go through all that turmoil and get through it, to see them get a breather, smile at each other.... You can see that they don't like hating the other person. They get to a point of forgiving to some degree.

Empowerment

An evaluation of the CDS mediation model is not complete without an effort to measure the results of mediation against CDS's highest goal. The vision of people learning to resolve their own conflicts has been a touchstone for CDS from the beginning. Readers have no doubt noticed this theme running in different colors through each chapter; it is not possible to write about CDS without referring to this central concept.

Many dispute settlement programs use the catch word *empowerment*. CDS was founded on that hope. Each of these excerpts from program literature illustrates a different piece of CDS's picture of empowerment:

> The goal is to help people retain control over what is happening in their own lives. (1984 program description)

> The mediation process introduces disputants to a new approach to conflict. Instead of an outside party deciding who is "right" and who is "wrong,"...the parties themselves develop a workable agreement. (1982 grant proposal)

> When people have actively helped build a workable solution to a problem their image of themselves and their feelings about others generally become more positive. And they may develop some confidence in their ability to deal with conflicts in the future. (staff notes, 1983)

> Mediation is based on the assumptions that all disputing parties have a legitimate problem, that they have the inner resources to find a solution, and that they will have a personal investment in making a solution work if they have been actively involved in creating it. (1982 grant proposal)

Mediators sometimes view the empowerment idea with a seasoning of private skepticism, saying they always hope that people have learned something, but they aren't sure. "I don't think empowerment will happen, but I keep my fingers crossed," says one mediator putting her finger on this ambivalence. She goes on:

> I'd like to see CDS provide a really good viable option to destructive modes of conflict. Society has methods of dealing with conflict which one way or another often wind up using force or punishment which are destructive to the social fabric. It is important to provide alternatives that will not automatically sow the seeds of new conflict, which in turn create new seeds, and so on.... The program says "Yoohoo! There's another way out here and it doesn't hurt so much." We can always hope that concept will spread....

Mediators like this woman see empowerment in a cultural context; the obstacles to changing society's inbred patterns loom large. Some people are more optimistic. They focus on satisfaction in small changes in individual lives. "A drop in the bucket" is a phrase which crops up in many mediator interviews. One woman who used it explains:

> By taking people through the process in a regimented way, it increases the potential of them using those problem-

*solving skills themselves when other things come up.... I
don't know if it's age or wisdom, but I feel more and more
that efforts to work with individuals and relatively small pieces
of the world makes more difference.*

One of the problems with broad goals like empowerment is trying
to measure them. Are people really empowered? To approach an
answer, we start with three points which summarize CDS's definition
of empowerment:

1) Taking responsibility, not expecting someone else to fix it, seeing
yourself as part of the problem.

2) Finding confidence and energy, breaking through hopelessness
and helplessness. Feeling "I can do something about this."

3) Learning new skills for coping with conflict.

CDS philosophy explicitly states that true empowerment means
these three points of change will carry over into future attitudes and
behavior. The CDS handbook states: "CDS provides a model for
settling future disputes. People see that they can work through their
own problems with each other." (Beer, et al., 1982: 2)

The replies of thirty families to CDS's post-mediation questionnaire
and information from disputant interviews and follow-up calls shed
some light on each of these three aspects.

Taking responsibility. One of the factors mediators note at the
Turning Point is that people begin to acknowledge their complicity
in the conflict. Many never admit fault but are able to change their
conception of "they are the problem" to "we all have a problem."

The survey showed a fairly even split between finger-pointers and
those who implied that the situation was a mutual problem. Nine
families who answered the questionnaire blamed the outcome of
the mediation on the other party and wrote of themselves as helpless,
innocent victims of the neighbors. They wrote comments like these:

*It was not the [mediators'] fault, the people we were
disputing with just do not care about anything but drinking
and making noise.*

The problem is my neighbors' attitude. They are impossible!

Eight others made comments, usually about the value of hearing
both sides, which acknowledged that all parties had a problem. One
woman wrote that she was glad that they had a chance to discuss
"different world views." That was the closest anyone came to
admitting an active role in the dispute.

Taking responsibility remains a difficult measure of empowerment. Not only is it hard to define; there is always the complicating possibility that the "stubborn" party is correct: it *is* the other party's fault. While many disputants make statements like, "Look, we have to live next door to each other," or "I know I have a hot temper and I blow up when I shouldn't," many other people sit through two hours of mediation, reach agreement, and on their way out the door tell the mediators, "I don't know what their problem was. We've never done anything." Most likely, people go out with the same attitude they carried in. Those who are conciliatory are willing to look at their own role; those who are feeling abused leave feeling used or exonerated.

The negative interpretation of taking responsibility is accepting blame. The CDS model, as Baskin (1984) correctly judges, ultimately places blame on the individuals. The underlying current whispers, "If you knew how to handle things better, you wouldn't be here." Although this is evident in observing CDS mediators and listening to their shop talk among each other, the survey responses of disputants do not show signs of embarrassment or shame. People speak forthrightly with anger or with satisfaction. They seem to retain their conviction that they are innocent, nice people who try to be good neighbors. Reactions during follow-up calls are often more reserved, however.

Confidence and energy. The second aspect of empowerment, also a slippery concept to measure, is how people feel about their ability to cope with conflict in the future. Certainly, disputants come into a mediation session at a low point of self-confidence. Whatever ways they have tried to fix the situation have not worked. Mediators take the opportunity during the Closing Statement to send people away on a note of praise and confidence.

Do people really feel energized and proud of what they've accomplished? The questionnaire asked, "Did the mediation change your feelings about how you handle conflict?—More confidence, the same, less confidence." Of 28 responses, half (15) of the disputants felt "the same," which given the briefness of mediation is not unexpected. Only 3 had less confidence (no agreements in these mediations), and 10 said they had more. There was clear correlation between renewed confidence and the perceived success of the mediation; 8 of those "more confident" parties had reached a satisfactory agreement. Apart from this small evidence, energy and confidence are hard to measure; most of us gratefully put resolved problems behind us, and if it brings renewed energy, we probably do not connect the two.

Learning new skills. The third and most observable facet of empowerment is the learning of more effective ways to handle conflict. A few disputants come to mediation with strong conflict resolution skills. Such people understand the usefulness of neutral parties. Some are familiar with negotiation tactics or handle upset people with gentleness and skill; mediators find them crucial allies in persuading other participants to reach agreement.

Most disputants are less sure of themselves. They explain that they tried to respond to conflict in an "adult," "calm" way, that they went next door to talk things over. Watching them in the mediation session, though, their lack of skill is evident. Under pressure, they do not practice the basics of conflict resolution: they cannot listen and speak without threats or outbursts, they fail to understand how the other side perceives the situation, and they are often unclear about their own feelings and motives.

Because the disputants come in with varying levels of skills, the questionnaire looked both at what skills people reported actually using and whether the mediation had influenced their behavior. The accuracy of these responses is limited, of course, since people often talk one way and behave another.

Disputants were asked "*Since* the mediation, have you ever used any of the following ideas during an argument with someone?" Out of 36 people, some of whom did not answer the question at all, the following number of "yesses" were recorded:

12 — Suggesting that each person take a turn of uninterrupted time.

6 — Writing down things everyone agrees to do.

17 — Listening *without breaking in* to someone who is angry at you or criticizing you.

16 — Refraining from calling someone names or cursing them out.

21 — Speaking frankly and directly to a person that annoyed or angered you.

The uneasiness many people express about agreements—either worrying that the agreement will not hold up or feeling that writing decisions down is unfriendly—is reflected in these figures. Indeed, it is questionable whether even six people have used this technique. Speaking directly has more respondents than any other. This may or may not be a positive sign, as the written comments suggested that for some people "speaking directly" does not mean speaking with discretion!

One third (12) of the 36 said that the mediation influenced their decision to act in these ways. Almost that many (10) said that the experience of mediation changed the way they handle conflict or difficult people. These 10 are, again, not necessarily affirming CDS's empowerment goals, as the following comments on how the mediation experience changed their tactics reveal:

Yes, if you want results get a lawyer.

Yes, avoid them.

The figures show that some people probably *do* learn something about conflict resolution skills and their personal attitudes. Comments during disputant interviews and on the questionnaire support this. One man, for instance, said that following the mediation, his household began routinely using Uninterrupted Time during house meetings. In the CDS survey, a man wrote that he learned "it pays to listen and not get mad." Others, describing what had changed, said they now "try to talk without getting angry." "Speak more directly—not as afraid of other person's feelings." Another said she "learned to be more patient."

Impressions of the mediation also give a clue to what people learned. Many liked the opportunity to talk things out, a good sign, but one counterweighted by those who still believed the mediators opinions to be central. A few complained that the mediators believed the lies of the other side or that mediation was superficial. More said that a judge or a psychiatrist was the only way to deal with "those people." Other disputants praised CDS for agreeing with the righteousness of their position. People experience mediation differently; the various reactions to the session mirror the mixed reports about satisfaction, confidence, and skill-building.

While participants may never think of what they have learned in such grand and radical terms as "empowerment," learning to negotiate better is probably of general interest to most people. Nevertheless, when disputants learn new skills from the mediation, it is for them a side issue, an opportunity which they may or may not notice. No one has been recorded saying, "I'd like to come learn how to cope with this kind of frustration better." Resolving the problem and protecting themselves are the disputants' two overwhelming concerns. Empowerment is CDS's agenda, not the participants'.

Disempowerment? The correspondence between satisfactory agreements and increased self-confidence, which we noted earlier, also suggests that empowerment may come not in learning specifics but in seeing results. Disputants gain confidence that talking matters out can really resolve conflicts.

After listening to disputants' post-session comments, an opposite pattern also emerged from "successful" mediations. "I don't know how you people do it," a businessman said, shaking his head after a not unusual mediation session. "You people have the patience of Job. I'd never be able to pull it off. Hats off to you." The mediators have done something incredible. Pleased astonishment shows in disputants' faces as they take their leave. "God sent you to us," said one woman. A staff member writes ruefully, "It feels good to be told you just performed a miracle, and it's hard to resist the temptation to believe it."

Could it be that a mediator's very skill undermines the goal of increasing the disputants' future self-confidence? Instead of glimpsing their own power, some disputants leave the session thinking that only talented, better-than-I-am experts can solve problems. After all, someone occasionally reasons aloud, the situation has improved drastically in two hours. And I haven't changed anything in three years of trying! The question for mediators is how to use their own power in such a way that the disputants begin to understand the large part they themselves played in working things out. For some mediators this empowerment is more important for the disputants' future than the particular terms of settlement reached at that particular time.

Empowerment remains a matter of faith. Will the pregnant teenager and her parents approach the coming decisions about abortion, money, and child care with more capacity to hear each other out? The program never heard from the family again. Does Mrs. Pratt really call her neighbor when a guest's car is blocking the drive, or does she complain to the police as before? Who is to know if the seed experience of one short intense evening will ever take root? CDS believes it is worth a try.

Part II

You have decided to mediate in your community. Intensive training has helped hone your third party skills. But where do you find disputes to resolve? So far this book has concentrated on the mediation process. Developing a mediation framework, however, is only the beginning of third party work. To organize any program takes many more hours a week than the time spent actually mediating. Intake, that is handling all the calls and correspondence before a mediation, is a large job. Hours are taken up with publicity and education and, always, the search for money.

A dispute settlement program's special organizational problems center on one key fact: Community mediation's purpose and its methods are unfamiliar—one might venture to say even alien and unwelcome—to the public. If you stop for two minutes and list current conflicts between people you know, probably you can think of at least three situations where a neutral person could help and where neither party would think of meeting with a mediator. No community is short on disputes, but many disputants have tightly shut doors. The challenge is trying to open them just a crack.

The second part of this book, therefore, looks at mediation in its wider setting: the choices Community Dispute Settlement made in forming a program; the place of mediation in the suburban community; the conflicting desires to help people live both fairly and peaceably with each other.

Seven: The Program Model

The appearance and soundness of a house are determined by the frame and foundation which hold it together. Any program model is shaped around goals and philosophy, whether or not those are consciously laid out. The form is further set by external factors such as money, location, connections with the community, and staff skills. While everyone agrees that a sound foundation of practice and purpose are basic to building a sturdy program, the young community mediation movement is still experimenting with organizational blueprints.

Whose house will stand? Whose house will fall? FSP has helped several programs besides its own CDS project, each with a slightly different program model. Some never got off the ground, others had a short life. A number are doing well. Before we compare and contrast the experiences of these programs, we first take a detailed look at CDS's own house.

An Overview of the CDS Program

The following overview of CDS's structure shows where the program fits along the spectrum of mediation services presently offered in North America. Because each community has a different set of "givens," we make no attempt to evaluate one model of dispute settlement program over another but hope that walking through CDS's decisions and their consequences will give readers a useful example of how one group handled the practical considerations of spreading mediation services throughout the communities in its region.

CDS has not changed substantially since it began in 1976 as an FSP project. A 1985 thumbnail outline of the CDS model differs in only two ways: the location has moved from the countryside site of the FSP office, and more importantly, the organization has become independent of FSP and the Society of Friends. The current CDS organization can be described by these characteristics:

Area served: A suburban county divided into small communities of many economic levels—from crowded row houses to expensive developments which are rapidly spreading across old farms to the west.

Constituency: Delaware County (population 555,000) but concentrating on neighbors and families referred by the district (lowest level) courts. Most come from the more densely populated areas of the county.

Location: The FSP-sponsored program was housed in the western end of the county in the FSP office. CDS moved in 1982 to a storefront in Darby, one of the poorer communities close to the Philadelphia city line. Preliminary interviews have always been conducted by telephone, though mediations are scheduled in the disputants' neighborhood.

Numbers served: 322 total calls requesting help in 1984 resulted in 46 mediations and 16 CDS-assisted resolutions which were not mediated. Caseload was tallied differently before this year, hence earlier figures are not comparable. In 1983 34 disputes were mediated. Under FSP, the program mediated 25 or fewer cases each year.

Funding: From 1976 to 1982, Philadelphia Yearly Meeting, the regional Quaker organization, paid the staff and operating expenses. Since mid-1982, funding has been through grants and donations. To date, disputant contributions have been insignificant. Recently, CDS has become a United Way agency, which has stabilized its funding.

Fees: The program first asked a donation of $5 on the theory that people have more respect for themselves and the mediation if they have contributed. Now the suggested contribution is $10–$25 from each side.

Budget: 1984: $35,000; 1985: $42,000. For 1984 this averages out to $109 per case, $760 per mediation, and $564 per mediated or resolved dispute. The figures for 1985 are higher: $247, $954, and $736 respectively. Before 1982, costs were integrated into the larger FSP budget and cannot easily be estimated. For two years the organization survived on a month-to-month basis.

Mediators: All are volunteers, mostly women, white, college-educated. Successful completion of the twenty-hour FSP mediation training and subsequent apprenticeship is sufficient qualification. The active pool has been, for any given year, approximately twenty-five people.

Staff: Two FSP staff members worked approximately half-time each; the independent program now employs one full time and one half time staff. They are responsible for intake and follow-up, accounts, seeking and administering grants, maintaining an active group of mediators, and outreach.

Oversight: Formerly the FSP committee, now a fifteen-person board of directors which meets monthly. The executive committee of the four officers makes interim decisions. Board meetings are open to any CDS volunteer or visitor and are run by consensus.

A day at CDS

How do the characteristics listed above translate into daily workings? What happens inside CDS doors? Another way to describe the basic appearance of the program is through the eyes of a staff person, as in this sample day in the Darby office.

Jim arrives at nine o'clock. Parking along Main Street is already full and the trolley is edging past the cars as it turns the corner in front of the small office. In the window, a cheery yellow poster reading "COMMUNITY DISPUTE SETTLEMENT PROGRAM" is surrounded by small hanging plants. Otherwise it looks like a strangely empty shop. Inside, the large room has four desks, one filing cabinet, and a bookshelf loaded with brochures from other agencies. In the back, an old electric typewriter and a mimeograph machine sit by piles of scrap paper. Near the door is a sitting area with a table and some comfortable second-hand chairs. Yellow fabric hides the wall and a dark red used carpet covers the stained and ripped linoleum. It took ingenuity and several weekends of work to make the old store less dingy.

The answering machine has many messages, some from disputants checking on mediation session schedules, one from a reporter wanting to see a live mediation, two from local court secretaries, one from FSP asking about the neighborhood meeting held the night before. Anne, the other staff person, is in Philadelphia talking to foundations about yet another round of proposals and then has an appointment near the CDS office with a senior citizen agency. Jim settles in with a cup of coffee.

The first return call to a new inquiry takes thirty-five minutes. The man is so outraged that he harangues Jim with every detail of a three-year dispute. Is he willing to let Jim contact the neighbor? Yes. Jim wonders if the man really understands what mediation is about and tries again: "You'll have to sit in the same room, Mr. Barnes, and the mediators will not *make* your neighbor do anything...." He types up a standard letter of inquiry to the neighbor before making the other calls.

At eleven o'clock Jim finally has time to check today's "to do" file: two follow-ups and one daytime mediation needing one more mediator, preferably a younger man. The follow-ups aren't home. After four calls to volunteers, Brad agrees to mediate.

Finances are tight. Careful updating of the books takes over an hour. This is interrupted by an older man calling to inquire about CDS on a judge's suggestion. Jim crooks the receiver against his shoulder and fills out an intake form. The man is overwrought and Jim has trouble getting him off the phone. While he listens, he begins to put together a folder for the mediators in tonight's case in Collingswood: contracts, evaluations, scrap paper, donation envelopes, a copy of the intake information, directions to the church....

Two women come in off the street wanting legal advice. Jim tells them how CDS can help and gives them a flyer for the Domestic Abuse Program. The phone rings again. This time a woman says abruptly that she and her husband have received the program's letter, they see no problem, and intend to ignore their daughter's complaints. She does not wait for persuasion but hangs up on her last word. "Well," thinks Jim, "At least it was short."

After lunch, Anne arrives full of energy. Pleased with her morning interview, she calls the head of the Board to tell the news. Then she and Jim talk over the large neighbor dispute which is dragging on for the third month. Should CDS cut its losses? The mediators need to come in for an update and strategy session, they decide.

One call to the police: Have any cases come in that CDS should follow up? Another to a board member: Can she speak to the United Presbyterian Women next Thursday? And it is time to head home. The phone rings as the door locks, and Jim smiles to himself as the answering machine clicks on.

The New Idea

Immigrant community elders. Parish ministers. Business arbitrators. Conciliation Courts of the 1920s. Utopian religious experiments. Alternatives to our court system are nothing new. As Jerome Auerbach (1983) has documented, dispute settlement outside the framework of law has a long tradition in this country. For programs starting up in the 1960s and 70s, however, mediation was a new and exciting idea.

As one of the earlier community mediation programs, CDS followed the growth of Neighborhood Justice Centers and court-sponsored programs with interest. Everyone was searching for models. Each mediation program reflected the organizer's own background. Labor models, characterized by strong mediators and frequent caucusing, were adapted by some (notably IMCR in New York City). Lawyers and arbitrators brought their own professional slant to other programs. In other cities, social workers and counselors approached the mediation model from their experience in healing interpersonal relationships. Here and there, notably in San Francisco and Pittsburgh as well as at Friends Suburban Project, community activists designed dispute settlement models.

When a special American Arbitration Association training was arranged in Philadelphia, the women who had been considering starting a dispute settlement program in Delaware County jumped at the chance. The AAA model was only partly suited to neighborhood mediation, and they soon struck out on their own. The immediate questions were those of sponsorship (FSP was one of several interested organizations), program goals, and development of an appropriate, workable mediation format.

There were high hopes for the program model. Staff member Johanna Matteus summarized many of these in an FSP memo several years after the program began. CDS should set an example as a democratic and empowering service, she wrote. Its organizational structure should reflect the mediation philosophy of shared decision-making. As a social change organization it would strategize about how to raise consciousness and provide information. Eventually it would expand services to teach democratic decision-making and to help people prevent conflict by learning to negotiate. This was, to her, the essence of working with the roots of community disputes. Another related task would be training strategically important groups in conflict resolution and prevention skills. The whole CDS project would concentrate on recruiting people wanting to work for community change.

Sitting through long hours of court during their years in juvenile justice advocacy, the founding group of CDS had watched Delaware County district justices handling streams of neighbor and teenager problems. Now the new program was ready to serve the community. If this mediation idea worked, Community Dispute Settlement would soon be inundated with quarreling households. They immediately organized two mediation training courses which covered different sections of the county. Would CDS have enough volunteers to handle the case load?

Getting volunteers to mediate proved no problem. In the succeeding years interest remained consistently strong, with training requests coming from many communities in Pennsylvania and nearby states. The new program also found that most mediations did end in agreement, that disputants were pleased with the results. The soil looked rich: there were ample disputes, a crowd of eager mediators, steady funding, and a process that promised to work well. A little watering and...like mushrooms, mediation programs run by local people would spring up throughout the neighborhoods of Delaware County. At the 1980 annual Philadelphia Yearly Meeting of Friends, FSP presented its year of work on a large bulletin board with names of active communities lettered on a field of large white mushrooms. This image became a tenacious program goal.

The sharp sunlight of experience slowly faded the vision from an expectation to a wishful hope then to myth. As most mediation programs outside centralized urban districts have since discovered, the US public is not flocking to their doors. Educating referral sources and building a reputation are taking time. The number of phone hours spent arranging just one mediation also came as a surprise. Persuasion proved more difficult than running the actual face-to-face session. This faint feeling of frustration has shadowed the program from the beginning. Why aren't people using something so plainly in their best interests? As we look at different aspects of setting up a community program, eventually we must return to this problem as the puzzling core question all community mediation programs need to answer.

Most of the professionals and community groups FSP trained have kept the mediation session format FSP developed. Their program models, however, were often distinctly different from CDS. As mediation takes hold in new places, forms will continue to change. This experimentation with models is helpful for a field still in its childhood. In evaluating one program model, we do not yet need to ask, "Is it the best way?" The question is more "Is the program making a positive difference in the community?" In measurable terms, this means asking how closely the CDS program meets its twin goals of 1) settling community disputes and 2) improving people's skill in handling conflicts.

Different Program Models

We begin by describing the common organizational patterns adopted by mediators in their search for legitimacy and survival. Across North America, mediation programs now have so many forms that we will only summarize the categories here, with a close look at where CDS fits into the larger picture. Following that, we will look at the many decisions a program makes and evaluate CDS's own response to these issues.

Public programs

Court-based. Many programs are funded directly by cities, counties, or states as adjuncts to their court systems. Two documented early experiments show how different such services can be. One is a storefront center affiliated with the local court in Dorchester, Massachusetts, which uses local mediators for one-to-two hour mediation sessions scheduled at the parties' convenience. The other is the Columbus, Ohio, Night Prosecutor Program where law students practice third party skills. The average session in this program lasts about thirty minutes, and the agreement covers primarily the subject of formal complaint. Most cases are funneled through these mediation hearings before the court will hear them. Many problems are referred to social workers and agencies, and often their representatives sit in on the sessions.

Several states have started systems of regional mediation programs affiliated with the court system. Another trend is the use of mediation in juvenile courts and for divorce settlements. Increasingly, judges recommend or require mediation for custody and visitation decisions. Frequently, these mediators are directly employed by the courts and work in the same building.

The court models have the advantages of a large, reliable, at-hand case load, somewhat secure funding, and public oversight. They have more clout to bring disputants to the table and to agreement. (A letter on embossed official stationery from the local judge "asking" parties to mediate next Wednesday at 3 p.m. before a hearing is scheduled looks as formal as a subpoena.) Binding agreements can be enforced by the court. In state-wide systems, staff and volunteers enjoy opportunities for training, conferences, consulting, and assistance with organizational problems. As with any public program, however, politics can suddenly raise or lower a program's fortunes, as the Dorchester Urban Court program discovered when a disapproving judge took the bench.

Community programs

Community-based programs are private, non-profit programs specifically organized to settle local disputes. Mediators may be professionals, students, or community people. Usually they volunteer or receive small stipends. At the core of the organization are a few enthusiasts convinced that the value and pleasure of resolving conflict is worth their hard work. The Atlanta, Georgia, Neighborhood Justice Center is one of the earliest and best known examples of community-based dispute settlement. In many states, numerous small projects are making headway. We do not read as much about these programs in mediation literature because they are less able to fund detailed evaluations or to publish their experiences. Some are isolated from other groups, developing organizational structure and policy on their own.

Social service programs. Some of the larger, more established programs like Atlanta have become agencies, with the larger budgets, professional staff, community status, and organized publicity and grantsmanship that "agency" implies. Newer or smaller programs might better be called "service organizations." The FSP-trained all-volunteer Dispute Settlement Plan of Chester County, which holds only occasional mediations, is an example of a service group. As a program of the local YWCA, it receives phone answering service and office space but otherwise employs no staff. For seven years its activity has been low, but steady. The yearly budget is under a thousand dollars. When someone in the community wants mediation, the program is there.

Community Dispute Settlement has many of the hallmarks of a social service agency: paid staff, an office, formal records, required training for volunteers. Yet the image of an agency doesn't quite fit this program. CDS still squeezes by on shoe-string funding. It presents itself as a project run by a small, dedicated group offering a service not because the community asks for it so much as because they believe in its potential and importance. The distinction is admittedly somewhat fuzzy, but it does reflect the perceptions CDS holds about itself.

Another subset of the community-based programs are the community panels. Community ownership and control over disputes is the idea behind these groups. Three to five trained local people from different segments of the community mediate together. Mediators try to represent the concern and the will of the community in these models. San Francisco's Community Boards Program is the most publicized example. China's much described mediation system is also based on the idea of panels of elected community members. *So, Sue Me!* by James Yaffe (1972) tells (delightfully) the story of New York City's Jewish Conciliation Court, a mediation/arbitration panel of three which settled disputes for a generation in one immigrant neighborhood.

Programs using panels can choose a combination of mediators who reflect the norms of their constituencies (as once juries were intended to?). They live around the corner; what happens to this dispute matters to them. A program like CDS, however, which finds itself in amid crazy-quilt suburban neighborhoods doesn't serve one group or one community. The public forum has less authority when mediators are unknown people with unknown opinions and unknown position in the community.

One service within an agency. La Comunidad Hispaña has long fought for the improved rights and welfare of the Hispanic agricultural laborers employed in southeast Pennsylvania's mushroom industry. After their staff and board received mediation training, they added mediation to their repertoire of intervention skills, settling differences between workers and employers, within families, in the court rooms, and in schools. The Problem Center in Cambridge, Massachusetts added a mediation component to other problem-solving and counseling services, deciding which approach best suits each case. The Human Relations Commission in Philadelphia has a department which responds to complaints in the city's neighborhoods. One-tenth of such disputes are mediated; the rest are handled by phone or by visits to the area. In Pennsylvania, Chester County's Services for Senior Citizens uses mediation skills to handle problems in Senior Centers and to help their clients negotiate with neighbors, home care workers, or even their own families.

Agencies which offer mediation as one of many options can handle cases with greater flexibility than a one-service neighborhood dispute resolution program. Often their funding base and referral network are broader. They have better access to professional expertise, to people who can help in training and in administration.

Problem-centered. Dispute settlement programs sometimes choose to concentrate on a single type of dispute. In Cambridge, Massachusetts, the Childrens' Hearing Project concentrates mostly on truancy, using adults and teens to mediate between student, parent, teachers, and school administration. The Federal Community Relations Service intervenes in disputes involving civil rights issues. Chambers of Commerce and the Better Business Bureau offer consumer mediation services. The Mennonites' Victim Offender Reconciliation Programs bring victims of crime together with the offender to work out restitution. CDS follows the work of such programs eagerly, learning from these variations of generic mediation which are designed specially for certain types of situations. The Children's Hearings Project, for instance, has as part of the mediation a thorough follow-up schedule, with the program checking often to see that the school is keeping its agreement.

Professional service

In addition to community-based and court-based models, a third is gaining rapid popularity: professional mediation services. These may be in-house programs, private practices, or skill-centered consulting.

In-house. Few organizations have their own mediation service yet, although personnel departments and company ombudspersons sometimes serve that kind of third party capacity. The largest program is probably at the University of Massachusetts in Amherst. This group handles complaints from both the University and the local community.

Private practice. The most visible third parties, and probably the fastest growing of all mediation services, are those professionals who specialize in conflict resolution which requires extensive knowledge of the content of the dispute. Labor-management, divorce, and environmental disputes are areas usually handled by career mediators. Educational disputes promise to be another, particularly work such as that Claire Gallant has done in Connecticut with special education (Gallant, 1982). Organizational development consultants have been mediating internal business disputes for a long time, though without using that terminology. Some of these professional services are similar to mediation agencies described above, but the client fees are substantial. The practitioner needs more educational background and probably in the near future some kind of certification. These professionals help legitimize the community mediation idea (indeed, small programs often ride the coattails of the more familiar and respected image of labor mediators). The addition of specialized mediators to CDS's roster might help fund neighbor mediations. One program in Boulder, Colorado, took this tack for survival several years ago. Though they are doing well financially, they have had to drop "barking dog cases" entirely. So far, CDS has not been tempted to specialize; to date we know of no environmental or divorce mediators in the Philadelphia area yet making a living exclusively from mediation.

Skills-centered. Professionals and agencies commonly include workshops and consulting as part of their mediation practice. Mediators from various mediation services have also started marketing their own training programs. A few community programs have concentrated their primary efforts in this area of education. One program in Pittsburgh trains and supports neighbors who already find themselves in the middle of their friends' disputes. Since CDS became independent, Friends Suburban Project, too, has increasingly focused its work in dispute settlement on training and on writing.

Where does CDS fit?

CDS's community-based organization has never been seriously challenged by its volunteers or by its funding and referral sources. From the beginning, the grassroots image has had appeal. CDS wanted peacemaking with visible results. Helping people regain control of resolving problems and spreading services to other communities through inexpensive training were ideas which suited FSP's style. Empowerment, alternatives, and nonviolence could each be addressed with minimal financing and a small number of capable volunteers. The other options of court or agency sponsorship, training programs, or professional services have been brought up from time to time but always rejected.

Despite close relations with local courts, CDS has consistently shied away from even considering official affiliation with the criminal justice system. Since its founding in 1968, Friends Suburban Project had been active in prison work and court-watching, in advocating for teens in trouble with the law, and in advising a citizens' committee fighting police abuse. The Project's interest in mediation was as an alternative, not as an adjunct, to the system. The people they saw in court needed a way out. The coopting of mediation by courts, they feared, would probably lead to one more pre-trial bureaucratic step for inconvenient or "trivial" disputes. The CDS founders believed that coercion would subvert empowerment and lessen the likelihood of mutually satisfactory agreement because parties would be pressured to give in so that the court could see some contract. Confidentiality and privacy might also be hard to maintain. There is some evidence to the contrary—high pressured court mediation agreements do often hold. Though most disputants show little concern about confidentiality or privacy, today these views are still a firm part of CDS philosophy. (Chapter Nine discusses these issues at greater length.)

When it became independent, CDS briefly considered the possibility of sponsorship. The idea has been rejected mostly because no one has found an acceptable affiliate. "We have always held tenaciously to our freedom to set our own policies and procedures," says staffperson Anne Richan. The main concern has been the matter of appearing impartial: In programs which customarily intervene as advocates, counselors, or crisis teams, is the neutrality of the mediation portion of the program jeopardized?

During the years when FSP was running CDS while maintaining a busy schedule of mediation training, the staff found mixing the two activities difficult. Training is time-intensive, whereas program maintenance demands a steady daily pace. When staff was absorbed in the immediate need to design and run a workshop series, the important details of processing mediation cases were often put off longer than they should have been. And training is not merely a matter of expertise in content; it is a skill in its own right. A changeover to skill-oriented programming requires changing the staff's work style and developing trainer competence. For CDS today, training could be an attractive and distracting opportunity for money-raising, professional prestige, and community education. So far they have not chosen to add an educational component to their services.

In its tradition of spinning off experimental offspring programs, FSP set up CDS as an independent organization once its future in the community seemed stable enough to risk the break. FSP budget cuts forced CDS out of the nest somewhat prematurely, but the program survived. The difficult organizing issues of money, location, staffing, and board structure took many meetings to work out. Nevertheless, transition was easier because the board did not have to implement a new program in all its aspects from scratch.

Despite the many forms a mediation service can take, most are still on the margins of the community. Professionals and the wider community of potential disputants and mediators frequently do not know about dispute settlement programs or how to use them. CDS is, for the moment, content with its low-key community-based program but unhappy with the correspondingly low profile which means few disputants are finding their way to mediation. What changes will help draw people to take better and more frequent advantage of its services? Some of these other program models may gain the community presence or the financial security mediation needs to flourish as a permanent community service.

Major Program Decisions

Once a program model is chosen, whether it be public-supported, non-profit community-based, or professional, a host of interconnected decisions follow: staff structure, outreach, what groups the program will serve, processing cases, and the role of mediators are some we discuss here. Organizational details reflect and influence the effect a program has in the community; the value of the mediation CDS does behind closed doors cannot be separated from the public role it assumes.

Who runs the program?

In envisioning the CDS organization, Friends Suburban Project made one mistake in its calculations. The program has proved much more staff-intensive than expected. Office coverage requires daily presence and a memory for dozens of details; few volunteers have the necessary blocks of time or the staying power. Outreach is also a never-ending task for staff, even with volunteer help. Visits to potential referring organizations need follow-up calls and revisits. Public education means speaking in front of community groups as often as possible, mostly on weekends and evenings. Publicity also rides on a barrage of words, and somebody has to write them. Being present in court to talk to people on the spot or taking the time for home visits to potential participants are also time-consuming but bring in more cases. FSP has therefore consistently recommended that new programs try to arrange for paid staff.

The Chester County program mentioned earlier has remained a volunteer program by joining the YWCA. The YWCA supplies file space and a person to answer calls. These are referred to the volunteer who is on duty that week. This person calls from home, and sees from scheduling through follow-up any dispute which comes in during her week. The system works fairly well. Outreach is the hardest task to cover. As a result, mediations average only one a month.

Some programs also give mediators a stipend. As one would expect, this gives them leverage over the mediators in training requirements and in critiquing performance. It also indicates respect for the skill such work requires. CDS has never considered paying volunteers except for reimbursing mileage and child care, and even that small amount is not often requested. An office and paid staff take too much money to make mediator stipends a serious consideration. Seen another way, CDS was founded in the tradition of the suburban woman volunteer; its mediators did not expect money and therefore CDS has never thought to include such a line item in its grant proposals.

Whatever the choice, the program has to assess realistically how much to expect of volunteers. For CDS, this has meant understanding how much free time mediators can commit, which as women return to full time jobs outside the household becomes less each year. Board members must have substantial time to give the program, but there are several smaller organizational tasks which lend themselves to the volunteer with few hours to spare outside of actual mediating. Volunteers have been most helpful in public speaking, writing newsletters, one-time projects, and consulting with staff about difficult cases.

In the light of the interests and availability of mediators, the group must decide how many paid staff people the program needs and can afford. Finding the right ratio is a major decision for programs with insecure incomes.

The search for referrals

Many mediation programs find themselves climbing a mountain of public ignorance with minimal funds for advertisement or networking in the community. Maintaining an outreach plan which consistently attracts a range of referrals is the biggest problem for most community mediation programs we have seen. Occasional visits to the dozens of local referral sources are not enough to keep mediation numbers high; after a few weeks, the new idea of using a third party from outside slips the minds of busy social workers, police, and judges. Suburban programs which report ten or more mediations a month usually have one or two sources whom they cultivate, and these supply the large majority of their cases. For CDS, the courts (about a dozen sympathetic judges) are the prime funnel. A small center supported by volunteers cannot manage regular contacts with a large number of sources. It has to concentrate on the most productive connections.

One crucial factor in the most successful programs we have worked with has been a director who has extensive community contacts and often an intensive, long-standing connection with a key referral source: a district attorney in one case, local police (through years of collaboration on neighborhood self-protection programs) in another. CDS has recently seen an upswing in both referrals and mediations after hiring a new staff member who worked in the county district courts for many years. She knows many people well and does not hesitate to plug CDS's services. Has this made the number of calls jump or is persistence paying off?

One question is whether funding for more staff or advertising substantially increases the use of alternative dispute settlement. Statistics from programs FSP has trained suggest that other factors are more important. The hiring or increase of staff has led to more careful procedure and more hours spent on fundraising and outreach. Referral numbers rise very slowly. Sporadic public advertisements (TV and radio, newspaper, brochures in public locations) have brought six or seven disputes to CDS attention each year. Skillful publicity may make a substantial difference; CDS does not have sufficient evidence yet to know if this is true. Certainly the publicity mediation has received in the media these past several years seems to be making some dent; more trainees and more disputants have heard of mediation before they find CDS.

Another factor in attracting referrals is flexibility in marketing. Many people who see mediation as an admission of failure can be enticed to try a "clearing the air" session or "just having a neutral person there" during a meeting. Sometimes consulting by phone about a person's options or running a workshop in their organization can open the door later to third party intervention. Although beginning programs are wise not to offer too many services at once, dispute settlement can take many forms besides face-to-face formal mediation. A wider look at the group's role as local conflict resolvers can help relieve the urgency to generate mediation numbers for foundations. Is talking with someone about how to handle a difficult meeting sufficient intervention? Could we be useful as go-betweens?

Constituency

There are three aspects of choosing a constituency: geographic region, type of dispute, and kind of disputant.

Community Dispute Settlement was designed to serve the entire county mostly because it was a convenient, definable unit. The founding mediators had worked on other county-wide projects before. When the program became independent, there was discussion about narrowing it to those areas around the borough of Darby that provide the bulk of mediation cases, but CDS was anxious to draw in as many people as possible. Neighborhood lines were hard to draw, caseload was too small. The board decided to continue county-wide service but to put its emphasis on the Darby area.

Unrestricted by any need to find disputants who could pay or to serve any particular sponsoring institution, CDS has been free to concentrate its dispute settlement skills where it wishes. From the beginning, the program limited its intervention to disputes between individuals, mostly those between neighbors and within families.

From time to time larger situations are referred to CDS. These can involve whole neighborhoods and require some different techniques, but are never turned down for reason of size. Community groups occasionally request CDS services. Two high schools and a few small businesses have also been clients. These interesting cases notwithstanding, the interpersonal emphasis of the program remains overwhelmingly dominant.

The considerations behind this choice of constituency will sound familiar by now. Concern for the way people and problems were treated by the court combined with a belief in the importance of reaching individuals led to a program centered on interpersonal disputes in neighborhoods, rather than to an effort to change systems and organizations. For most of the new mediators, settling family and neighborhood disputes is where they want to give service. Most of them are nervous about any conflict involving many people or requiring a different approach than the customary two-hour mediation session. Other areas of mediation demand specialized knowledge, but even the newest volunteer has knowledge of family and community life.

Although CDS records show periodic interest in cultivating sub-group constituencies such as Quakers, the Hispanic community, tenants, or schools, this did not happen. FSP's background in advocacy work with teens did give the new CDS program a flow of disputes involving this age group, though it tapered off as the connections with juvenile justice agencies grew more distant.

The program has wide but clear guidelines for accepting a case for mediation. Most disputes which lend themselves to CDS mediation have:

1) An apparent incentive to settle for both sides. This can be the necessity of living or working in proximity to the other person, or more specific desired solutions (as a when a landlord wants the tenant out and the renter wants the deposit back).

2) A situation where specific behavior can be (reasonably) changed.

3) No need for professional knowledge (environmental, labor, financial, legal, psychological, medical) beyond what disputants can easily research themselves.

4) A willingness to sit in the same room with the other parties and attempt to work things out.

These guidelines are loosely applied. The staff considers their own sense of the parties, as well as other signals. Situations involving abusive behavior or addictions are usually guided elsewhere. On rare occasions, cases revolving around particularly difficult people are turned down if the person is judged by CDS (*not* by the other party!) to be incapable of negotiating. One woman, for instance, wanted the neighbors to stop climbing on her roof and beaming waves through her walls. Another person had come to mediation before, and the staff knew no discussion would help her. CDS rejects referrals on the basis of evaluating personality only a few times a year. Unfortunately, such characters are usually discovered in the session! Still, the price of inclusiveness is worth it. Time after time, seemingly impossible people have been able to reach workable agreements.

The success rate of CDS mediations and the dedication of the mediators indicate sound screening practices. Once disputes reach the table, the problem is usually amenable to solutions. Mediators report that they have mediated few or no cases which they found inappropriate to mediation, and then it was often a matter of unpredictable personalities or hidden agendas.

CDS is always looking for more sources of income. From time to time the staff and board consider expanding within the framework of community and family dispute settlement. In deciding on new directions, some possibilities have slipped by—an oil company willing to pay for mediations with poor customers with large back bills, for instance, eventually gave up the idea because the CDS board could not determine how to maintain the appearance of impartiality. Any new constituency will require reworking CDS's dispute resolution methods and its public image. One such opportunity came in early 1984 when the area's largest landlord, a realty company, asked CDS to be available whenever the company could not resolve a tenant dispute itself. (Tenant/landlord mediations have always been accepted by CDS, but local rent laws offer few incentives for non-resident landlords to negotiate.) This sort of relationship with agencies and businesses is probably one direction of the future.

The limits of constituency are restricted as well by mediation's weak radio signal. CDS staff believes that the county is presently under-served because people who are wrapped up in the intense world of disputes do not know the program exists. Working with a greater variety of disputes—whether that means divorce, internal organizational conflict, or matters of public policy—might help spread the word and widen the base of community support for CDS. The nagging financial and publicity problems might benefit from such flexibility. On the other hand, caution and overwork suggest concentrating on increasing referrals from traditional sources.

Where to locate?

When CDS set out to find a new home, the main topic of board meetings for several months was deciding in what section of the county the program should locate. Media, the county seat, was the headquarters of most agencies and many law offices. It was near to most mediators' homes. But the program had been working more in the eastern part of the county where most district justices who supported the program preside. FSP had long had dreams of a storefront program like the ones in Dorchester, Massachusetts, and Venice, California. If people could drop by the office, the program would belong to them more, it was said. Attracting local residents as mediators and board members would be easier. Although the prospects for income were shaky, the location committee recommended signing a lease for an old drugstore in Darby. From there it was only one block to a trolley and bus transportation hub; anyone in the region could get to the office.

A few board members were nervous about opening an office in such a depressed area. The staff soon discovered that most people thought CDS only served the Darby area because it was not in Media with all the other county-wide agencies. The dreams of community involvement have not materialized. A few walk-ins, mostly irrelevant to dispute settlement, come in, and some disputants do stop by to talk directly with the staff after initial phone contact. There has been no correlated gain in numbers of mediations or in volunteers. Class differences and the difficulties blue-collar and poor families have in finding spare time were not affected by the program's move to their Main Street. Darby residents remain as removed from the workings of CDS as ever. When a possibility of inexpensive space near the Media courthouse came up a year later, the staff and the board were all eager to follow up the offer until the space proved unavailable.

Scheduling and preparing people for mediation

The scheduling of mediations can cater either to disputants' convenience or to program efficiency. CDS has chosen the former. Setting up each session at a time and a place acceptable to the disputants and finding available mediators means *much* more staff time. At a minimum, if all schedules mesh and both disputants and first-called mediators are willing, the office makes six phone calls. The phoning more typically takes several days of arranging and rearranging. The average court-referred mediation takes a week to set up; others need more than two.

Disputants restricted by tight schedules, young children, or night work appreciate the flexibility. Many people take someone to court expressly to punish them by at least forcing the opponent to miss a day of work. Such tactics do not work with CDS mediations. Negotiating the arrangements is a signal to the disputants that they will be helping to make all decisions and that resolving their problem is more important than CDS getting through with another case. If the case load becomes significantly larger, this policy may change.

Dispute programs seem often to differ more in how they work with disputants before the mediation than in what happens during the session. Some disputants only receive notice of a hearing. Others have preliminary interviews at the dispute resolution center. The Christian Conciliation Service sends out pages of pre-mediation workbook exercises. CDS makes home visits only for large neighborhood cases. Normally, the office communicates with disputants by phone or by letter. This demands less time from the disputant and on occasion allows them to save face. On the other side, it loses people who either respond better to personal contact or who do not have telephones.

On record

Record-keeping is a sensitive matter. Programs vary from the one in Chapel Hill, North Carolina, which in the beginning stored no records ("We are *not* an agency keeping files on people") to others which maintain detailed case histories. As with most institutions, CDS has gradually improved its forms and its file system. Typed descriptions became intake forms. Lists became numbered case logs. Loose scraps of paperclipped telephone messages became a page recording the gist of every conversation with the parties.

Periodically, as files become more sophisticated, CDS has to decide again what information should be kept and in what file. For many years the case file included only the telephone log, a brief intake form, a copy of agreement, and notes from follow-up. If a mediator chose to report, that information was to be kept without names for training and writing purposes. Disputants were asked for name, address, telephone (they are not always willing to disclose these basics—suspicions run deep in hot disputes), where they heard about CDS, convenient hours for mediation, and a description of what is happening.

Until 1984, no demographic information—age, race, ethnicity, income, etc.—was collected. It was considered interesting but intrusive and ultimately irrelevant to resolving most cases. Staff has only partly conceded to the funding pressures for demographic statistics; the mediator now notes the information after a mediation but does not ask disputants questions. Recently, CDS began keeping written evaluations of every mediation session. These are cross-referenced but filed separately from the case file after follow-up. Filing, as we all know, is the last job that gets attention in most offices, and despite program resolve to keep personal information and descriptions of what happened in a mediation out of people's case files, quite often the folders contain much more than the agreement, phone log, and case outline.

Confidentiality

Maintaining records means controlling access to their contents. Conducting negotiations as a neutral party means keeping discreet public silence. Certainly one of the stickiest mediation issues is confidentiality. What do responsible mediators report publicly? When should they be silent?

Most professional discussion of this has centered on what a mediator can say to a court when asked to testify. FSP decided from the beginning not to divulge information if subpoenaed. The only testimony a CDS mediator has given in court (and there has only been one such instance in eight years) is that the parties had reached an agreement, a matter which CDS considers public. Disputants are told that judges will be notified that the parties did or did not agree on a contract. No details are revealed about the nature of the solutions, how people behaved, or what was said.

One of the surprises has been that disputants show little concern about program confidentiality. CDS is carefully constructed to provide a privacy denied by court procedures. Confidentiality is a cardinal commandment. But disputants rarely ask about confidentiality before or during a session. "The whole neighborhood knows already," say some. Others are more than happy to tell anyone who wants to hear. A present staff member remarks with some amusement that most of her callers object to confidentiality. They are angry when the program refuses to relay information to the other party or when CDS will not tell the judge that the other party was "uncooperative." Our disputant surveys also revealed a number of such complaints from disputants who left mediation without agreements. Confidentiality nevertheless remains a firm official policy.

Maintaining this commitment is most troublesome when talking to agencies, judges, and journalists; the line between protecting disputants and capturing interest crucial to the program's continuation is a difficult one. If the magistrate chats with you as a colleague, do you pretend you don't know the situation or tell him you can't discuss it? Does this matter when the case is no longer in court or was handled by a different district justice? Another gray area that CDS confronts regularly is the reporter who will only write up "real" cases with "real" photographs, and when refused, presses for the details that might identify the disguised stories the program gives out.

We are trying to promote the idea of third parties. What do we ourselves write in our books and press releases? Presentations to potential referral sources must be lively. Mediators must show that they know the ropes, that they can handle difficult cases. Composite stories (unless told as true ones, which creates the appearance of disregarding confidentiality) just don't sell as well. It is the quirks of real cases that are memorable and that convince the audience of your experience.

In theory, mediators say nothing which could lead others to pinpoint the participants, nothing which would jeopardize their standing in the community or before the bench. In reality, CDS mediators draw the line in different places—and sometimes sneak across their own lines.

Because the mediator's knowledge is potentially damaging or embarrassing, the FSP *Mediator's Handbook* specifically outlines what confidentiality means for the individual mediator: Notes from the mediation are destroyed afterward. Any record of the mediation in a mediator's own records should not include names. Parties' names should not be used outside the mediation except with CDS staff and co-mediators. The session is not discussed with referral sources. The dispute and the session should be described to others in a way which does not suggest the identity of the party. If any authority asks a mediator to reveal information, the mediator should discuss the matter with CDS staff and board first. If a particular case would be useful for wider publication or research, the mediator can ask the parties for permission. (Beer, et al., 1982: p.22)

In practice, CDS mediators talk freely with each other about cases. In a small program like CDS, it is these stories which keep the pool of volunteers energized. Shop talk reminds mediators of their "mission," and helps them learn from each other's experiences. They praise and encourage each other for skills the public is not likely to see. After the tension of dealing impartially with a dispute, they release their desire to laugh, to complain, to pass judgement— all those actions forbidden to the mediator during a session.

Selecting and evaluating mediators

Selecting mediators for specific cases has been difficult for CDS staff. The main problem is eagerness. Everyone wants more cases! How can CDS give everyone a fair turn with only four mediations scheduled a month? Loyal volunteers deserve mediations—but so do new, potentially skillful mediators coming into the program. CDS loses all but the most determined trainees because too few opportunities for beginning mediators surface in the weeks immediately following training. The staff looks over the list of phone numbers, trying to decide whom to call. Certain people are more available during the day; men are always in short supply; tough mediations require at least one tough mediator. There are many considerations to weigh besides giving everyone a turn.

Inevitably, a core of mediators who are most active has developed. Edith Primm of the Atlanta program reports, interestingly, that she tried assigning mediators randomly, without judging who was better at X- or Y-type mediations, and found the results as good as her previous hand-picking. CDS has tried several assigning schemes, but they do not last long because often the staff is lucky to find any mediator free at all.

Another problem which remains is finding a satisfactory procedure to evaluate and advise, or in extreme cases take off the roster, a volunteer who is a weak mediator. It is easier to rebuke an employee than to criticize a regular volunteer who is donating personal time and money. No one is appointed to evaluate mediator ability. Staff cannot be put in the position of judging mediators who sit on the board which hires them, especially when some new staff members take mediation training for the first time only after they are hired. Likewise, the Board does not want to examine fellow Board members or other volunteers. Many are personal friends. So the issue is brought up from time to time and left unresolved. This problem is a direct consequence of the way CDS was organized as a group with many cross-alliances and with dispersed authority. Most other mediation programs claim to have operating procedures for critiquing and, if necessary, dismissing mediators.

Meanwhile, without a formal, open system of mediator evaluation, the CDS staff simply calls people whom they believe are competent and available. They schedule less capable mediators with more skilled ones. These subjective judgments are formed through one or two co-mediations with a person, stories from other mediators, and the staff member's personal reaction to that individual.

Survival

FSP has trained many groups who planned to start a community program. Many projects vanished as fast as they appeared. Harrisburg's volunteers were suddenly sidetracked by the Three Mile Island incident. Woodbury's would-be coordinator took another job. Chester had had one successful program in the early 1970s, but politics prevented a subsequent project from getting started. Other training groups in New Jersey and Pennsylvania, despite good intentions, never mobilized the resources and energy necessary to start a dispute settlement program. Hopes outran time, interest, and funding—a common phenomenon in any community organizing.

Beyond the ordinary difficulties of starting community projects, there may be obstacles peculiar to mediation programs. Looking at several groups connected in some way with FSP, two of which folded and four of which (including CDS) are active, several key factors for survival emerge.

In Wilmington, Delaware, mediators planned to help with tensions over court-ordered desegregation, but school officials preferred to handle problems using their own in-house resources and the transition came with less turmoil than anticipated. Without a specific problem to tackle and without any staff to search for other referral sources, volunteers drifted to other activities, though still expressing a wish to mediate.

FSP learned one lesson from that experience: mediation services cannot count on selling themselves to given parties, especially when crossing into the turf of professionals. An ad hoc third party with no track record and no connection with recognized institutions has little chance of formal entry to any public dispute. Without the expectation of mediating other conflicts, nor the mechanisms to begin such service, the would-be mediators found themselves with no disputants.

Lest this recital sound too gloomy, we hasten to add that several FSP-trained programs besides CDS have found a useful place in their communities, in particular the all-volunteer Dispute Settlement Plan in neighboring Chester County, the Bucks County program north of Philadelphia, and Dickinson Law School's program in the rural central Pennsylvania county of Cumberland. None of them are as large as CDS in budget or in caseload, though the new Bucks County program may eventually grow to the same size. But all of them show promise of surviving. Why?

It is interesting to note that each of these programs is affiliated with a well-established organization, the YWCA, a social service project working with the elderly and neighborhood crime prevention, and the Dickinson Law School, respectively. These organizations provide both financial benefits and an umbrella of legitimacy. Even with few cases and rapid student-mediator turnover, the Dickinson program can be sustained over thin spots by the school's ongoing sponsorship. Furthermore, the social service agency and the Law School have pre-established connections who can refer regularly; in one case mostly police officers, in the other, local judges.

Each of these programs, like CDS, has a county-sized base and a wide definition of cases they will consider mediating. All started with groups of trainees, many of whom knew each other beforehand as neighbors, as Quakers, as students, as volunteers in other programs. Could this be a factor in sustaining interest and group energy? Certainly it affects the ease of organizing when members see each other daily or weekly in other contexts.

Indeed, the story of the Lansdowne Mediation Program, the longest-lived of all FSP's trial community projects, suggests that a tie with a known local organization, a large population base, and a cohesive group of fifteen or more volunteers are probably critical to survival.

In 1979, FSP decided to try out its mushroom theory of expansion by starting a satellite program serving one community in the county. The borough of Lansdowne was chosen for several reasons. The local district court and the police chief had been consistently referring disputes to CDS; the local Friends Meeting agreed to sponsor the program; and a local woman trained in mediation was interested in directing it. The Meeting was granted regional Quaker funds to experiment with a "community resource for conflict resolution."

The director set about organizing a small group of mediators, incorporating the program, and advertising throughout the borough. A year and a half later, the Lansdowne Mediation Program had no funds left, and it was reincorporated into CDS. Despite dozens of outreach visits which brought in several referrals a month and personal visits to potential disputants, not one mediation had taken place.

Reading back over the staff reports and board minutes, one has the sensation of watching the program breathe on a respirator. The October '79–June '80 Progress Report, written for a funding proposal, fills a page with lists of the program's activities. They organized board and training sessions, they found money, they wrote by-laws, printed brochures, and visited countless groups and agencies. No mention is made of the program's purpose: "We want to mediate!"

What happened? There was a lot of work to be done and not enough people to do it. One staff person on minimal salary was not enough to cover the needed outreach, much less scrape together funds, coordinate volunteers, organize the program structure, take incoming calls from disputants, and arrange mediations.

Then too, the program had a string of bad luck with referrals. Either the disputes had been resolved before mediation (sometimes due to the program's intervention), or a disputant could not be persuaded to come. Any program has a large fallout between inquiry and mediation; the smaller the community, the smaller the referral base and the fewer the mediations. If the number of mediations remains insignificant, funding becomes an increasingly ominous problem.

The handful of volunteers were dedicated, but they were only a handful. Organizing demanded unending work. How can a group maintain its enthusiasm and commitment if they have no chances to mediate? Though CDS and Chester County groups have long had this same problem, there have been enough mediations to retain most volunteers and sufficient numbers to share the burden of organizational tasks. Feelings of discouragement and overwork made public relations with a smile difficult, and the less energetic community response in turn disheartened the Lansdowne program more.

The director says in retrospect:

> *Enthusiasm. Yes, that was the central problem. You can hire people to do something tangential to their interests, but volunteers have to get out what they come in for. They got into the program to mediate, not to have board meetings. I was the program. The office was in my house. Separating out program failure from personal failure was impossible. It was lonely working in an independent office. You are dealing with people at their least happy, at their worst, and you need to have people around to offer support.*

As with any organization, there were political and personal difficulties. In retrospect, none of those factors seems enough to explain the absence of cases. Lansdowne Mediation Program volunteers and FSP kept saying "If we do more effective outreach, if we change intake...."

It is revealing that since the program remerged with CDS, the few cases from that borough come from the same police chief who supported the program before the local experiment was tried. Part of this may be a matter of class; other regions of the county with similarly high income levels also have fewer per capita referrals. Lansdowne also has increasing numbers of poor residents who have left Philadelphia, however, and these people did not use the service either.

By now, we assume that any community that small (less than 12,000), no matter what its social and economic level, is unlikely to support an independent dispute settlement program until third party services become widely integrated into our ordinary ways of coping with conflict. San Francisco's nineteen neighborhood centers are supported by a central organization. The budget for each center is more than CDS's. For the time being, suburban mediators who want to work in their own neighborhoods probably need to find themselves a niche within another local organization.

Says the Lansdowne director:

> There wasn't a group of people in the community who decided they wanted it to happen. There were a smattering of individuals, and there were a number of organizations that thought it was a good idea. No one opposed it, but no one was passionately attached to the idea either. The Meeting gave money but no referrals. The district justice (who had referred in the early days of CDS) had many fine things to say, but he didn't refer a single case.

To summarize, these experiences with programs in different regions indicate the importance of:

1) Connections with a legitimate organization;

2) A spigot of referrals;

3) A reliable source of funds;

4) A cohesive group of mediators large enough to split up the work of organizing;

5) Paid staff if the program is handling more than about three mediations a month;

6) A sufficiently large local population with incentive to mediate— either because living situations breed disputes or because community institutions are unable to resolve many interpersonal disputes.

These factors have also influenced CDS's history as an autonomous program. FSP had offered legitimacy and reliable funding to its fledgling program. Yet credibility gained through six years of work in the community was not sufficient to ensure smooth transition. For a while after it became independent in mid-1982, CDS's future was precarious. The problems centered on the second factor listed above: no predictable income and too few sources for cases. (True, referrals were as irregular as before, but the secure funding had made this less critical when it was one of many FSP projects.) Mediations averaged only three or four a month. Foundations would not consider second requests. Referral sources weren't interested or simply didn't refer. Budgeting was month-to-month.

The program had several things operating in its favor, however, including an established reputation, a wide population base, supportive district justices, experienced staff, and a capable, devoted core of over twenty mediators—all those elements which had seemed to be crucial to the success or collapse of other dispute settlement programs. After a year and a half, the picture began to change as persistent fundraising and talking to county agencies paid off. The program received another impetus through the outreach work of the new staff member who through her court work has acquaintances in every corner of the county. This, along with acceptance into the United Way, has given the program promise of a more stable future.

Where from here?

Obtaining that spigot of referrals and funds means compromise, of course, and in CDS's case, survival seems linked to developing an agency model of community service. How much has the CDS program model helped or hindered meeting its goals?

Many goals have been met in a small way even if the results are not measurable. Delaware County residents now have another alternative to the court system if their primary aim is to settle a dispute, and many courts give this information to them when they come in to file suit. CDS has been able to keep the service private, inexpensive (for the user), and quick.

CDS has not been able to spread out to a broader base of mediators or disputes; in particular, it has not found entrée to larger community problems or to special constituencies. As Eileen Stief remarks:

> *The most important thing that has come out that we have learned is that if you choose the kind of model we have, you're not going to be very busy, but you keep your values intact. And the mediation work you do is satisfying and well done.*

Is the goal of independence from the system fatal to developing a strong program? As long as money and cases are tied to the benevolence of larger institutions, the answer may be yes. Community Dispute Settlement, if it survives as it is currently designed, is likely to continue its low-profile role in community life.

It will provide a useful service to those who find it and educate some people in the county about better ways to approach conflicts.

True, CDS has been slowly expanding its services and trying some new tacks for finding referrals. Yet since Quaker sponsorship ended, CDS's approach to dispute settlement has not altered much at all. Nine years have seen only small increases in the amount of mediation business (1 mediation per month in the beginning years, now 3.8). This suggests that unless a major change in organization occurs, CDS will probably not process the large numbers of people or mediate those community-wide disputes which bring broader recognition.

CDS is not the only mediation organization which has settled into a routine. Sally Merry's research (reported at the 1984 National Conference on Peacemaking and Conflict Resolution) on various kinds of mediation centers shows a disturbing tendency for programs to freeze into institutional patterns prematurely. "This is the way we do things." The programs restrict themselves to certain kinds of disputes; they mediate in a set style and format; they select and train volunteers in a given way. The people who give vision and form to the program eventually move on, leaving an organization which faithfully continues to reproduce the original models.

Merry comments that in such a new field, we are all uncertain of what we should be doing and how. The temptation is to build walls around a small territory. It is easier to deal with a defined clientele and method than continually to face the uncertainties of change. She found few programs developing the flexibility to use different kinds of intervention for different situations. CDS cites tight funding, limited volunteers, and the difficulty of finding sufficient cases as reasons for treading the known paths. Those same problems could just as easily be cause for moving in new directions, however. Habit and lack of confidence are probably two unnamed and weighty factors.

As programs move into second generation leadership, their founders are acknowledging that they have to let their projects go. One person likens this to parenting. Some aspects of the program may far exceed initial expectations. In other ways it is a disappointment. One thing is certain, though. The program will never turn out the way the founders planned it. As a small organization whose members have many cross ties with each other, CDS's transition has been gradual. It is not yet clear whether those lingering bonds with early staff and volunteers continue to give the program energy or whether the second generation will experiment more freely as the first group leaves.

   Some other community programs have developed different and interesting perspectives on the idea of community participation in dispute settlement. Some train case developers who persuade people in their neighborhoods to try mediation. One director says her program tries to be "the eyes and ears of each neighborhood." By going out to keep their finger on the pulse, they have a full mediation schedule. Still other groups are concentrating on creating support groups across neighborhood lines which help members intervene within their segment of the community. Churches are returning to the traditions of reconciliation. In the larger world, increasing awareness of the role of culture, race, and class in conflict resolution is altering the way mediators approach disputes. These new directions can help us shake our convictions about how mediation ought to happen. They challenge CDS to continue redefining its definitions. What do we mean by "resolution," and what are we resolving for whom? To do this, we will need to step back and look again at the concept of community and where mediation can usefully fit into that wider picture.

Eight: The Community

"Community Dispute Settlement" the program calls itself, trying to carve out a corner among dozens of other groups which work to improve their surrounding neighborhoods. What does the "community" part of the name mean? The term seems to apply loosely to the people who use CDS. Sometimes "the community" includes the mediators. The word has political and romantic overtones, implying both a united, active stance and a network of interdependence and friendship. On one level, we know that those perceptions are far from the reality of suburban neighborhoods. At another level, like the myth of the outsider, the concept has a powerful pull.

Several aspects of community are important to examine in relation to CDS and mediation. Most of these revolve around the critical question of who is permitted access to community disputes. We look at the response of professional groups to CDS as well as the attitudes suburban neighbors hold about conflict and community. Wider issues of impact on community—justice, peace, and social change—will be addressed in the final chapter.

We have watched more than one mediation program fail because it could not gain a foothold in the community. Funding and active use of the program, those two measures of legitimacy, never rose high enough to justify the service. Although nearly everyone agrees that there is need for skilled mediators in their communities, as we have seen, most of us believe that *other* people are the ones who need dispute settlement, that *our* particular problem can only be resolved by more extreme measures. Granted, part of this is a matter of improving program outreach and education. But why does CDS have to work so hard for such small results? To think about legitimacy and survival, we have to look at what this indicates about our suburban community, its structures for handling friction, and its attitudes toward resolving conflict.

The Professional Community

In earlier chapters, CDS disputants and mediators expressed their satisfactions and doubts about the program. Now we turn to those who benefit less directly: the primary supporters and critics of community mediation, those who work in the criminal justice and helping fields.

The relationship of CDS and the professional community is the most easily observed measure of mediation's place in the county. How do those in such prominent community institutions as local governments, schools, or the courts perceive CDS? The answers fall in a wide arc. Mediation is a threat to some, a nice, somewhat vague idea to most. A few have begun to see it as a valuable resource. When we examine CDS's search for a legitimate place in the community, each of these perceptions is an important piece of the puzzle.

The legal community

The courts and CDS have always had informal but fruitful cooperation. About one-fifth of calls for service are referred by district justices and their staff. During the past two years about half of those referrals from this first level of the Pennsylvania court system reached the mediation table. In the early days of the program about 65% of all mediated cases were sent from the court. That percentage under the independent program has hovered between 74% and 79%. In other words, although CDS gets many *inquiries* from sources besides the courts, three-fourths of its *mediations* are cases sent by judges. While we will look at the implications of these statistics for "voluntary" participation later, suffice it now to note the consistently close connections between CDS and the entry-level courts. Some district justices are more interested in CDS than others, yet half of the county district courts made referrals last year, with seven sending five or more cases.

Delaware County, the area CDS serves, has over thirty district justices. The eastern part of the county has recently consolidated its court facilities so that several district justices work together. The rest of their colleagues each command a small office and courtroom within their own area. These may be in a shopping center or in an elegant private home. The atmosphere reflects the voting population. One antique collector has turned his suite into a showcase for his best pieces; the bar and the gavel are fresh-polished brass. Old maps and a handsome clock hang on the walls. Across the county in the busier courts serving poorer clientele, the rooms are dingy and unadorned. In one, the secretaries work behind bulletproof glass.

Pennsylvania district justices are elected. No knowledge of law is required, and at present count, eleven in Delaware County are lawyers, the highest percentage in Pennsylvania. Currently, all thirty are men. The state trains both newcomers and old-timers annually. Since the job usually falls to loyal party members, politics is likely to sway decisions where the judge has discretion. When one neighbor comes in to complain about another, the district justice has the choice of proceeding with charges, helping the people work things out, or sending them to mediation. The attitudes of his constituents heavily influence that decision. Their satisfaction means votes.

Diversionary programs (court jargon for agencies where people can go instead of receiving a fine or jail term) are regarded with a wary political eye. The variation in response can be measured by the patchwork pattern of referrals.

Some courts decide that their constituencies are better served by referring their cases to professionals, whether it be Shoplifters Anonymous, Detox programs, or CDS. The six or seven district justices who use the program regularly are mostly those from courts with full calendars. They are glad to hand over their most persistent cases to CDS and believe they do their constituents a favor by having "experts" help them resolve things without anyone ending up with a court record. The justice who referred forty cases and reported that not one of the parties returned to court is an advocate of diversionary programs. While his figure of 0% recidivism is undoubtedly exaggerated, he is excited and pleased with the success of CDS's mediations.

A colleague reports that twenty of the neighbor cases he has referred have been settled; some of the resolutions were "miracles." He likes to write to both parties recommending CDS because, and he quotes another district justice, "trying to settle this type of dispute in the courtroom is like trying to do brain surgery with an axe."

Others believe that their voters want them to be judges and only judges. People have chosen to come to court and that is their prerogative. Several who preside over busy courts approve of CDS but confess that when they get up on the bench they are so overloaded with work that they simply forget. In a few of the outlying courts with smaller case loads, the district justices take pride in settling most problems themselves. They know many of the litigants personally. This system is in its last days; economic and political changes are gradually forcing these small courts to merge into regional offices where people can no longer count on a hearing before the particular district justice who was elected in the disputant's own district.

"This is my job; I've done it for years. People expect me to solve these matters. I mediate in here every day." These are some of the remarks made by magistrates who do not refer to CDS. District justices in the richer, upper-middle-class sections of the county imply that their constituents would be insulted if they sent them to a community service agency, especially one located in the Darby area. They know most of the people in their districts, and often they give people in trouble backroom fatherly admonishment and let them go. Says one court secretary of one such old hand, "He has his own brand of taking care of things. He listens to the whole story, then gives them a little lecture."

Is there any tactful response to these officials who take pride in doing it all themselves? Says a lawyer who speaks on CDS's behalf to groups of judges and attorneys:

> The DJs [district justices] *and the township commissioners say "We've done it all these years." I ask them two things. First, do you have the time? I remind them that those aggravating ones come back five or six times. [Second] is that you make no friends that way. Both sides may be angry. You threaten and cajole them into doing what they want, but they come back three days later. If you send them to mediation, you don't have to side with anyone. And if it doesn't work, chances are they'll say it was CDS that failed, not you.*

One person interviewed cited a case example which supports the lawyer's point. When a district justice imposed the maximum fine, the defendant was enraged and voted against him. The opposing party was angry that the fine had been so low and also switched her vote. By providing real solutions for disputants in circumstances where there seems to be fault on both sides, one would predict that an elected magistrate could avoid making enemies of dissatisfied constituents. If the effort failed, presumably the diversionary agency would receive the brunt of the clients' anger.

The listening district justices nod in agreement, but no calls come in from their offices the next week. Either CDS has much convincing to do or we have not correctly grasped the needs of these men.

Lawyers

When CDS began in 1976, lawyers were slower to warm to the idea of mediation: "Bread and butter out of the mouths of young lawyers," went the joking but serious phrase. One lawyer admits to some embarrassment when his wife started mediating for CDS. He felt the program was competitive with lawyers, taking away cases from young attorneys who were barely scratching through. "I asked her some pretty sharp questions," he says with a smile, "but now my attitude has changed completely." What changed his mind?

> I became persuaded that even young lawyers don't want to get into these cases. It is a tough economic rub. It always takes more time than you can charge for because people can't afford the fees. The second reason is that having watched the results for a few years, I think [CDS] does a better job of resolving disputes. When the court declares a winner and a loser, the losers will try to get even again—only the next time they will be more devious.

He goes on to explain that when lawyers meet to arrange a settlement, the outcome may be fair but the clients feel cheated. They want to tell their story. It is even more important to them than winning the case. The whole legal system is designed for admission of proper evidence. The clients become frustrated. Community mediation ministers to the heart of the issues while allowing people the chance to scream at each other and to get matters off their chests. It costs them much less. Also, he says, attorneys make the process of settlement look mysterious because it enhances their professional image.

This man's observations seem to summarize the remarks of most lawyers who come in contact with CDS. They agree that the clients CDS takes on are the ones who swallow much of a lawyer's time with little monetary return. A secretary in a court which often refers to CDS reports that she cannot remember ever hearing negative reactions from lawyers when the office recommended mediation for their clients. As the Chapel Hill, NC mediation program staff wryly noted in an interview, opposition and ignorance seem to disappear at the same time.

Lack of knowledge is still a roadblock. A district justice finds the attorneys as ignorant about mediation as their clients, though not opposed to the idea. He warns that CDS has fallen woefully short on informing and cultivating the county Bar association, which he sees as a potentially key support for the program. A lawyer who mediates with CDS agrees.

*The word is not out very much, but in my experience, lawyers,
even the young ones, who know about it think it is terrific.
They soon learn what doesn't pay. Besides, there are lawyers
who...really care for the clients that come in. A lot of us don't
like the cost and delays in the legal system either.*

*One of my cases the DJ referred to mediation—his first
referral. The other lawyer hadn't ever heard about it and
wasn't sure, but the DJ said, "Look Jim, this is what we're
going to do." Then he invoked the number of a law that
didn't exist and said it allowed him to refer. The lawyer went
along* [with referral to CDS] *and the feuding families threw
a block party later on that year. It had been a children
problem, and they'd been in and out of court. The other
lawyer was convinced.*

Of course there are limits to the lawyers' support. Cases
appropriate for mediation which also can yield high fees are unlikely
to be referred. Lawyers remain primarily concerned with law. When
asked what cases would not be suitable for mediation, several
mentioned situations where there had been criminal acts, where
someone was "wrong," where certain behavior was illegal and had
to be stopped. They agreed that CDS disputants often enter the
court system with such claims but seemed to think that those cases
at their base had nothing to do with breaking the law. With both
lawyers and district justices, the cases which seem ridiculous, costly,
or bothersome are considered candidates for mediation. Cases
involving what they consider important violations or which generate
income are kept in their own jurisdiction. This self-interest is natural,
but they seem unaware that the division of cases into appropriate
and inappropriate for CDS is based as much on their own values as
on distinct legal differences.

As the lawyer volunteering for CDS pointed out, attorneys are also
concerned that so many people have little access to the courts, that
so often justice can be bought by corporations and wealthy
individuals. Most members of the county Bar already take one or
two free cases a year. The organization is considering schemes to
maintain basic legal services in the face of the federal attempts to
eliminate such programs. CDS is seen as a small way to help resolve
and to make more room for important cases. But more on the
implications of this outlook in the final chapter!

The police

Police departments would seem a logical place to catch disputes before they enter the treadmill of the court system. Police also have several reasons for favoring community mediation. First, local police units can never enforce all the laws within their community; they must choose which laws are most important. A program like CDS can take some recurring problems which do not involve serious crimes off their hands, situations where the right and wrong are confused anyway.

Second, a significant number of police officers are killed responding to family and neighborhood calls. Family and neighbor quarrels take away time from investigating and patrolling. They are rarely resolved by a police visit. Predictably, disputants complain that after reporting several incidents, the police are reluctant to respond. A mediation program which deals specifically with people who know each other would seem likely to get strong police support.

Yet from the whole county, CDS receives only nine or ten police referrals every year. The staff meets with police chiefs and juvenile officers. Mediators give in-service presentations. Why aren't the police sending people to the program? Even a nearby program which has organizational connections to many police departments reports that only two townships tell disputants to call the mediation center. The police are generally positive or, at worst, neutral about dispute settlement. Why hasn't the program captured attention?

One explanation is procedural. In this county, the police are responsible for following up any case they refer to an agency. If the person is ordered to the same agency by the district justice, then the court must check that the person has gone to the diversionary program. Naturally, the police are inclined to leave that responsibility to the judges.

Sheer disinterest and tedium are another reason. One policeman, who was on the beat in a poor section of the county for twenty years before taking an administrative position, explains that he had come to hate his job which was "more boring than you could possibly imagine." The worst shift was the 4 p.m. to midnight with its usual ration of drunks, addicts, and fights. This dreary routine sapped him of the incentive to help people more effectively. Even if he had had the interest, he probably would not have had the time. There are so many different agencies for so many services that it takes thorough study to size up any given situation accurately and then refer it appropriately. Except for Domestic Abuse and Crisis Intervention (which he used constantly), "you just forget about it." He said that he never heard any comments, negative or positive, from fellow officers about CDS.

A leading politician much involved with local police reforms is more blunt in his explanations: "Police departments are paramilitary organizations. They take orders, do what they're told to, and don't do anything they're not told to. You have to get to the police chief and see that he pushes his men hard to refer people to mediation." Palenski's study (1984) of the relationship of suburban police departments to mediation programs located in the New York City region supports this. He found that unless the department is involved in planning a dispute settlement program, it is unlikely to become standard operating procedure. Without a directive, officers will not bother referring. They believe their job is to maintain authority and control, not to give advice or help. The attitude in these New York City suburbs seems to be the same in Delaware County: Let the courts deal with it.

Even when an approving police chief makes the effort to encourage his officers to connect people with the program, few cases lead to mediations. Perhaps this is because the police come on the scene when tempers are hottest—few people want to consider talking things out with "that jerk" at such moments. Often when CDS phones three days later, everything has simmered down. The individuals no longer want to pursue the case.

Confusion about the program is hard to combat. As with all potential referral sources, presenting information well is not enough. For somebody to make referrals, he or she has to: 1) like the idea of the program, 2) intellectually understand how it works, 3) see it as outside his or her duties or capability, and 4) be able to look at a particular situation and say *This one* should be mediated." This ordinarily happens only when a person can watch what a program does, a true Catch-22 in a mediation program with few sessions and a policy of confidentiality.

Even in municipalities where police know about CDS, program files show that over and over disputants are told by the police to take the matter to court. Even when people say they want to speak to the other party, the police warn them not to. And people follow their authoritative advice.

A staff person who met weekly with a supportive local chief reflected on another reason the police connection was unproductive. She got police referrals, she said. One was a local crazy—if you drove down the block you could see which place it was; it was in shambles. The police were ready to try anything. Another time they referred a family violence situation where the police were tired of being called in. She received these insoluble cases simply because the police had no other place to turn. "The police didn't have bad intentions. The program just didn't match what they needed. It's not anybody's fault. The courts didn't know what to do with the worst cases either."

This also suggests that the police do not refer other, more suitable disputes because they don't feel a strong need for what the program can offer. The ones they felt confident about were probably the same ones CDS could have resolved—because there was still room for conciliation.

This confusion about what CDS can do, the habitual tuning out, the multitude of smaller programs clamoring for business, and the inappropriate cases which are referred, are three themes which also surfaced in our talks to political and social service personnel.

Politicians and officials

Apple pie and motherhood: Who can object to someone who settles fights? Not politicians, certainly! Public officials are often asked to intervene in voters' problems. Predictably, however, they do not often turn to CDS because they naturally want the political credit for solving these cases themselves.

Public approval has been easily forthcoming from boroughs and townships throughout the county. A few municipal councils make donations to CDS, and the program receives several thousand dollars each year from the County Council budget. Harmonious communities are in office-holding politicians' best interests, and generally, they are pessimistic yet glad to see the program trying to intervene in neighborhood problems.

A few large neighborhood situations which have stumped the local government have been turned over to CDS. Although the program makes headway with some of these, they are often, like those the police refer, the most intractable situations. In one case, a borough mayor called in frustration when one household continued to call her office with endless complaints. Two other referrals were neighborhood blocks which had been continually in and out of court. The distrust and divisions had proved too entrenched for each agency which intervened. Although small changes were evident after CDS came in, it is difficult to build a reputation on cases which are the least amenable to conciliation.

For the politicians, the police, and the district justices, politics is always a consideration when choosing to refer or to handle something themselves. Says one mayor who is hoping to involve CDS in landlord/tenant complaints which reach his office, "I have a wonderful track record with settling impossible cases." As a politician, he has "a tremendous gut feeling for what compromise is all about." In other words, conciliation is a good bit of his job. Lest they look like unsympathetic bureaucrats, elected officials cannot pass on too many problems which are brought to them.

Another reason that politicians don't send cases to CDS is one which the program seems reluctant to consider. CDS stays aloof from politics in a county that is highly political. Two people who currently refer cases to the program laughed when we brought up CDS's difficulty in finding mediations and asked what we expected. "Let's face it," said one, "the whole board is liberal Democrats...and vegetarians. There's not a three-piece-suit Republican in sight." They went on to point out that no agency in the county gets financial or referral support without Republican connections.

Turnover in government departments and in elected ranks makes continuing education a mind-boggling task. This becomes an overwhelming obstacle with the constellation of surrounding local agencies, where personnel are even more transitory.

Agencies, schools, churches

Difficulty in describing mediation and in maintaining regular contacts after an initial visit are problems wherever the program cultivates referral sources. The main sticking point is that resolving conflict is a matter of pride and of job security. Nowhere is this more evident than in CDS's relationship to other professionals in agencies, schools, and churches. Mediation could be an valuable component in many cases which come to the helping professions: divorced parents negotiating child-raising rules, gang fights, families caring for an infirm relative, or teenagers who are fighting with their parents. Agencies agree that dispute settlement is appropriate, but again, referrals drop off soon after outreach stops.

Professionals who volunteer with CDS bring very few cases to the program, if any. One social worker who mediates and serves on the CDS board admitted:

> Even if I worked in this county, I would never send cases to CDS. And you can't say I don't know about the program. It's too much trouble to refer and follow it through another agency's procedures. Every time the phone rings there is some new crisis. Mediation doesn't seem as immediately important.

Ministers, school teachers, and counselors are similarly approving but unresponsive.

This Board member goes on to explain two other reasons he believes agencies are unlikely to refer. First, most social services are at once overworked and struggling for more clients. They cannot keep up with the volume of troubled people coming through their doors, yet their financial survival, like CDS's, hinges on bringing in more. They cannot afford the time to refer someone with multiple problems to other places which only handle a piece of the need, nor, if the case is a simpler matter, can they afford to lose a client.

A second problem relates to organizational structure. While CDS can convince the director of a program that mediation is a good idea, the referrals only come when the direct line staff understand and become committed to working with CDS. It is interesting that one of the few programs reporting a high agency referral rate is Elmira, NY; apparently they offer in-service training to many of these groups, an excellent way to gain the cooperation of a program's staff. (Kowalewski in Volpe et al., 1982)) Continuity of interagency relations is also frustrated by the frequent turnover in these low-pay, high-burnout jobs which are quite often staffed by young professionals just out of school.

Cultivating these programs can bring in some cases: the most obvious evidence is the precipitous drop in teenager/parent mediations when FSP began to lose touch with its earlier program, Youth Advocates, and its juvenile justice network. On CDS's side of the referral problem, outreach procedures have been sporadic. Agencies and schools are such erratic sources that staff energy has been turned towards the district justices. There is no standard system for following up visits or keeping an agency informed about the status of disputes it has referred. From time to time, the cry goes up for more and better outreach, but the effort outweighs the results and the activity subsides to its usual pace.

CDS promotes the idea that a range of people can, in their spare time, learn to mediate. That same democratic ideal prevents social workers and counselors from referring to an outside program. If "anyone" can learn mediation, then professionals with years of training in human dynamics should be even better at it. Mediation is not a piece unto itself; it is one people-skill which belongs in any competent professional's repertoire. A referral implies the person or agency can't handle a case which the community expects them to solve.

It is hard for professionals to see how what CDS does differs from what they do. They say that in their jobs they too make people talk directly to each other. They stop interruptions, they concentrate on specific changes in behavior, they ask people to explain how they feel. What mediators have trouble explaining is the "magic" of what can happen when people go through the complete mediation process. That experience is qualitatively different from a discussion, a consultation, or a therapy session.

A minister who is a staunch supporter of CDS says that pastors are unlikely to send parishioners to mediation because "they feel threatened by all these agencies doing their work for them." Pastoral counseling is often the favorite part of their work. ("That's where we get to play God," he says with a smile.)

In nine years, this man has only referred one case to CDS. He likes the idea of mediation because it gives people a chance to work things out reasonably. His church is always available for mediations. Why then does he never send people to CDS for that kind of help? "Because we believe that family or personal problems are also spiritual problems...and so do our parishioners. That's why they come to us." Agencies necessarily lack the spiritual dimension that a minister sees as vital to true resolution. His explanations are silently supported by the complete absence of referrals from the many churches which regularly offer their social rooms for CDS mediations.

School counselors have to deal with paperwork, with getting one more student into college. If they get the opportunity to mediate they are glad to do something which deals with people-problems. They aren't going to pass along such cases to outsiders, particularly if they are expected by their bosses and the taxpayers to be handling all student conflicts.

Nearly everybody likes to solve other people's problems. We enjoy giving advice and helping people get along with each other. And who doesn't occasionally like to play those roles we looked at in an earlier chapter: judge, friendly advisor, reconciler, boss, or parent? Those kinds of people are *in charge*. They are respected. Being asked to intervene in a conflict is a genuine compliment.

We all believe that we are experts in human relations, says one minister and CDS mediator. How right he is! Many people tell CDS "Oh, I do that kind of work all the time." We are likely to ask someone else to act as mediator only if we don't like the people who have the problem. We should bring in a more neutral person when we ourselves are deeply involved, but as our stake in the matter rises, so does our unwillingness to have anyone else interfere.

Dilemma: CDS likes to picture mediation as something that most people can learn, and that most people already do. We have *volunteer lay* mediators, yet we want to win respect from *paid professionals*. Although from our training of professional groups we know that those who say "I've done this for years" are usually critically lacking in mediation savoir-faire, there is no delicate or convincing way to prove to professionals that CDS is more skilled than they are in this area.

Baskin (1984) comments on the professionalization of CDS's mediators as a move away from community responsiveness, as another way of again taking power and money away from the people who have the disputes and limiting who can work with those conflicts. But what is an appropriate path when our communities are inured to trusting "important" problems to professionals and when professionals are so insecure about their incomes, their reputations, and even their jobs, that referring to any volunteer lay group is seen as a dangerous sign of incompetence?

The professional community's reactions to CDS have been a mixture of approval and smiling dismissal. One district justice, when asked why he didn't refer, told the male CDS staff member, "We don't have any cases trivial enough for the Quaker ladies." A district justice helping make contacts at the higher court levels for the Chester County program said, "You can see they think you are bleeding hearts." This condescending image of a church-affiliated volunteer agency run by women may be the particular impression of a few, but more likely it illustrates the way many judges and lawyers perceive the program.

This diminutive status may be one reason for the shortage of referrals. Only a narrow band of cases reaches CDS. In contrast to some other community mediation programs, it handles few cases which concern money or damages, and almost none involving violence. Major disputes, such as splits between factions in a school board, a feud in a church near the CDS office, and friction between a condo complex and a neighboring night club, are resolved elsewhere. CDS is valued for its ability to resolve nuisance cases which, like tightly knotted shoelaces, seem trivial yet impossible to undo. The program has not been able to join efforts effectively with other professionals who see community conflicts cross their desks every day.

Mediation's Place in the Suburban Neighborhood

Suburban mediation programs like CDS are faced with persistent cultural patterns which often discourage the use of mediation. Political decentralization and the autonomy of individuals within the neighborhood both raise serious questions about how to make third party services easily available in a form that self-sufficient suburbanites find useful. The high value placed on rights, principles, and personal independence, coupled with the expectation that

188 / PEACEMAKING IN YOUR NEIGHBORHOOD

courts and officials must enforce them, is another large obstacle to the acceptance of mediation programs.

The diversity of CDS's suburban communities makes us wary of over-generalizing about mediation's possible place there. Before we look at specific roadblocks, we acknowledge the complexity of the population CDS serves: half a million people reside in Delaware County. Census maps (1980) of the county's municipalities show wide differences in such categories as median age, poverty and income, race, house value, population changes, and owner-occupancy. Only part of the county fits the image of the comfortable, single-home suburban life. Rural farms and wealthy estates in the northern and western sections are surrounded by acres of immaculate and spacious new housing developments. There are several large towns and two prestigious college communities, as well as communities comprised of apartments, old multiple-family frame houses, and less costly small homes. Along the river, Chester, a desperate, depressed city, and several decaying factory towns appear no better than Philadelphia's poor neighborhoods. In Darby Borough, where CDS is located, more than 14% of the population lives below poverty level. It is one of the most crowded of all municipalities in Pennsylvania.

As we have already noted, disputes come from the middle-income range of the county and somewhat from the poorer sectors, with almost no participation from the professional and wealthy inhabitants. Although the need for mediation may be greater in places where houses are closer and options fewer, in no community is CDS widely cheered as the ideal way to resolve disputes. Delaware County suburbanites—well-off or poor—seem to share a set of beliefs and social organization which discourage the use of mediation.

Rules and social norms

The vanishing village. Among Quakers, initial excitement about community mediation was first fueled by accounts of the traditional models found in the oft-cited example of the African moot (triggered by Danzig's article in 1973, and later expanded by Lowy's reports about Ghana). The appeal was the image of a tight-knit group resolving disputes through consensus after each party was allowed to blow off steam and present its side of the story. Less attractive to Americans looking at the possibility of mediation were the pressures of conformity in such societies and the mediator's authoritative, reprimanding role. (For those readers wishing an overview of the many fascinating anthropological studies in this field, see Merry, 1982.)

The structure of a suburban neighborhood is far from a village, but similar problems seem to pop up despite modernization, mobility, and revolution: dogs, for instance, and rambunctious children. One would guess that other issues which arise in many cultural variations might be the use of space, insults, participation in communal projects, vandalism and petty theft, and disagreements over ownership. In any society, living adjacent to others necessitates developing ways people can cope with troublesome neighbors.

To its credit, CDS never tried to transfer small-village mediation methods to the ever-moving kaleidoscope of its suburban community. Here, the neighbors no longer have much overt say in disciplining and directing people's behavior (if indeed they ever did). Few ties of kinship, employment, or friendship can be invoked to restrain disputes in our neighborhoods because those relationships occur away from the place we live. Even in poorer neighborhoods where several generations of friends and family live nearby, the existence of a legal system fundamentally alters the power of informal community pressure because the court is seen as a stronger, quicker recourse than personal persuasion.

This is not to say that all discipline comes from the law. Social norms still control the behavior of individuals in a neighborhood. Driving through the county streets, it is obvious that different neighborhoods have a distinct character which residents take care to maintain. The cost and location of homes presorts a community's residents; the choice of neighborhood announces what socio-economic level a family has achieved. One suspects that it is through identification with a certain social level that outward norms (maintain your lawn, join the PTA, exchange baked goods during holidays) are subtly but consistently imposed. The wealthier the neighborhood in Delaware County, the more homogeneous it appears. No one needs to come from next door to scold. Poorer neighborhoods in this county have more variety in race and class background. Open disagreement is more common. Neighbors sometimes feel free to yell at each other out on the street. Still, the idealized independence of the well-to-do neighborhood remains: "No one tells me what to do in my own home."

In many communities, rules about neighborliness are written into local ordinances. There are laws restricting where one can build a fence and how high, regulations about cutting grass, rules for when dogs can bark, laws governing trespass and namecalling. Since friendship between households is usually casual at most, when a social rule is broken and an initial confrontation doesn't get anywhere, neighbors soon turn to officials who enforce those rules: the court, the police, the township code enforcer, the dog-catcher, the board of health.

Rights

The lack of deep, long-term ties between neighbors increases the importance of establishing personal rights. In community disputes this means that people regard "the way people ought to behave" as constant. Individuals come in and out of the slots of "friend" or "next-door neighbor" but their interaction is predetermined. During mediation, disputants talk a lot about these cultural rules: about their rights, about being decent neighbors. Until the mediation is well along, they are less likely to personalize: "That really hurt my feelings." Mrs. Green will ask you to keep your children out of her yard because on principle children ought to respect a neighbor's— any neighbor's—privacy. This argument may or may not be bolstered with the personal fact that the noise bothers her when she naps. The importance of principle seems most clear in disputes from poorer neighborhoods. In a society which accords them little respect, the guarantee of personal rights is their final protection.

The rights that form the base of CDS's neighborhoods' unwritten rules are security, property, and family privacy. (See Chapter Two.) Duration of home-ownership and age, *not* relationships, seem to determine whose rights are more important. How long you've lived in a neighborhood is an important yardstick of your right to do as you please. Disputants invariably cite this fact within ten minutes of sitting down to the table. "We've lived here thirty-five years, and we never had a problem till they moved in." When they face renters across the mediation table, they plainly state that temporary people should have less say in what happens in a neighborhood. Other parties may be criticized for inheriting property; they have not *earned* the right to live there. Younger disputants usually defer to older neighbors out of respect for their age, but hold fast to the rights which come with paying for a house.

Getting "respect," an issue which comes up in nearly every mediation, signifies that the other party is not infringing on your rights. It is that nebulous and coveted acknowledgment from neighbors that you are a valuable person, that you have "made it." It is not a respect based on knowing someone well as a person, but on leaving the person alone.

Unnegotiable differences around "rights" usually pinpoint the place of interclass or intergenerational strain in a changing neighborhood. Throughout the county, these are the source of much friction; they run like a barely visible thread through many CDS cases. Disputants complain about the way children address adults, for example, or about neighbors who snub friendly overtures. The kind of assistance and consideration people expect from neighbors are rooted in beliefs about status and "proper" life-style. Newcomers and old-timers have different ideas about respectability. The upwardly mobile and their more settled or struggling neighbors resent each other. Mediations become battles over clashing values about what kind of people should live in the neighborhood, even though the issue being discussed is ostensibly an overhanging tree branch or where people park their cars.

Rights, then, as measured by respect, are the fences which give each household privacy and security. There are some areas of agreement on those norms and on whose rights have priority. Changing neighborhoods are less likely to agree on those accepted behaviors, however. As long as rules and rights take precedence over friendly relations, the custom of every-family-for-itself will push people into disputes with minimal pressure to work problems out amicably.

Isolation and independence

While the county does have neighborhoods where family and friendships form a strong sense of local identity, by and large this county's suburban neighborhoods are characterized by independence, retreat, and casual relationships. One disputant wrote:

> We have moved.... We believed we were doing a better thing [by moving out of the city] *and it turned out to be a mere delusion. We were so miserable and alienated from the lifestyle of, quote, "the suburbs." I will take city life and city people any day. At least I feel at home and live in an honest and caring neighborhood. My husband and I both grew up in a tightly knit Italian neighborhood, surrounded by our family and filled with our cultural identities. Believe me, we are not at all prejudiced, but there's no place like home!*

The sense of alienation she felt is not shared by other residents who consider that isolation a refuge. The importance of *home*, whether the disputants view it as retreat or as the center of a community of personal friends, lies at the heart of most CDS disputes.

What community needs are met by neighbors on the ordinary

street in Delaware County suburbs? Close cooperation and interaction is not highly valued or economically necessary. According to Baskin's findings (1984), survival in the ghetto still depends on a network of support, while survival in the suburbs, except in an occasional emergency, is not based on neighbors. A neighbor dispute does not put critical relations on the line: one's family life, one's job, one's friendships are usually unaffected.

The immediate neighborhood is not expected to provide friendships either. Neighbors may choose to be friendly, but if they want to remain distant, this is usually accepted with little complaint. "Mind your own business" is the rule. People do not often call CDS saying they want to mend a friendship with their neighbors. They say, "We used to be friends, but I don't care to speak to them ever again." They want to affirm their right to stay autonomous and unrestricted. Mediation is used to stop intrusion, not to help a geographic community live together as an effective working group.

The exception to the low importance of neighbors as friends and support is uncovered in disputes between children and in those between women (occasionally couples) who have raised children together in a neighborhood. As Useem, et al. (1960) document, young mothers who are home during the day form a support system for each other. They swap information, help watch children, lend a hand when the car breaks down, and provide each other with adult companionship. Taking an old friend and neighbor to court is traumatic, and many are glad for the opportunity to sit down with a mediator. Children, of course, form tight relationships. When these bonds between neighbors exist, mediation has sometimes resulted in emotional reconciliation and renewed cooperation.

From private to public

Caught up in the small, intense world of their battles, some disputants are quick to call in the police and the courts. Others, especially those with professional or community standing, are often reluctant to admit that they cannot get along with neighbors. They use family and friends to help them cope. In neither case is mediation immediately appealing—it is either perceived as too private (and therefore weak) or too public and formal. Two ministers from a community which started an unsuccessful mediation program described these opposing views when they tried to explain why their people didn't seek out dispute settlement.

A Baptist minister, who has since left, had a congregation of transients. He perceived people in the borough at the security level on Abraham Maslow's hierarchy of needs. They have left the city and "made it" but have not reached a stage of commitment to community. Personal experiences of right and wrong are more important than peace in the neighborhood. They think, "I've gotten out of West Philly and I'm on my way up to Springfield, Media, the Main Line. I'm just here for the meantime." They do not need to worry about survival so much anymore; they are busy securing their house, their yard, their driveway. What the community thinks is a secondary concern.

The rector of a church serving long-time residents said:

> *The old static borough network has a lot of third and fourth generation families who tend to deal with troubles themselves, within the family. Local therapists have come to me begging for clients. It isn't for lack of money; doctors are doing well. It's that everybody is an expert on human relations.*

In the first situation, people go to court easily; in the second, disputes may run underground for years. Pushed far enough, however, even those people will complain to public officials. At this threshold, upholding general principle (No one hits my dog) becomes more important than keeping up good relations. That transition, which we call the Great Divide, may prove to be a key factor working against community mediation programs.

On the one side of this divide is avoidance and accommodation. When relationships are important, calling in a third party (perhaps because it is equated with complaining to the police?) is considered insulting: "Why didn't you come tell me?" These strong feelings about the right way to treat a neighbor mean that most people put up with considerable annoyance to keep the atmosphere friendly. Eventually, some will try talking to each other. Most attempts to resolve neighbor troubles probably never go beyond this private effort.

When talking and ignoring fail, there is little incentive to maintain good relations. The neighbors' cooperation and friendliness is not vital to survival. If one family does not follow the customs of respecting privacy, property, and person, then the other feels little obligation to stay within the bounds of good neighborliness in return. The disputants fall back on laws which sketch out the unwritten social code. If laws are broken, officials are there to enforce them.

Once this dividing line into public territory is crossed, the dispute takes on an identity of its own. The situation becomes reframed for these bureaucracies as a violation of general principles rather than a matter of personal aggravation. For example, the issue moves from "basketball games keeping my baby awake" (My child and I are bothered) to the legal label "noise and harassment" (anyone should be punished for bothering others this way). If mediation is to be successful, the parties must be willing to return to an interpersonal view of the situation, to discuss the basketballs and the baby's sleeping hours. The grievant has to give up the benefits he or she may have sought from officials: attention from authorities, public proof of guilt and punishment of the other party, a chance to get even, and an affirmation that one's anger and actions have been justified.

It should not puzzle us that so few neighbors come voluntarily to mediation. They are caught. In the early stages suggesting outside intervention is "rude," "over-reacting," or an admission of incompetence. If they then move to redefine their situation in terms accepted by those who enforce the law, terms which necessarily require a concern with principle, with guilt, with fact-finding, vindication, and restitution, they can no longer opt for negotiation without losing face. Negotiation means backing down on principles which for months they have worked themselves up to defending.

Once the Great Divide is crossed it is hard to go back again. Mediation is ideally suited for that brief moment when parties decide the time has come to confront the situation head on, but before they have formalized the situation as a matter for public judgment and no longer wish to talk things out. The question is how to devise mechanisms to catch people standing on that dividing line.

Unlike city programs, which often mediate situations involving violence, issues of survival, and mental health problems, the majority of CDS disputes deal with the desire to hold onto a secure, respectable, and private home.

Mediation beyond the neighborhood: Communities of association

Despite the neighborhood and family orientation of most dispute settlement centers, these are only two sources of daily interpersonal conflict. Each individual in the suburbs belongs to a constellation of partial communities. That person carries many labels which identify those associations: Episcopalian, grandmother, supermarket manager, resident of Fair Oaks Townhouses, bowling team member, leader of a women's support group. Organizations, jobs, families, and churches were once subsets of a geographic community (although these groups and neighborhoods have always been much more mobile than our myths about "the old home town" would indicate). Now, neighborhood is only one membership in a list of many. The car- and telephone-centered suburban existence centers on social networks which are primarily connected to mutual interests, not to place of residence. In looking towards the future of mediation in our communities, this fact may offer clues about how it must be packaged to gain wider acceptance.

As you drive out from Philadelphia into Delaware County, the suburban neighborhoods have blocks of identical row houses. Gradually these streets give way to suburban developments, wealthier areas with widely separated homes on curving streets which go nowhere. Up and down the socio-economic ladder, we migrate in and out of those homes, jobs, churches, and activities. We even move in and out of our families. The twentieth-century community, as seen in the formation of networks and support groups or in the far-flung family, draws members from a widening region rather than from one town, one rural county, or one city neighborhood.

This fluidity and independence lessens the need for getting along with each other. Once a conflict has become heated, disputants often do not seem to care what the other party thinks of them. Many say that they plan to look for another job or home. They look for a way out, not for a solution or reconciliation.

Communities, whether neighborhoods or organizations, try to maintain continuity despite the turnover of members. They need ways (be that rituals, mediation, discipline, peacemaking, or team-building) to counter the expanding force of individualism which can so easily rip a group apart. The vagaries of interpersonal relationships still have profound influence on the effectiveness and well-being of the community.

While the suburban neighborhood no longer relies on close relations to thrive, the community of interest does. If members are angry, they will leave. If people are feuding, the work will not get done. Within the associational groups, therefore, mediation skills, though not labeled as such, come in handy time and again.

Communities of interest need dispute resolution skills to help members cooperate. As in quarrels with neighbors, the polite (even moral) first response to the other party is avoidance or talking things out privately. If the conflict festers, if the split in values is too deep to mend, then members turn to political and legal tactics. They hold secret Board meetings; they fire someone without due process; they railroad proposals through; they may sue.

Why is it that CDS has trouble gaining entrée to such organizational disputes, even though mediation is particularly suited for confronting conflict without destroying relationships? Again, the evidence overwhelmingly suggests that formal mediation programs with their outside mediators are too removed for most such community disputes. In addition to the usual hesitations neighbors describe, an organization has the more complicated task of outwardly maintaining public face while inwardly protecting a maze of friendships which enable members to work together for the group's common goals. Bringing in an outside consultant or mediator is both a public admission of weakness which can threaten the cause and a private statement that things are so bad that relationships and possibly the status of some members are at stake. Some people resent the implication that their group is too incompetent or too cowardly to work matters out themselves. Although from time to time organizations request CDS mediation, nearly always another faction of the group rejects the proposal. Also, judges may send reluctant neighbors and families to CDS, but not organizations or businesses. So the main channel for mediation programs, court referrals, is ineffective.

Even so, the interpersonal tensions and the need for ongoing cooperation make these communities of interest ideal candidates for private, tailor-made mediation which respects the friendships and traditions of the organization as well as the law. If the potential role of mediation programs remains doubtful, one productive direction for spreading the use of dispute settlement is to train insiders to mediate. CDS mediators who belong to other organizations have been pivotal in resolving internal conflicts there. Two CDS mediators in personnel work use the mediation format regularly when employees and supervisors confront each other. Three others have assisted in the reorganization of dance associations. A carpenter works with customers to develop one design everyone can agree on. Another helped keep her food coop together. One said her mediation had helped her son and daughter-in-law through a rough time in their marriage. Each person we interviewed had some tale to tell. Usually the place they intervened was within their family, at work, or in groups and churches where they were members.

Many communities do not take the time to develop systems for addressing conflicts. If someone masters the skills of conciliation, however, that person can cope with interpersonal problems wherever she or he becomes a community member. Unless a group practices mediation and negotiation before a dispute grows too bitter for in-house resolution, our communities of shared interest will grow brittle and disintegrate under the strain.

To summarize, then, CDS competes with professionals in the criminal justice, political, and helping fields for the right to intervene in local disputes. It has found a small niche in neighborhood conflicts, where it addresses the tensions inherent in suburban values. Among associational communities, CDS intervenes indirectly through its mediators who have membership in other groups and through FSP training courses.

Choosing: Rules Or Relationships?

There is always tension between the community's need to work out more amicable future interactions between members and the community's obligation to run a just and predictable system where behavior beyond set limits is consistently and publicly condemned. The school building has been spray painted several times this summer, and the windows broken. Is it more important to punish all vandals equally or to stop the vandalism and pay for clean-up? Two families are harassing each other and up the street more households are getting involved. Maybe they should be urged to talk things out. Maybe they should both be fined. Those involved have to negotiate with the community about which outcome is more desirable: justice or good relations. Do they want to follow legal precedent, or do they want to negotiate a compromise? Are rights more important than friendliness? Is community order more prized than cooperation?

The community also has a variety of possible reactions to a dispute. If Mr. Jones calls Mrs. Smith rude names and makes unproven allegations, the response of others will depend largely on context. Mrs. Smith may be encouraged to sue for libel. Another community might pointedly ignore the incident, a third might praise Mr. Jones for "telling her off." A fourth community may arrange meetings to discuss the problem. In a fifth, the community might rally around the two sides for a feud; in a sixth group, Mr. Jones might be expelled...and so on. The triggering event has meaning within a complex framework, and it is this which determines what dispute resolution procedure is chosen. The communal organization, goals, and values determine the battlefield.

When the surrounding community responds differently than the contending parties expect, the feeling of betrayal, not just by the neighbor now, but by the people who are supposed to *do* something, is explosive. Many disputants come to CDS furious. Their elected officials have shrugged off their requests. Their neighbors have refused to talk. The minister has said that he doesn't want parishioners to bring their conflicts into the church. When they wanted to talk things over, the police advised them not to. When

198 / PEACEMAKING IN YOUR NEIGHBORHOOD

they went in to file charges, the judge threw the case out. Whether disputants like it or not, the community *does* track its disputes and determine the range of options a person has.

Communities resorting first and foremost to the courts are advocating rules and order over relationships. The parties may hate each other for years; that is *their* problem. But the rules have been publicly upheld and reinforced. In this environment, the content of the dispute is most important, and the decision may set a precedent for other people involved in the same type of situation. The more interchangeable people are in the communal network, the more likely rules rather than relations will be the organizing force for continuity and for restraining individuals who cause trouble.

Mediation is biased toward regaining harmony. The community advocating mediation is choosing a process which favors stability and good relations. This comes out in statements about getting along together, neighborliness, self-discipline, consideration of others, talking things out. The desire for harmony, a quality often opposed to changing behaviors and norms, is one reason mediation agreements tilt towards the status quo. The nature of the dispute— dogs, assault, theft, vandalism—is considered secondary to well-working relationships. The goal is a community where most everyday problems are resolved quickly and simply so that people can live and work together without constant tension.

Mediation is, therefore, one effective way to resolve disputes within groups when future cooperation or cohesiveness is a feasible goal: notably, families, schools, churches, businesses, and organizations. It helps the group adapt to new ideas and circumstances, it improves the cooperation and hence quantity and quality of the community's work. Mediation is a strong adhesive for mending a fractured group, but it cannot become the glue which alone binds a community together. Without an overriding purpose and commitment from members, resolving internal disputes is empty effort.

The irony is that mediation seems best suited to precisely those situations which do not come to outside intervenors. Mediation is ideal for working out problems between people in relationships, and those problems with complex and emotional histories. It allows for honesty, flexibility, and compassion in a way that formal structures do not, and therefore carries with it the possibility of continuing relations. If conciliation has any significance, it must reunite and transform.

Even a cursory look at CDS and other mediation projects shows that people who actually come to the program are mere acquaintances, that the mediation forum is used to reinstitute the conventional rules of interaction and distance which keep next-door-strangers from interfering with each other. Yet surely mediation fails to offer meaningful service if it is routinely employed to help people distance themselves from each other. Separation resolves tensions by circumventing them, which does not in the long run enhance growing, cooperative community. For CDS to continue mediating in suburban neighborhoods, however, it must offer what disputants want, and they want walls. As Robert Frost's New England farmer dryly reminds himself as he and his neighbor pile up the stones between their properties, "Good fences make good neighbors."

Spreading the skills

Even if mediation does not answer the mainstream desire for independence and personal rights, as a human activity and as a formal service, it still has a place in the community. The task is to promote both the informal and the professional mediator so that the community benefits from the availability of one and the special skill of the other.

The ability to intervene in a dispute is a privilege, the prerogative of the wise, the elder, the expert. Trust and friendship mean a great deal during emotional disputes; feuding parties are likely to pick as intermediaries people whom they know are sympathetic and trustworthy. From counseling and analysis to support groups, matters of personality and relationships have only recently become the province of professional help. A new class of intervenors, a layer between lawyers and the lay person, arouses suspicion from both directions. Legal and social service professionals want to retain their right as trained, experienced experts to the privilege of mediating. Everyone else wants to be the person that family and friends turn to. People in conflict want help from someone they know. CDS mediators, in the pattern of professionals, are appropriating a position of respect on the basis of training, not on who they are as individuals.

Remember those people in the neighborhood who were conflict resolvers—the church secretary, the janitor? In small communities people are self-reliant and often self-schooled in many tasks which help people cooperate and accommodate. When a group reaches critical mass, it begins to specialize. In the process, mediation, that is, our ability to change and heal ruptures in other people's relationships, has become in some ways a diminished art. Third party skills are learned in bits and pieces from individual trial and error. We have already noted that CDS mediators find few role models in their communities. No one is raised to take over the mediation function. Women have been taught these skills for use in the home and in relationships, but they are not expected to use that approach authoritatively in the public sphere. In the USA, we seem caught in the middle, unwilling to relinquish personal conflicts to professional intervention and yet frustrated in our attempts to help ourselves.

People who turn down a mediator's services in favor of dealing with a problem themselves are not necessarily avoiding conflict. Often they seem to be following an instinct which says that they have the inner capacity to heal and to change. In community groups, members become treasurer or publicity chair even if they have no credentials for the task. When people take on different roles more easily, organizations suffer some in quality but can gain in cohesiveness and confidence. Handling disagreements and eruptions becomes just another matter everyone learns to cope with. Even though groups sometimes reach a point where tensions cannot be resolved without intervention from outside, most often conflicts are handled well or ineptly by the parties themselves. Perhaps muddling through a conflict without resorting to specially trained intervenors is risky, but when it works, it is satisfying.

Far more critical than educating a group of professional mediators, then, is the renewal of confidence based on real skills so that communities can use mediators who, as members of the disputing group, have ready access to the dispute. If, as CDS evidence shows, mediation empowers the mediators more systematically than it strengthens the disputants, then the argument for training lay mediators, lots of them, is that much more convincing.

Spreading the skills is needed, and it is happening. The personal focus is still no substitute for institutional programs which, like the law, educate as well as take action. Every local area has these institutions, political and informal, which resolve problems. The very existence of programs like CDS puts the ideas of mediation and conciliation in front of the public, even those who never think of using the service. Besides increased awareness, the program adds a practical service to a community's resources. There are always situations which escalate beyond control. Mediators have experience far beyond the ordinary number of disputes that most people are ever involved in.

Professionals are important at the point where a body of knowledge is too big for everyone to learn. Some kinds of mediation need expertise in the subject matter as well as in facilitating negotiations. Complicated disputes with many parties take much time to resolve. A visibly neutral presence is sometimes essential for many reasons, among them providing safety, focusing energy on resolution, and restraining nasty or unethical behavior. Trained professional intervention makes sense here as an option for those parties who either lack the internal resources for resolving such conflicts alone or who prefer outsiders. The challenge is developing skilled and experienced mediators who work for formal programs while encouraging others in the community to try their hand at helping out friends and neighbors in conflict.

Good community is like good health. A person works towards well-being in the way that he or she lives. It is a state of balance and growth which is not definable or complete at any one point. We each do a dozen things every day which help our bodies stay healthy; with luck we do not have to visit the doctor very often. Likewise, we each contribute in small actions towards the living community. If you pick up around your house every morning, the annual spring house-cleaning becomes manageable. Disputes left uncleared leave a mounting pile of dirt and clutter in the community; tackling the mess becomes that much more difficult. The dispute itself is not the disease, however. Like a fever, it is a symptom which signals deeper social tensions. Any community struggles with forces pulling it apart; the discipline of daily reconciliations and daily problem-solving are persistent ties that hold us together and push us onward.

Nine: Dreams of Justice, Dreams of Peace

CDS's primary service is resolving small-scale disputes. Its work focuses on changing the individual; its vision of wider community influence is usually described as a ripple spreading from those individuals applying newly learned conflict resolution skills in their families and communities. The collective attempts of mediation programs to bring about greater peace, justice, and empowerment must be seen in a larger perspective than the outcome of individual mediations. CDS also influences society as a part of a nationwide dispute resolution movement. Within this societal context, we turn to the final question: What are the implications of CDS's successes and failures?

   The Quaker founders had several dreams for CDS. They hoped that mediation would provide a genuine alternative to the criminal justice system. They envisioned a burgeoning network of mediation programs as people eagerly sought to resolve their disputes and to help others do the same. Mediators would be peacemakers in their communities. Freeing people from disputes would bring fresh organizing energy to neighborhoods. When we evaluate the minimal impact of CDS in Delaware County and from there look at its role in the struggles for justice and significant change, the disappointments are particularly strong.

Dream 1: Alternative to the Criminal Justice System

   Continuing frustration with our cumbersome legal system gives rise to a motif found in most pro-mediation literature, that of alternatives: alternatives to overworked courts, alternatives to expensive and dragged out proceedings. The early projects of the

Law Enforcement Assistance Agency (LEAA), the American Bar Association (ABA), the American Arbitration Association, and others arose from a desire to reform the lumbering juggernaut of the legal system. Mediation programs taking this viewpoint define success at least partly in terms of the potential relief to the criminal justice bureaucracy, in particular its magistrate courts.

The concept of alternatives usually goes beyond finding another place to farm out court cases. The mid-eighties has seen a gradual shift in focus from decongesting the courts to building other dispute resolution mechanisms. Projects like the ABA's Multi-door Courthouse operate in tandem with the courts to extend the range of services available to people with complaints.

More radical proponents of mediation want to circumvent the whole criminal justice system. During the Vietnam War, the New Left resisters found themselves in court and in jail. They saw first hand the vagaries, the ludicrousness, the outright brutality of the criminal justice system. Some of this indignation led FSP members and others around the country to create alternatives beyond the perimeter of the entire system. Emily Sontag indicted the courts in FSP's first article about mediation:

> The impact of the justice system can be substantial on the individual. Working people already hard pressed financially are burdened by the court process. Bail money must be raised. If the individual does not meet the standards of Legal Assistance or the Public Defender's Office, he/she is saddled with a sizeable fee for a private attorney. If the verdict is adverse he/she may face a fine plus court costs.... Every day in court means a loss in wages. Predictable court continuances compound this problem. Sometimes a job is lost....(FSP, 1979)

Friends Suburban Project wanted as little connection with government institutions as possible. Since 1968, FSP had experimented with alternatives: group homes and a youth advocacy program. They had tried direct reform within prisons. Court-watching, reform school hearings, and a group organized to prevent police abuse—all had tested the effects of public monitoring. Most of the results were minor and temporary. By the time FSP started CDS, the staff began not only with an analysis of current community need but with an outspoken bias against the entire institution of criminal justice. LEAA funds were available from the U.S. Department of Justice, but the staff would not consider requesting government money. The goal was not only to keep people out of the courts and the police stations but to keep the legal arm from reaching into neighbor and family disputes.

Whether reformers are insiders trying to improve the legal system or community organizers trying to circumvent it, their interest in mediation has one source in common. The push for alternatives reflects two decades of a decline of faith in institutional solutions and the persistent fight to center power in smaller, more local systems. Mediation appeals to people who want to do something on their own territory. It is a project that takes a manageable amount of time and money. Ideally it returns a measure of control to the local people. Neighborhood mediation, like decriminalization and deinstitutionalization, is an idea born of this decentralized approach.

Mixed results

Are the alternative dispute resolution projects seeing the changes they hoped for? Certainly, as we have seen, mediation does offer some individuals a workable alternative to the courts and the police. CDS and other programs do satisfactorily resolve interpersonal and intergroup disputes which are otherwise handled by the law. Both the accused and the plaintiff have more control over the outcome.

As for changes in the court system, no one is surprised to see mediation making a negligible dent in its massive problems. Predictions that mediation would provide relief to the legal system have not been realized. Mediation has not provided a measurable remedy for problems of cost, efficiency, recidivism, and reduced court load. As dispute settlement becomes a profession, practitioners are increasingly arguing that if mediation resolves disputes, it has value whether or not it benefits the burdened courts. Even so, CDS and most other programs mention the judiciary's concerns, such as overloaded court dockets, in their public relations. The perception that mediation relieves crowded courts remains politically important in the effort to win community approval, so we are likely to hear these claims for some time to come.

For community-based mediation centers, activity is generally much lower than in court-connected programs. The disputants may save time and money, but the program's cost per mediation is high—in CDS's case over $700. By measures of case volume or the effects of empowerment, programs like CDS have proved, at best, an alternative to litigation for a tiny fraction of the community.

Community-based programs have managed to sustain autonomy from the courts, although that separation is neither easy nor clear-cut. Given the dependence of CDS on court referrals, how independent is it? We have slowly come to understand that CDS in fact lies *within* the boundary of the legal system, extending the borders of criminal justice so it can be more consensual and less adversarial. Most crimes and problems are quietly absorbed by the community. They are ignored, hidden, or forgiven. Mediation gives the courts and the police one more avenue to handle those disruptions which otherwise go unchecked or end up addressed unsatisfactorily in the wrong forum. The power of the justice system stands in the shadows behind the mediators as they persuade people to conform on their own before the court has to employ rougher sanctions.

"Like a magnet, the legal system draws everything towards itself," says FSP's Charles Walker. Courts co-opt fringe programs and absorb them into the institution. CDS, like other struggling independent programs, has found itself cultivating closer relations with the police and district justices who first hear complaints—the front line of the criminal justice system. Working closely with the courts has tempered the program's anti-system bias. CDS has learned by experience the limitations of mediation and, correspondingly, the usefulness of the courts in resolving some kinds of disputes.

Despite FSP's criticism of the injustice perpetuated and sanctified by the legal system, it had only a vague idea of the power of that system to mold experimental programs into yet more agencies dependent on political largesse for survival. Nor did FSP take into account the power of the public's beliefs about law and personal rights which lead them to resist mediation. Today CDS has settled slightly left-of-center, portraying itself as a new institution, but relying on old established ones. Carefully guarded independence notwithstanding, CDS has become an adjunct to the district courts in the eyes of the district justices and disputants who use it. Because so many disputants are sent by district justices, founder Eileen Stief says, "We haven't created an alternative to the courts. We've become an alternative to the courtroom."

The price of separateness has been limited activity and a threadbare budget. Outside the stone battlements of the system, there is little economic protection and community recognition. Inside the gates, survival means conforming to the norms of those in power. Whether, or more accurately in what form, mediation programs continue will depend on the mood of those running our legal institutions.

Dream 2: Many Groups Will Flock to CDS Doors

FSP expected a rush of enthusiastic participation to greet the new Community Dispute Settlement program. Not only did they worry about training enough mediators to meet the demand, they expected communities to request help starting their own neighborhood centers. By now the personal and cultural reasons that individuals decline mediation need no review. Gradually, FSP has come to see the larger political issues behind that consistent reluctance.

We arbitrarily divided these overlapping political concerns into four categories for discussion, leaving the fifth major issue, control and pacification, until we look at Dream 3:

1) For richer, for poorer
2) Protection: legal and physical
3) Access to courts
4) Coercion

For richer? For poorer?

A famous and wealthy artist who lives a few miles from the FSP office has been in court with his neighbor for months. They are fighting over damming the river which runs along their properties. Beside the road a roughly lettered sign stands in the marshy field: "Site of the dispute between X and Mr. Y...." The local newspaper reports each court round and quotes the attorneys on both sides. In the end, (the newspapers are silent) something is resolved, the sign comes down.

Yet apartment dwellers who complain about noise or slashed tires or obscene gestures are often scolded by authorities. "Why can't you settle things like adults?" Lawyers can only afford to take a limited number of such local disputes; courts are annoyed by them; the police stop answering calls or respond perfunctorily. People referred to CDS are sometimes upset that officials do not think their problems significant, while the rich man down the road who also complains of property damage and business loss can hire expensive lawyers to carry his case up the ladder of appeals.

Referral sources sometimes use community mediation programs as a dumping ground for "petty" complaints. One man was upset that his case had been deflected to mediation because the police and the judge considered it trivial. He wrote CDS before his mediation, enclosing photocopied legal correspondence:

> *Read this document carefully and you will clearly see that this was not a community dispute but rather it was a despicable criminal act which can only be settled in a court of law.* The affidavit ends, *We have our children at our in-laws*

because the last thing W said was, "I'll kill you—you can bet on that." We want only one thing—peace and to be left alone.

This man doesn't ask for vengeance. He doesn't want money. His letter does not ask that the man be jailed or fined. He just wants officials to take his fear of his neighbor seriously and help him end the problem.

For several years, mediators used the term "minor" disputes. The American Bar Association Committee on Dispute Resolution and other groups have since dropped it from their titles. Other words also subtly carry the label which says "petty dispute." *Inappropriate* cases and *overcrowded* courts, for instance, are terms which suggest that neighbor and family disputes are not important enough for court time and attention. (Forer, 1984; Abel, 1982) Weeding mediation cases out of the court calendar perpetuates the ranking of disputes by social class rather than by content: if you are important, your dispute is important. If you are unimportant, mediation is good enough. One suspects that even careful attention to vocabulary is not going to convince disputants that community mediation is as valuable as going to officials.

Protection: legal and physical

Many critics worry that mediators cannot protect the parties physically, legally, or emotionally. Asking people to talk freely may endanger participants as much as if they signed unfair terms of agreement. Sometimes there is much at stake; a job may be on the line, or an important relationship.

Not infrequently, disputants voice fears of physical attack during or after the session. Ideally, mediators should halt a session when one party *unwillingly* risks future harm by speaking out. In practice, however, it is hard to judge whether a person is freely choosing to risk retaliation.

The possibility of retaliation arose in two CDS mediations where a neighbor had threatened others with a gun. In one, the man turned over his weapon. In the other (mentioned earlier in the book), the family tiptoed around the offended neighbor so that he would have no more cause—except that his first threats had been over the minor matter of people walking on his grass along the curb. The program agreed to mediate because each time it was the threatened party who wanted to meet with the gun-waving neighbor. Fortunately, no violence followed.

The lauded informality of alternative dispute settlement means that the protections of a courtroom are not there either. Ordinarily impermissable hearsay evidence and outright lies are allowed to come up unchecked. There is no way to force disclosure of relevant information, such as financial assets. Private words with the mediator are not privileged; likewise, anything said at the table can be repeated in court. A disputant who is emotionally vulnerable or is unaware of the law can be at the mercy of the other side, as in the one case previously mentioned where a woman gave up part of her court-ordered child support. Parties are often persuaded to drop charges—the main legal leverage they have during mediation—and if the agreement fails, it may be difficult to bring the matter back to court.

The loose rules in a mediation are also its advantage: in private dispute settlement people can soften the rigidities of the law. The agreement can adjust to the peculiarities of the disputants' situation. (They can agree to let dogs bark past legal hours or forbid children to play in the driveway, for instance.) Voluntary participation and voluntary agreement do provide an escape for someone who does not like either the proceedings or the results. As long as charges are pending, a dissatisfied party can still return to court.

We have at times used these arguments to brush off disputants' concerns about the mediation process. The people who decide to litigate are not convinced. The fact remains that those who do come to mediation are taking a risk, whether or not they are conscious of that choice. Justice is possible in a CDS session but cannot be assured.

Access

Liberal opponents see mediation as second-class justice. The problem is not necessarily the quality of dispute resolution, however, but restricted access to legal rights. The poor will be shunted off to speedy, mandatory dispute settlement, these critics say, and denied due process. Those on the economic fringes will become further distanced from the law.

In particular, groups which have battled through the courts for basic civil rights are justifiably afraid that when the political pendulum swings against them, as it has recently, diverting cases to mediation lets courts off the hook. Some commentators believe that the extension of civil rights during the past two decades has gone far beyond what the society is able to deliver. Mediation becomes a nice way to hear out grievances without giving a controversial legal ruling. Instead, a third party encourages complainers to be "reasonable" and "cooperative." It follows that even if the mediator is relatively impartial, the act of mediating is not politically neutral.

Mediators become gatekeepers for the courts, acting as the secretary who pleasantly deflects unwanted visitors.

Looking specifically at CDS, when district justices send people to mediate, the complainant can still elect to press charges after the mediation. Furthermore, CDS cases almost never involve fundamental civil rights issues. The very existence of the program, however, serves to legitimize mediation as a diversionary option for problems the court does not wish to hear.

My day in court: we all want to know that we can have it when we need it. The question of access is probably most important to CDS disputants as a cherished entitlement in and of itself. (That the district justice will dispense justice once they can tell him their story is taken for granted!) When a wrong is done, they want to know that someone will set it right. When people or institutions with status give them an unbiased and attentive hearing, it affirms their legitimate right to be upset. Indeed, Tyler's 1984 study finds that litigants mostly want to be heard, that the outcome of the case is secondary to this in determining whether people thought their court experiences to be fair.

An elected district justice who refers to CDS only occasionally explains that his constituents will not vote for a magistrate who refuses to listen to them, who cannot himself solve their complaints. These people have prepared for weeks, he says. How can I tell them when they come up to the bench that I want them to go away and talk to each other? It may be more effective, but it isn't what they want. In a different part of the county, mediator and court secretary Brenda Dunn agrees. "I can't believe the sea of humanity that comes through this office every day. They don't seem to care what happens at the hearing. All they say is, 'I just want to tell the story to *my* judge.' They've elected that judge from their people. He acts like a father confessor to them. They want to be heard."

CDS disputant surveys indicate high regard for mediators' attentiveness, friendliness, and impartiality. Once people have crossed the "Great Divide" into the public sphere, they nevertheless seem to prefer an intervenor with more authority. Even when the mediated contract answers their stated needs, mediation is often seen as a poor substitute for official action and as a substitute court for the poor.

As Folberg and Taylor (1983: 249) remark, however, cries of "second-class justice" are based on a romantic notion of the legal system. Disadvantaged and even middle-class groups already have little access to the expensive courts. Meanwhile richer people, like the two men with the dam who can afford representation, are tied up in long, costly, and often unsatisfactory court proceedings. Ironically, the people who feel pushed aside into mediation may get better results. Nevertheless, many disputing parties do make choices based on ideal notions of justice—"I am entitled to this"—not on pragmatic considerations. (Merry, 1985)

In further paradox, the advent of divorce mediation services appears to have turned the access issue on its head. Now there is concern that only those who can afford to pay for mediation can get that superior service, while the rest of the population must rely on judges! At second glance, however, the argument is still essentially the same: All citizens deserve a full choice of dispute resolution options, regardless of their financial means.

Coercion

CDS began with the conviction that voluntary attendance was vital. *Voluntary* is a fuzzy, relative term, however, which does not help mediators decide how much parties should be pressed. Because mediation programs have failed to draw in substantial referrals, many must rely on judges or officials to pressure disputants into coming. The longer FSP has worked with community mediation groups, the more troublesome this issue has become.

A mediation program can find customers in three ways:

1) self-referral, where people come to the program independently, with no negative official consequences should they decide not to mediate;

2) optional participation, where authorities present disputants with the choice of mediation;

3) mandatory attendance.

While CDS naturally has welcomed people who come on their own initiative, most who call the program have been given two choices: try dispute settlement or appear in court. The program still frowns on mandatory mediation but its definition of voluntary participation has stretched to encompass anything but outright refusal. CDS was designed to circumvent neatly and inexpensively the frustrations people experienced in court. The embarrassing truth is that the people who were supposed to benefit from this empowering, informal forum must at times be ordered to attend.

This is not to say that coercion has no place in conflict resolution; most of us need some push to tackle unpleasant interpersonal problems. CDS regards those pressures which play on internal motives as generally appropriate: Is there a need and desire to settle?

Are people weary? Avoiding court? Fearing retaliation or the possibility of losing a friendship? The staff urges callers to weigh consequences, hoping that the opportunity to talk things over will prove appealing. This approach convinces a good number, including people who were ordered to attend.

Allowing the courts to arm-twist the less willing is a giant step removed from this kind of persuasion. Since CDS's inception, "suggesting" mediation has been routine practice for some district justices. Some present it as a wise option, but most say, "Don't come back until you've talked to CDS." For those community programs where people supposedly come out of choice, mediator Richard Salem asks, "What is voluntary? People don't say no to judges." (Speech, Athens, Georgia, 1983) And once courts adopt such programs, as they have in several states, judges can recommend mediation with warnings that "uncooperativeness" will be taken into account if the case comes back before the bench. People used to getting the short end of the bureaucratic stick do not need big hints.

Recently some courts have started issuing written judicial orders diverting litigants to the program. Some at CDS see this merely as the paper equivalent of a verbal recommendation. A CDS staff member points out that disputants don't know much about mediation or are too intent on winning in court to look at other ways of constructively settling their disputes. Once they are at the table, they discover that the session is useful. Afterwards, she says, they tell CDS that they are grateful for having come.

The program's survival means maximizing the case count and the number of agreements reached. The muscle of the legal system is hard to fight; it is no accident that most self-referrals do not come to mediation, whereas a high percentage of district justice referrals do. The logical conclusion is that the more judges insist that people try mediation, the better. Otherwise, there's not enough business.

During the session, the authority of the criminal justice system is also invoked. Mediators remind recalcitrant disputants that if they don't come to agreement, the court may hold it against them. This is true. It also relies on the judge's power to require submission and underlines people's duty to do as they are told.

Apart from the threat of court action, pressure on disputants to participate continues during the mediation session. Again CDS tends to assume it knows what the disputants need. As we discussed in the Mediation Model chapter, some of those assumptions center on the process: parties are expected to talk directly, for instance. Of particular concern when discussing the issue of coercion is the contract. CDS mediators cajole people into reaching specific kinds of agreement, such as dropping charges or speaking together when another problem arises. Likewise, CDS mediators will sometimes sidestep demands and issues if that discussion could blow apart the rest of the agreement.

The disputants' vulnerability to the mediators' directions makes the concept of mandatory mediation even more troubling. Not only may people be forced to attend, they may find themselves maneuvered into accepting the mediators' idea of an acceptable contract. Despite talk about people upholding agreements they have crafted themselves, results from court-mandated mediations (or programs which foster the illusion of force) do not show less compliance than voluntary programs. If people will not follow the carrot, the stick works, too.

The return to legal forms. As more people are forced to try mediation before the judge will give them a hearing, the need for legal protection will also increase. Some mediators and some programs already exercise a degree of authority and intimidation of participants which is causing a backlash of protest from advocates. If someone ordered to mediation believes that his or her rights and safety are in jeopardy, lawyers will soon insist on coming with or negotiating for that client.

The scenario unfolds in predictable order: Rules governing admissibility of evidence in mediation, confidentiality, mediator qualifications and accountability may be legislated. In short, mediation programs allied with the courts may either find themselves meting out weaker justice in a semi-court setting with semi-protections, or else they will fade away altogether as the advantages of privacy, flexibility, and informality are circumscribed to the point where parties are better off using formal adjudication.

Dream 3: Peacemaking in Our Neighborhoods

FSP cast itself in the role of peacemaker, trying to respond to the neighbors who told us over and over, "All I want is peace." Peace—between households that simple word can cover anything from isolation and stand-off to heartfelt reconciliation. CDS can, at best, bring people the kind of peace they want. Most of the time, disputing parties settle for a civil separation, a peace which reinforces the dividing lines between people.

Seen in the larger perspective, working for this kind of peace can be a double-edged effort. Mediation techniques can bring conflict out in the open for a group to address head on, or they can be used to put out flash fires of rebellion. Do community mediators help their neighbors find a new peace or encourage quiet resignation?

Pacification and control

Diversion to mediation can be used to suppress "trouble" in several ways. It can restrict access of some groups to customary routes of public recourse. Unpleasant or irresolvable issues are removed from the public eye. More details of people's lives can be controlled.

When a program aspires to bring about peace between groups, it is tempting to define "tensions in the community" as the problem. But whose tensions are we reducing? The unease of those in control? Historically, tensions have been essential in getting attention from the powerful. Mediation which seeks to ease the discomfort prematurely is not making peace, it is guarding the ruling house.

Sidetracking. When disputes involve parties of distinctly unequal status, the repressive potential of mediation surfaces. Disrupters are roped off from other potential protesters by negotiating behind-the-scenes. Wider problems are conveniently pigeonholed as individual situations. The momentum of individual anger is cut short, making it less likely to explode in public. Mediation is a good way to shove problems into a dusty corner.

Domestic abuse cases are a good example of the destructive consequences of dealing with disputes as isolated problems. Actions of violence become negotiable. There are rumors, for instance, of an agreement reached in one mediation program in which the wife agreed not to nag and to have supper ready on time while the husband promised not to beat her again! From the perspective of women's rights advocates, diverting abuse cases is a backward step in a long fight to make the law treat abuse as criminal behavior. Mediation puts the dispute back into the private rooms of the family where the system can ignore it, thereby placing the blame, or at least the burden, on the woman or child while condoning the man's violence.

Conflict brings visibility. Agreeing to meet with a third party usually removes the problem and its solution from public view. Mediation appeals to those who dislike fighting and want to resolve matters quietly. For disputants who want to bring out their grievances where everyone can hear them, whether that be the old man who shouts at passing children from his porch or tenants angry at high rents and unrepaired plumbing, the invisibility of dispute settlement proceedings is a drawback.

Let's take as an example a family harassed by neighbors because they are in some way different. Mediation may help everyone reach a degree of understanding. The harassment may stop. On the other hand, this means there is no build-up of public pressure which could help other households in the same community that are experiencing similar troubles. They may not even hear that other people like them are having the same difficulties. At worst they may be pressured to acquiesce to mediation "like so and so was willing to do." Even though CDS often recommends mediation, the staff believe that their responsibility is to point out the consequences of the different paths people can take. The choice between visibility and restoring peace belongs to the disputants.

CDS handles few situations which clearly affect the wider community. (Remember, the program does not mediate domestic violence disputes and rarely intervenes in interracial situations.) There are certainly cases where the scales are tipped: Adults sometimes use mediation sessions as weapons to silence teenagers. Mediations between neighbors of different classes can also be painfully one-sided. Community mediators do not often intervene in large-scale community conflicts, but they do help regulate access to justice and public attention by accepting individual cases which, in the aggregate, society is reluctant to rectify.

In the end, CDS accepts cases one by one. The program decided to mediate a high school conflict between two black and three white teenagers because all involved agreed that the fights did not reflect school-wide interracial tension. It usually declines requests between individuals and companies or government agencies, because once staff has reviewed the situation, they decide that advocacy is probably a more useful tack.

Extending social control. Pressuring individual disputants to participate in mediation and to reach a given range of outcomes is an even more serious problem when we look at the community-wide effect of such pressure to conform. The concern of Abel and those authors he includes in his books (Garth, Harrington, Santos, et al., 1982) is that mediation, like therapy and reform movements, subtly expands social control beyond the boundaries of the law.

Mediators can poke official fingers into heretofore personal matters. Instead of tossing a case out when no law has been broken, the judges refer it. Officials can insist, through ordering mediation, that you prune your bushes more diligently or hang your clothes on the other side of your yard. They don't have to tell disputants directly what to do because although the forum is participatory, its outcomes are also predictable.

Critics also see mediation camouflaging itself as neutral and personal when in fact it enforces obedient behavior. Abel (1982: 270) speaks of "relaxed coercion," pointing to those same factors we mentioned in the Mediation Model chapter: no robes, donations rather than fees, the use of church social rooms, talking about help with *problems* instead of lecturing or intimidating, and so on. This gentle approach means lighter punishment as well, Abel says, with restitution, apologies, or promises of changed behavior instead of fines or prison. While the process is less coercive than the formal ones, its deceptive friendliness is dangerous; disputants plunge in without the shield of due process to protect them if the mediation fails. They are given the illusion of deciding their own future, even though the actual choices are few.

Furthermore, as mediation becomes more ensconced, the selection of mediators by the justice system or politicians becomes a means of control. Any appointment process weeds out nonconforming candidates. Even when skilled and fair people fill these court-mediator positions, politically chosen mediators (as recent experience in the Philippines shows) have difficulty remaining immune from the pressures of the government.

Peacemaking and pacification—the two words have the same root, but head in opposite directions. No mediation program can ever be certain that its peacemaking is not also promoting undue social control. Nevertheless, we can look for signs that our mediation is having an empowering effect in a situation. Perhaps one key is watching for genuine participation. Another is whether each party sees the outcome as beneficial. Unlike pacification, peaceful relations grow out of respecting the needs of everyone. Such concord is a real decision of disputants, neither imposed nor made in desperation.

Dream 4: Social Change

The founding group envisioned the mature CDS program as a springboard for organizing the community. Carving out a secure spot among many county agencies did not seem significant enough. CDS could be a starting point for new ways, new perceptions, new activism. Quakers have often taken on third party roles in international reconciliation. Helping both sides is a way to form critical connections and build trust for future projects. FSP was waiting to see where this community program would lead. How would the concept transfer from international situations to their own backyards?

* * *

The housing project's parking lot was muddy and dimly lit. Sharon preferred to park her sports car out front under the street light, but the engine warming bothered the neighbors. They called the police so often that the commissioner finally told Sharon she could use the no-parking area on the other side of the street. Everything was fine for a while. Then another commissioner, running for re-election, informed her she was to move her car out of the no-parking zone. The dispute began all over again.

After more than an hour of mediation, they were getting nowhere. Then Sharon volunteered that she was afraid to park in the apartment lot on nights when she left home at 2 a.m. for work. Out on the street, her boyfriend could watch from the window to make sure she got to the car safely. No one had asked her before why she put the car on the street. The other woman was instantly sympathetic; she too had stopped going out after dark in their neighborhood. The discussion was friendly after that, but still no one could think of a solution. Finally, one of the mediators suggested they try to change the no-parking zone. One reported later, "Suddenly the room was full of enthusiasm and energy, everyone smiling and talking." They left, planning as a foursome to visit the commissioners.

From disputes to community organizing

Sharon and her neighbors identified several neighborhood problems: safety for women at night, poorly lit parking areas, and the inconvenient no-parking regulations. They turned their personal dispute into joint lobbying for public solutions. FSP had hoped to see mediation foster many of these small efforts to improve the community. Disputants would begin to discuss their larger neighborhood problems and take action. Mediators would be inspired to work on some community issue. If they found a pattern of teens victimizing old people living alone, for instance, they could use that information to start organizing.

On a grander scale, the program was seen as returning democratic control to neighborhoods and circumventing the evils and inefficiencies of the police and courts. The ideas of Paul Wahrhaftig and Ray Shonholtz about community ownership of problems also influenced FSP. In their thinking, a neighborhood justice system which remains separate from agency and government control "resusitates individual and neighborhood civil life." (Shonholtz, 1984: 15) Local people take charge of local services, thereby restoring the neighborhood's capacity to control its own conflicts. A truly community-rooted program counteracts the message that people are incapable of addressing problems without the assistance of professionals. Efforts are made to spread skills and services throughout each subgroup of the community. FSP also shared Wahrhaftig and Shonholtz's idea that local conflicts are worth talking about. Since individual troubles often stem from larger problems (for example, irresponsible landlords, high teenage unemployment, unresponsive public agencies), Shonholtz's San Francisco Community Boards hold public mediation hearings to promote consciousness-raising which may spur collective action.

From the beginning, there were signs that the CDS model FSP was developing would not reach these goals. In May 1979, FSP staff member and community organizer Johanna Mattheus wrote with disappointment of CDS: "It is not a program that will automatically effect change in our social structures. Mediation, as a service, does not attack the basic roots of the problems we come in contact with. (The service it provides though is human and important.)"

This criticism appeared frequently in FSP memos and minutes, as did the addendum "but what it does is useful," but no plan for how to redirect the program was forthcoming.

During staff meetings there were arguments on both sides of the social change issue. "CDS is becoming just one more diversionary arm of the court system." "The service is in itself social change. That's what empowerment is about." The discussion always ground to a halt around the polarities of the organizer's position of advocacy and the mediator's officially non-partisan stance. There were several problems: the restrictions of the confidentiality policy for both community and CDS, mediating without taking sides, and maintaining a public reputation for fairness and impartiality.

Confidentiality. Unlike programs using public sessions, CDS limits potential opportunities for consciousness-raising or community organizing to a few individual disputants and two mediators. Confidentiality not only hinders community access to the mediation session, it especially restricts the mediators' ability to organize further action. How can CDS reconcile its promise of privacy with the organizer's need to bring issues out for public debate? As with consumer refunds, the particular complaint may be satisfactorily resolved, but the perpetrators are free to repeat their behavior with the next person. Systematic injustices stay hidden.

Even so, most CDS staff felt that responsibility towards disputants meant passing up chances to organize. The program promised them a private alternative to airing dirty linen in the public courtroom. How could mediators openly cite the case details without violating that?

Advocacy and impartiality

"You cannot be mediator and advocate at the same time without jeopardizing the impartiality necessary for this work," Eileen Stief argued. She recalls talking to a pastor about mediating between the church and local teenagers. The church's playground had been opened for neighborhood use after agitation by the parents and social workers. Now they were having problems with younger children being chased away. If FSP had been clearly identified with opening the doors, she says, mediating would have been impossible.

One program's experience indicates that these concerns may not always be important to disputing parties. An advocacy group well known for its persistence in radical community organizing on behalf of Hispanic farm workers, La Comunidad Hispaña used skills learned in FSP mediation training more often than anyone had predicted. Their advocacy made them visible; they were seen as influential with their constituents and they were bilingual. One mediation was actually initiated by mushroom farm owners, who usually see this agency as a thorn in their side. However, the program felt the inherent tensions between impartiality and advocacy. Political activism was their first concern. They have altered the original format substantially, using it more as an on-the-spot skill to cope with crises within the Hispanic community. As advocates, they use mediation skills to structure negotiations with landlords, bosses, public agencies. They no longer advertise separate mediation services, nor make claims of impartiality.

The non-partisan position inhibits social change in other ways as well. The commitment to refrain from value judgments about "good" and "bad" solutions helps mediators submerge the impulse to push for what they believe are fair outcomes. CDS presents itself as secular and apolitical. The potential educational function of mediators (as found in socialist or traditional mediation systems) is consequently restricted.

Organizing starts with empathy and passion. Maintaining an image of neutrality implies distance between mediator and disputant, as well as between mediator and the situation. The position of outsider impedes getting to know the people who bring disputes, and professional detachment warns against emotional involvement in the issues disputants raise.

Impetus to organize. Another roadblock to organizing communities around dispute issues turns out to be the disputants themselves. They are distinctly uninterested in the links between their problems and other people's except to validate the truth of their own claims. Those who do see the connection usually find it one more reason for hopelessness: "Everyone has trouble with vandalism. Not much you can do about it." For the most part, there is little sign of broader thinking among CDS users. Disputants are more likely to see their cases as unique situations of individual victimization. They express surprise (and some regret) when mediators say that their dispute is like many others. They are not curious about those other people. Understandably, they do not want their problems dismissed as "one of those common driveway cases." Mediation is a solution to personal discomfort and invasions of private space. The object is to be left alone, not to begin organizing.

Sharon did go to the commissioner with her neighbors. Their request was rejected immediately by the disinterested official. They didn't push any further. The car noise continued to bother the other family. But this time, aware of Sharon's problem, they reported that they were putting up with it quietly and that Sharon had treated them most considerately since the mediation.

Sharon and her neighbors were unable to influence the authorities, but they were able to break down the fear which had paralyzed them for months. The problem had not changed, but expectations, feelings, and hence responses had. Some would argue that this illustrates how mediation forces people to meekly put up with aggravation. From the disputants' point of view, however, the fear and rage which for months had dominated their daily lives were gone.

Then too, people who decide to speak out sometimes succeed. In a more recent mediation, an elderly patient who was discharged without warning and with no assistance in getting home persuaded his doctor to investigate the inadequate patient-advocate system at the hospital and to speak to each one of the personnel who had contributed to the problem.

Personal vs. political

Separating action and context also discourages social change. CDS's individual approach to settling disputes and its accompanying psychological analysis of conflict puts wider social factors in the background. Even when mediators are careful, it is difficult not to convey the thought that people who generate this much trouble either have not behaved appropriately or else are too incompetent to settle their own affairs. The embarrassment disputants show about attending mediation suggests that they share this judgment. In their book about America's working class, Sennett and Cobb (1972) eloquently describe how we each internalize our place in society and turn our anger at our powerlessness against ourselves. We convince ourselves that we individually deserve our troubles. Ideally, mediators hold both the individual and the broader context of disputing behavior simultaneously. They work to enable people to take responsibility while recognizing that in many ways their situation is ultimately not their fault.

CDS mediations do not explore the social circumstances underlying individual complaints nor those factors which deplete people's political and emotional resources to deal with them. CDS mediators do show a grasp of the societal forces which bring disputants into conflict. In justification of the narrow focus of mediation sessions, they accurately point out that in two hours the systemic roots of conflict are too big to tackle. The disputants are probably not interested anyway. Those who see disputes as symptomatic of political and economic inequities argue that such an individual approach makes mediation as pointless as rebuilding stone houses along a fault line after each earthquake. They say that the therapeutic approach leaves the disputant with a sense of being at fault and without an understanding of the wider forces at play. Yet the political approach sets people up for frustration—they want things to change today—and can reinforce the victim role. Effective change requires both understanding of broad social forces and the ability to take personal responsibility for acting.

The organization's position in the community

The creation of mediation programs potentially *dis*empowers community people by removing yet another function of friends and family to the realm of professional knowledge. Community self-reliance is undermined by the belief that its residents are incapable of fixing their own problems and by the habit of relying on agencies.

Since helping is, as we have said before, primarily a one-way flow downward, the pattern of one group doing good for those less fortunate is hard to combat. Another organizational impediment to social change has been the continual focus on keeping the program alive. There is scant time or money to experiment with different tactics. As with many small dispute resolution programs, CDS depends on foundations for funds and the courts for referrals, a reliance which makes political action all the more difficult.

Today, no one at FSP expects any surprising turnaround in the patterns of nine years. The last wistful hope for social change is vested in empowerment, a change for individuals with remote chances of cumulative effects. Consolation comes in the belief that CDS does add a useful human service to the community's resources, that it does help people develop conflict resolution skills. FSP's Charles Walker wrote CDS founder Betsey Leonard in 1978, "CDS is part of several currents of thought and action: decentralization, working out solutions as close to the people involved as possible.... It seems to me CDS is not so much a *salient* in the process of social change as an accompaniment, a logical extension."

Looking Back

Putting to rest dreams for CDS is not to dismiss CDS as a failure, for on its small scale it has pleased many users, but to face those things we have omitted and the fruits of that oversight. The program should not be faulted for large dreams or for falling short of them. These ideals were never substituted for responsible organization; along the way CDS has set modest objectives and moved carefully. The program has established itself in the county's social service community. Nonetheless there are places where different choices might have helped FSP come closer to its dreams for dispute settlement and community empowerment.

Involving the community

Perhaps the most disturbing mistake which the program made was failing to connect its rhetoric about community control with systematic grassroots organizing. Because the cases were few and because its members were often good friends, there was less impetus to seek out new groups of volunteers. For legitimacy and funding, it turned to other professionals, judges, and foundations, creating a service which would win their support.

This is somewhat surprising. FSP had long experience in community organizing and in the past had not hesitated to openly challenge powerful institutions. This time, because it was creating a positive alternative rather than fighting the abuses of the existing system, FSP was not attentive to the potential negative side of its own actions.

Assessing need. The principle organizing step we overlooked was gathering information and opinions from people around the county. Instead, the program made its own judgments about what was needed. No one asked people in other neighborhoods how *they* preferred to handle difficulties. CDS just assumed that they would welcome a chance to escape from courtroom procedures. Knowing that most people would rather talk out a problem first, we banked on that desire to bring people to the table, unaware that the hurdle of seeking an outside intervenor is a high one. Even after the expected wave of enthusiasm turned out to be a low-tide ripple, the program still did not approach disputants for advice.

Proponents and critics of mediation both make assumptions about what people need—be it dispute resolution or confrontation or radical social change. Even if the program spent many hours talking to people in various sections of the county, it is possible that it still would not put a finger on what the community wants. Just looking at the behavior of CDS disputants shows that what people want, what they think, and what, under strain, they actually do in a conflict can be contradictory.

Marketing. It is always easier to know what your own group will accept. It is interesting to note that when FSP later developed its Friends Mediation Service, it was immediately adapted to the Quaker community. "Sounding board services" and "clearing-the-air sessions" were more palatable than "mediation." Instead of a CDS-style agreement, Friends Mediation Service used the Quaker practice of writing a concluding "minute." Go-between work, consulting with one party, and training were seen as possible options.

CDS has not given much thought to tailoring its service and public relations to the different constituencies in the county. Few areas have strong neighbor bonds and therefore, with no neighborhood program center, CDS has cast a wide geographic net. This has not been sufficient. To draw in more cases, the program must figure out how to cross socio-economic lines, and how to get access to disputes within suburban organizations.

Theory. Why has the program gone in a direction it never planned to go in? That pattern was set quite early when FSP planned CDS. Missing were the theoretical underpinnings needed to create a program which could attract and sustain community involvement.

There was no plan for how the undefined "community" was to take over direction of the program. No one had a practical model for moving from individual complaints and individual empowerment to collective action. Caught up in the daily operation of the program, we just hoped it would happen.

Perhaps organizers tend to resist the cautious and pessimistic theorizing of the academic world, yet without it their projects often spin their wheels. Mediation programs need a social construct which explains such things as:

1) What is a dispute? Why do we want to settle them? Who is pushing mediation and why?

2) What purposes does the legal system serve in this community? What can mediation do that the courts do not?

3) What kind of social change is possible or desirable?

4) What communities do we want to empower? How do *they* want to be empowered?

These questions form the crux of the critiques of such writers as Abel (1982) and Cain and Kulcasar (1982).

From the beginning, CDS failed to examine potential obstacles and implications of using mediation. It tried to educate and persuade, as if the problem were just community ignorance of mediation and not our own incomplete analysis of how communities respond to conflict. Survival as a radical institution requires careful analysis and deft footwork. Without sufficient understanding of neighborhood structure, of community needs, and of our own motivations, FSP ended up creating a social service agency, although that had never been its intention.

Organizational problems

Money. CDS presents its problem primarily as one of money. The independent program was designed in the belief that it would always run on a low budget. Uncertain financing led to a situation not uncommon for small businesses and organizations: those who pay shape the program by setting guidelines for receiving more funds. Recently foundations have been asking CDS to prove its cost-effectiveness in comparison to the court, for instance. This puts the program in the position of competing. Eventually, it could even force the program to dovetail its activities with the court to save money. The search for money also restricts CDS's ability and willingness to try new ideas. A large portion of CDS staff time is tied up in writing grants, keeping records, and making reports. The hard work to establish more regular funding has paid off. The outlook for CDS's survival is increasingly positive. Perhaps this greater stability will free the Board and staff to try out different program directions.

Merry and Silbey (1984) pr 'dict that court-based mediations, which set up bargaining sessions t, at are quick and do not unsettle the present power structure, will eventually crowd out less economical and potentially radical community-based programs which take a more explorative approach. They foresee the simpler, faster, less threatening model becoming standard.

Community mediation programs will have to make thorough, careful plans to withstand this trend. Edith Primm of Atlanta's highly successful Neighborhood Justice Center insists that even if the organization is nonprofit and providing a good service, running a program is running a business. Whether they develop a social service or turn to community organizing, mediation centers need that ability to generate money aggressively.

Institutionalization. The early days were filled with talk of community and empowerment. It was hard to think of many things that could be wrong with conciliation. After a while, organizational concerns about establishing a secure financial and referral base became overriding. The program has gradually come to rely on predetermined formats. There is one basic mediation process; ways of recording and selecting cases have been standardized; methods of outreach follow established patterns.

Developing a routine has increased staff productivity at the expense of adaptability. Unusual cases or ones outside county lines are often turned down. As it can less afford to accommodate disputants, such as those who have unusual complaints or who do not own a telephone, the disputants must match the program's criteria and follow the program's standard mediation plan.

Inevitably, institutionalization brings with it a spirit of caution. CDS has maintained its autonomy and its principles by staying small. It has taken few risks. As Eileen Stief says regretfully, our hands are clean; they show no streaks of political dirt or calluses from battles fought.

Future Directions

Essentially the independent CDS has centered its energy on one goal: to help more people in the county discover the benefits of mediation. The objectives keep the program on a straight trajectory:

the plan is to expand, not to change, what it has been doing since the mid-seventies. After nine years, mediators and program staff continue to work with enthusiasm to realize that vision.

As we have seen throughout this book, mediation encompasses a range of forms and can be used for widely varying goals and outcomes. It is in that sense of adaptability and multiple uses a tool, though never a neutral one. ("Injustice via technique," murmurs one critic.) (Robert Cover, 1979: 914) Acknowledging that mediation is always employed consciously or unconsciously as a way to change people's behavior does not mean that it should not be used, only that it has its own limits and consequences.

CDS can go in several directions. It can *politicize* by working its way firmly into the criminal justice and political system. If the powers that be regard it as their own program, CDS stands a good chance of generating many more cases and obtaining significantly more financial support. The cost would be giving up several of the program's values (liberal, participatory, empowering) and relinquishing more control to groups with different philosophies.

The program can swing in the opposite direction to become aggressively *community-centered*, developing extensive networks in the neighborhoods, with program decisions based on what those volunteers want to do in their own communities. This either means shifting to a new pool of mediators and/or working more directly in present mediators' neighborhoods.

Mediators facilitate only a few CDS sessions each year. Their skills have much more impact among their own networks. CDS could decide to shift towards 1) expanding the number of people in other community networks who have conflict resolution skills and 2) possibly sponsoring discussions of community situations and disputes: meeting with a Town Watch group, for example, or as some dispute settlement programs have, starting support groups of neighborhood problem-solvers.

The cost of training and problem-solving with a corps of neighborhood residents running the program is high, too. Again, CDS would face another group of people with different values. The ways of handling incoming disputes would probably change, as would the structure of any formal sessions. Such a format also requires extraordinary community development and fundraising energy.

Chances are that CDS will continue to wend its way between radical principle and political co-optation. It is likely to choose economic practicality, seasoned with the optimism about bettering disputants' lives which has been a hallmark of the program.

Kernel of Radical Change?

Before giving up on mediation as a positive force for community change, we return to FSP's third guideline, one less mentioned in this book, yet central to the whole operation: nonviolence. Contrary to the popular notion of nonviolence as passive suffering, the word encompasses action as well as attitude, action based on the principle that the means and the ends are one and the same. Mediation can be both a way and a goal for building a more nonviolent and just society.

Just as disputes will always be with us (one imagines that even Utopia has barking dogs), so will the time-tested practice of using intermediaries. Easy access to third parties is a useful option for any community. There are times when people do choose to settle something rather than to fight. There are disputes which needlessly drain energy from more important tasks. Mediation has value simply because it is often able to resolve such situations. It does not need to be relegated to the status of a trash basket for the courts.

Political activists tend to be lukewarm about putting mediation on their agendas. Strategies such as provocation, sticking by principles, and arousing emotions can seem to be the antithesis of mediation's search for harmonious solutions. Granted, as FSP has learned, that mediation is at best a minor tactic in advocacy and protest, there are other ways it can be put to good use. Third party skills belong in every organizer's repertoire; the more alternatives we have for addressing conflicts, the more flexible our responses to different situations can be.

Using George Lakey's progression of social change, as laid out in his *Strategy for a Living Revolution* (1968), we can locate several areas where mediation (and conflict resolution skills generally) can play a part. Those stages in developing a nonviolent society are empowerment and consciousness-raising, organizing, confronting, non-cooperation, and parallel institutions.

Empowerment and consciousness-raising. We have already discussed mediation's empowering role at length. Suffice it to note that mediating in the community can help people frame their issues from new perspectives and gain greater assurance in their ability to deal with conflict. Ideally, the mediation experience is a launchpad for future actions. In our experience as trainers, when people learn to confront others and make themselves go through with it, they gradually conquer their fears of doing so. It may be that successfully facing another party across the mediation table to work out immediate personal matters frees people to tackle wider community problems. Emotionally, the slate is cleared of distracting irritations; intellectually, people can become more aware of their own behavior and attitudes. On a practical level, they can use tactics they experienced in mediation for tackling other difficulties between people.

In a public setting, mediation brings out information for and from the community. A tenant who brings forward a complaint, for example, may find others in the audience who have had problems with the same housing director. Neighbors realize that the welfare family down the street is going through hard times and needs sympathy, not harassment. Likewise, communities can press members to mediate when innuendo and bad feelings indicate submerged problems which should be brought to everyone's attention.

Organizing. Anyone who has been involved in any movement for change knows how much of the time is spent coping with ideological and personal differences, coordinating between groups, and straightening out misunderstandings. While some of these issues are not amenable to negotiation, notably those centering on different values, FSP has intervened in a few disputes (and witnessed many others) between political activists. Mediation can grease the wheels when friction is no longer a challenging disagreement but has turned into hostile acts which undercut the mutual goals of those involved.

Since neighborhood organizing in the suburbs is frequently a short-term action around a specific issue, such as school policy or zoning, maintaining good relations between members is less critical than mediating between diverse interests and approaches. Skill in confronting, in supporting people, in solving problems, and in consensual approaches (the four basic skills in FSP mediator training) can strengthen any collective action by wide groups with divergent views.

Confrontation. Anyone who believes mediation to be a sweet and pacifying procedure has not experienced a full scale mediation. Most are fireworks sessions. Few people are willing to lay themselves out like a rug for the other party to walk over. Mediators expect vehement disagreement and blatant antagonism. Mediation can be a highly confrontational session where parties can say more than they have previously dared. And for once the other party is a captive audience because the mediators insist that each person listen without interrupting. Outside the constraints of legal discourse, parties can choose what will be on the agenda. Issues can be presented as part of a different world view.

Of course, the main drawback to using mediation during times of confrontation is that powerful parties will not come on the challenger's terms, or may not come at all. Restrictive terms can make mediation into a farce in which the weaker party knuckles under but publicly appears agreeable to the conditions of subjugation. Before confrontation in a mediation session, the disadvantaged party must be certain they have a say in who mediates, what the rules are, and who has access to information revealed during negotiations. Admittedly, these are big "ifs" when one party has little leverage over the other. Even if the dominant party agrees to sit down to negotiations, it may be presented on a "we'll talk to you if you promise to be good" basis.

Another difficulty is public image. Any group that publicizes its absolute adherence to principle will find it difficult to explain why they are negotiating with the enemy. Richard Salem's story (Salem, 1984) of running between Jewish and Nazi leaders before the Skokie march is an excellent illustration of how the need to negotiate conflicts with the leaders' need to appear unswervingly principled. For this reason, mediations are often secret. In the international sphere especially, private mediations and public protests are staged in tandem; each has its uses.

Non-cooperation. When a group decides to break away from an established institution, it needs to find ways to take care of its internal disputes. Mediation is certainly one option. The experiences of socialist and workers courts with community mediation-style forums give warning here, however: Mediation necessitates a degree of impartiality which is difficult to maintain and is therefore easily corrupted into summary justice or into a puppet court.

Parallel institutions. It is in designing institutions for the future that CDS's experiences become particularly important, for two reasons. One is as a caution. The other is as a model for settling differences.

Those who are working for a more just, nonviolent, and participatory society cannot afford to ignore the weak influence of CDS and other mediation programs on their communities. CDS has had mild success in repatterning the way its mediators and a few disputants handle interpersonal conflict, but it hasn't touched the core values which foster disputes in the first place. The drive to punish and to be vindicated is fiercely resilient. Nothing has eased our desire for privacy, for an authority to listen to us and decide for us, for protection of property and reputation. What answers will new institutions provide for whole cultures carrying these deeply inlaid attitudes? What substitute rules can they offer a multiethnic, interracial, and highly mobile society, especially one with vast inequalities of wealth?

Mediation today is a test model for larger institutions of the future. Cumbersome and unreliable as they may be, negotiations led by skilled and impartial facilitators (i.e., mediators) are a cornerstone of any nonviolent society which seeks peaceful yet forceful ways to survive conflicts. Experiments like CDS, despite the possibilities of misuse and co-optation, serve an educational function of making that concept more visible and more valued.

Like the ministers, lawyers, and social workers CDS talks to, political leaders at every level claim that they mediate all the time, yet their ignorance of process and issues is appallingly apparent. Some in the peace movement, too, fall into this casual assumption that a belief in peace means the ability to bring it about, that if we know the parties and understand where they are coming from, our intervention will be useful. In technique, even CDS and others with experience in community mediation still have much to learn. CDS mediators have learned a few tricks of the trade, but, like most beginners, we repeat the same moves over and over. We are often unsure how to handle the curve balls of unusual or complex cases. Small local organizations like CDS give mediators a chance to build up a repertoire of experience which can be accessible to the larger community.

If mediation becomes widely used, communities must decide how to keep control of that forum. Mediators are people, often strangers, who are privy to information given in trust. Deliberately or not, their ideology sways the nature of the discussion and the agreement. When impartial parties answer to powerful institutions, or when they need to earn a living from their skills, those interests inevitably affect the outcomes.

To allow a variety of mediating institutions seems the safest way to safeguard the disputants' access to appropriate intervention. Throughout this book we have argued for dispersing mediation skills as widely as possible and against walling off yet another field of expertise. Widespread training programs would allow many people to use mediation when and where they see fit.

Conclusions

Community mediation has many flaws in conception and organization. At worst, it adds little to our quest for greater justice and leaves a false peace in its wake. True, this simple, practical process can address certain kinds of injustice. It forestalls escalation of violence. Yet our society has already twisted that potential, bending the premise of voluntary participation, using mediation to shunt off unwanted people with unwanted troubles. The more we become involved in dispute settlement, the more ethical issues emerge.

For FSP, a group well versed in local criminal justice issues, it has not been easy to find acceptable balances between justice, peace, and order. Like most other groups, we draw our own dividing lines and live uneasily with the gray areas. Despite all the hesitations the criticisms in this chapter raise, the mediation session still holds promise. Looking at *justice*, the large majority of people do reach at least partial agreement and say that it was fair. By building mutual respect and developing specific agreements about behavior, mediation can establish a basis for *peaceful* relations. As for *order*, an agreement is the disputants' statement of how they wish to live within the bounds of their community.

Descriptions and theories do not quite convey the *essence* of a mediation experience. There is a sense of mystery about what happens behind those doors that remains as compelling as it is inexplicable. The Quaker founders of CDS hold that, at some level, justice and peace grow from solutions rooted in spiritual change, and it is these glimmers that often illuminate mediation sessions. Something vital is happening.

The most exciting mediations are those where people are guided through both conciliation and fair negotiations. The inner *and* the outer upsets are heard and resolved. The Turning Point and the euphoria which can follow settlement demonstrate the latent positive energy which mediation can release. The decrease in hostility documented by Sontag (1980) marks a modest change. If this finding is accurate, mediation may promise to help us remember the humanness of ourselves and of our adversaries—our capacity for generosity as much as our habits of mistrust and misunderstanding.

So in an erratic way, we have, after all, been peacemaking in our neighborhoods—sometimes during a mediation session but more often in the parts of our lives outside CDS's jurisdiction. We are adding skills to our communities and raising awareness of unfamiliar ways to resolve disputes. On occasion, we are able to turn an ugly conflict into a more cooperative and productive situation.

It is tempting to draw grand conclusions from small matters—a friendly third person helps two or three people straighten out a frustrating and emotional conflict. Yet what is an insignificant reconciliation? One person says to the other, "I'm sorry this happened. We had no idea you were ill." "Yeah, I get carried away sometimes, I admit it." "It's nice to be speaking again." Confidence returns to people who thought themselves powerless. Hard emotional work and dormant good will break through what once seemed an impasse. A new empathy for the other side is coupled with a few specific agreements about changes. Both the practical and the emotional aspects of reconciliation go hand in hand—mundane changes but visible, hopeful ones.

This book has been full of stories. Where there are stories, there is meaning; where there is meaning, stories spring up—something happens worth retelling. Our interest in these small incidents and their small resolutions hints at the enduring importance of conciliation to the human community. "They haunt me sometimes," says one mediator, "there are ones I still wonder about. What happened to them? You never hear." The long-range effect of mediation is elusive; the process of peacemaking leaves many loose ends. Long after the incidents are over, images of the people linger: the funny ones, the pathetic—and those who were unexpectedly touched by the spirit of reconciliation.

* * *

The old woman's hands shook through the whole mediation. Her husband was angry about many things in the neighborhood. He seemed to blame thirty years of aggravation on the small children next door. It was hard to make him understand. The young woman started to cry. "I try so hard to respect you. I've done whatever you ask. When you had the police come, it took my heart out." Her husband sat silent beside her, his dark eyes grave, watching. The older man talked a long time. Eventually he agreed to the usual: everyone would speak to each other politely. The mother would come over to retrieve any balls. The mediators left the room to write the final draft of the contract. We could hear them talking.

"My parents were newcomers here, too."

"Raising children is a hard job; I know how it is."

"I used to be an engineer at the shipyards. I can't do much but a bit of gardening now. That boy of yours, he's a good boy. And good looking, too."

The mediators came back in. The young woman signed the agreement first.

"If you can be nice to me just once, I can be nice to you a hundred times," she said.

Everyone shook hands. The two women kissed each other. As she was leaving, the old woman took the mediator's two hands in hers, tears in her eyes. "Thank you so much," she said, still trembling. At the door, her husband turned. "I'm through with fighting the neighbors' battles. From now on they'll have to fight their own," he said, "We just want to live our last years in peace."

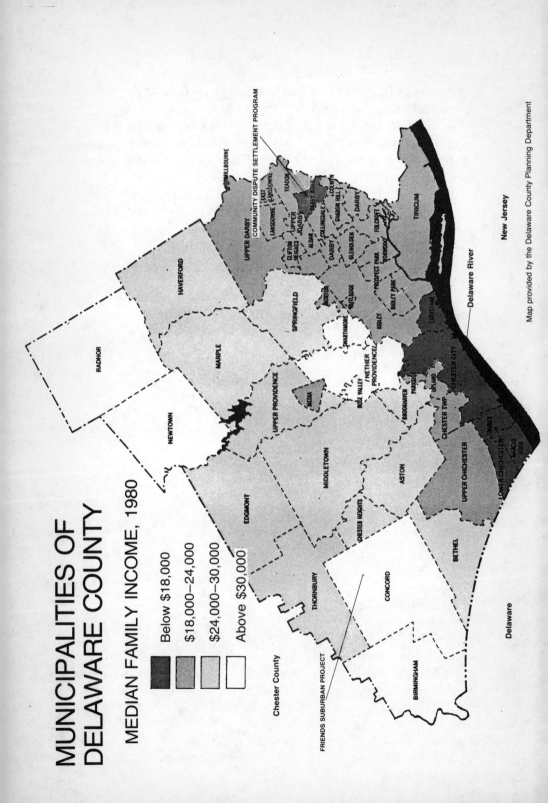

MUNICIPALITIES OF DELAWARE COUNTY

MEDIAN FAMILY INCOME, 1980

Below $18,000
$18,000–24,000
$24,000–30,000
Above $30,000

Map provided by the Delaware County Planning Department

New Jersey

Delaware River

Delaware

Chester County

COMMUNITY DISPUTE SETTLEMENT PROGRAM

FRIENDS SUBURBAN PROJECT

MILLBOURNE
EAST LANSDOWNE
YEADON
UPPER DARBY
LANSDOWNE
DARBY BORO
ALDAN
CLIFTON HEIGHTS
COLLINGDALE
SHARON HILL
DARBY TWP
COLWYN
DARBY
GLENOLDEN
FOLCROFT
PROSPECT PARK
NORWOOD
HAVERFORD
SPRINGFIELD
MORTON
RUTLEDGE
RIDLEY PARK
TINICUM
RADNOR
MARPLE
SWARTHMORE
RIDLEY
MEDIA
NETHER PROVIDENCE
EDDYSTONE
NEWTOWN
UPPER PROVIDENCE
ROSE VALLEY
BROOKHAVEN
PARKSIDE
UPLAND
CHESTER CITY
EDGMONT
MIDDLETOWN
ASTON
CHESTER TWP
TRAINER
UPPER CHICHESTER
LOWER CHICHESTER
MARCUS HOOK
CHESTER HEIGHTS
THORNBURY
CONCORD
BETHEL
BIRMINGHAM

Bibliography and Sources

References & Selected Bibliography

Abel, Richard L., ed. (1982) *The Politics of Informal Justice. Volume 1: The American Experience. Volume 2: Comparative Studies.* New York: Academic Press.

Adler, Peter S. (1984) "The Balancing Act of Mediation Training." *Training and Development Journal* 38 (No. 7): 55–58.

Alper, B.S. and Nichols, L.T. (1981) *Beyond the Courtroom: Programs in Community Justice and Conflict Resolution.* Lexington, MA: Lexington Books / D.C. Heath.

Auerbach, Jerome S. (1983) *Justice without Law?: Resolving Disputes without Lawyers.* Oxford, UK: Oxford University Press.

Baskin, Deborah R. (1984) *The People Next Door: Community and Mediation in the United States.* University of Pennsylvania unpublished PhD thesis.

_____ (n.d.) "Problems Faced by Community Mediation Programs in Using Models Implemented in Other Contexts." *The Friendly Agitator.* Concordville, PA: Friends Suburban Project.

Beer, Jennifer E.; Stief, Eileen; Walker, Charles C. (1982) *Peacemaking in Your Neighborhood: Mediator's Handbook.* Concordville, PA: Friends Suburban Project.

Buckle, Leonard G. and Thomas-Buckle, Suzann R. (1982) "Doing unto Others: Dispute and Dispute Processing in an Urban American Neighborhood," in Roman Tomasic and Malcolm M. Feeley, eds. *Neighborhood Justice: Assessment of an Emerging Idea.* New York: Longman.

Buzzard, Lynn R. and Eck, Laurence (1982) *Tell it to the Church: Reconciling out of Court.* Elgin, IL: David C. Cook Publishing Co.

Cain, Maureen and Kulcsar, Kalman (1982) "Thinking Disputes: An Essay on the Origins of the Dispute Industry." *Law & Society Review* 16 (No. 3): 375–397.

Coleman, J.S. (1957) *Community Conflict*. New York: The Free Press.

Colosi, Thomas (1985) "Negotiation in the Public and Private Sectors." *American Behavioral Scientist* 27 (No. 2): 229–253.

_____ (1983) "A Model for Negotiation and Mediation in the Public and Private Sectors." Conference on International Negotiations paper presented at the U.S. Dept. of State, Washington, DC

Coogler, O.J. (1978) *Structured Mediation in Divorce Settlement: A Handbook for Divorce Mediators*. Lexington, MA: Lexington Books/ D.C. Heath.

Cook, Royer F.; Roehl, Janice A.; and Sheppard, David I. (1980) *Neighborhood Justice Centers Field Test: Executive Summary Final Evaluation Report*. U.S. Department of Justice, National Institute of Justice, Office of Program Evaluation.

Cover, Robert M. (1979) Foreword to *The Yale Law Journal* 88 (No. 5): 910–915.

Danzig, Richard and Lowy, Michael J. (1975) "Everyday Disputes and Mediation in the United States: A Reply to Professor Felstiner." *Law & Society Review* 9 (No. 4): 675–694.

_____ (1973) "Toward the Creation of a Complementary, Decentralized System of Criminal Justice." *Stanford Law Review* 26: 1–54.

Davis, Albie M. (n.d.) "Resolving Conflicts Creatively: The Dispute Resolution Movement." Unpublished paper.

_____ (1983) *Mediation: An Alternative that Works*. Salem, MA: District Court Department, Trial Court of Massachusetts.

Davis, Robert C. (1982) "Mediation: The Brooklyn Experiment," in Roman Tomasic and Malcolm M. Feeley, eds. *Neighborhood Justice: Assessment of an Emerging Idea*. New York: Longman.

_____; Tichane, Martha; Grayson, Deborah (1980) *Mediation and Arbitration as Alternatives to Prosecution in Felony Arrest Cases: An Evaluation of the Brooklyn Dispute Resolution Center*. New York: Vera Institute of Justice.

Delaware County Planning Department (1984) *Census Analysis: Analysis of Delaware County 1980 Census Data*.

Deutsch, Morton (1973) *The Resolution of Conflict: Constructive and Destructive Processes.* New Haven, CT: Yale University Press.

Felstiner, William L.F. and Williams, Lynne A. (1980) *Community Mediation in Dorchester, Massachusetts.* National Institute of Justice, U.S. Dept. of Justice.

_____ (1978) "Mediation as an Alternative to Criminal Prosecution: Ideology and Limitations." *Law and Human Behavior* 2 (No. 3): 223–244.

Felstiner, William L.F. (1975) "Avoidance as Dispute Processing: An Elaboration." *Law & Society Review* 9 (No. 4): 695–706.

_____ (1974) "Influences of Social Organization on Dispute Processing." *Law & Society Review* 9 (No. 1): 63–94.

Fisher, Roger and Ury, William (1981) *Getting to Yes: Negotiating Agreement without Giving in.* Boston, MA: Houghton Mifflin Co.

Fiss, Owen M. (1984) "Against Settlement." *Yale Law Review* 93: 1073–1090.

Folberg, Jay and Taylor, Alison (1984) *Mediation: A Comprehensive Guide to Resolving Conflicts Without Litigation.* San Francisco, CA: Jossey-Bass Inc.

Forer, Lois G. (1984) *Money and Justice: Who Owns the Courts?* New York: W. W. Norton.

Friedman, Anita (1973) "Mediations." *Issues in Radical Therapy* 1 (No. 2): 2–11.

Fuller, Lon L. (1971) "Mediation: Its Forms and Functions." *Southern California Law Review* 44 (No. 2): 305–309.

Gallant, Claire (1982) *Mediation in Special Education Disputes.* Silver Spring, MD: National Association of Social Workers.

Garofalo, James and Connelly, Kevin J. (1980) "Dispute Resolution Centers Part I: Major Features and Processes." *Criminal Justice Abstracts*, September 1980: 416–439.

_____ (1980) "Dispute Resolution Centers Part II: Outcomes, Issues, and Future Directions." *Criminal Justice Abstracts*, December 1980: 576–611.

Gilligan, Carol (1982) *In a Different Voice: Psychological Theory and Women's Development.* Cambridge, MA: Harvard University Press.

Gosling, Jonathan and Mahendran, Janaki (1984) *Report of Visit to U.S.A. 1984.* London, UK: The Newham Conflict and Change Project.

Greenberg, Jerald and Cohen, Ronald L., eds. (1982) *Equity and Justice in Social Behavior.* New York: Academic Press.

Gulliver, P.H. (1979) *Disputes and Negotiations: A Cross-cultural Perspective.* New York: Academic Press.

Hallman, Howard W. (1984) *Neighborhoods: Their Place in Urban Life.* Beverly Hills, CA: Sage Publications.

Hamilton, Debra L. and Zelermyer, Karen (1982) *West Virginia Project on Mediation Final Report.* West Virginia Supreme Court of Appeals.

Harrington, Christine B. (1982) "Delegalization Reform Movements: A Historical Analysis," in Richard Abel, ed. *The Politics of Informal Justice: The American Experience.* New York: Academic Press.

Haynes, John M. (1981) *Divorce Mediation: A Practical Guide for Therapists and Counselors.* New York: Springer Publishing Co.

Himes, Joseph S. (1980) *Conflict and Conflict Management.* Athens, GA: The University of Georgia Press.

Hofrichter, Richard (1982) "Neighborhood Justice and the Social Control Problems of American Capitalism," in Richard Abel, ed. *The Politics of Informal Justice: The American Experience.* New York: Academic Press.

Howard, Dorothy (1983) *The Disputes Resolution Program of the Philadelphia Commission on Human Relations: An Evaluation.* Unpublished Report.

Kessler, Sheila (1977) *Creative Conflict Resolution: Mediation.* Atlanta, GA: National Institute for Professional Training.

Kolb, Deborah M. (1983) *The Mediators.* Cambridge, MA: MIT Press.

Kraybill, Ron S. (1981) *Repairing the Breach: Ministering in Community Conflict.* Scottdale, PA: Herald Press.

Lacey, Paul (1982) *Quakers and the Use of Power.* Wallingford, PA: Pendle Hill Pamphlet No. 241.

Lakey, George (1968) *Strategy for a Living Revolution.* San Francisco, CA: W. H. Freemen and Company.

Laue, James H. (1982) "Ethical Considerations in Choosing Intervention Roles." *Peace and Change: A Journal of Peace Research* 7 (No. 2/3): 29–41.

_____ and Cormick, Gerald (1978) "The Ethics of Intervention in Community Disputes," in Bermant, Gordon; Kelman, Herbert C.; and Warwick, Donald P., eds. *The Ethics of Social Intervention.* Washington, DC: Hemisphere Publishing Co.

Lerner, Melvin J. (1977) "The Justice Motive: Some Hypotheses as to its Origins and Forms." *Journal of Personality* 45 (No. 1): 1–52.

Marshall, Tony F. (1984) *Reparation, Conciliation and Mediation: Current Projects and Plans in England and Wales.* Research & Planning Unit Paper 27. London: Home Office.

McEwen, Craig A. and Maiman, Richard J. (1984) "Mediation in Small Claims Court: Achieving Compliance through Consent." *Law & Society Review* 18 (No. 1): 11–49.

McGillis, Daniel (1984) "Who Should Pay?" *Dispute Resolution Forum.* National Institute for Dispute Resolution: 1, 5–8.

_____ (1982) "Conflict Resolution Outside the Courts: Implications for Applied Social Psychology." Also an untitled paper covering similar material. Unpublished paper.

_____ (1980) *Neighborhood Justice Centers.* Cambridge, MA: ABT Associates, Inc. Washington, DC: U.S. Department of Justice, National Institute of Justice.

McGillis, Daniel and Mullen, Janet (1977) *Neighborhood Justice Centers: An Analysis of Potential Models.* Washington, DC: National Institute of Law Enforcement and Criminal Justice, LEAA, U.S. Dept. of Justice.

Merry, Sally Engle (1985) "Everyday Understandings of the Law in Working-Class America: Legal Ideology and Control." Unpublished paper.

_____ (1985) *Mediating Family Conflict Outside the Courts: Teaching Parents and Adolescents to Negotiate: Report on the Children's Hearings Project.* Cambridge, MA: Children's Hearings Project.

_____ and Silbey, Susan S. (1985) "Mediator Settlement Strategies." Unpublished paper.

_____ (1984) "Dispute Resolution Ideologies: Confrontation and Consensus." Unpublished paper.

_____ and Silbey, Susan S. (1984) "What Do Plaintiffs Want?: Reexamining the Concept of Dispute." Unpublished paper.

_____ (1982) "Defining 'Success' in the Neighborhood Justice Movement," in Roman Tomasic and Malcolm M. Feeley, eds. *Neighborhood Justice: Assessment of an Emerging Idea.* New York: Longman.

Moore, Christopher (1983) *A General Theory of Mediation: Dynamics, Strategies, and Moves.* Rutgers University Ph. D. thesis. To be published.

_____ (1982) "Code of Professional Conduct for Mediators." Denver, CO: Center for Dispute Resolution.

Nader, Laura (1984) "The Recurrent Dialectic between Legality and its Alternatives: The Limitations of Binary Thinking." *Yale Law Review* 132: 621–645.

_____ and Singer, Linda R. (1976) "Dispute Resolution." *California State Bar Journal* 51 (No. 4—July supplement): 1–19

National Center on Women and Family Law (1984) *Mediation and Family Law Materials*. Unpublished collection of papers and news articles on mediation and women.

National Institute for Dispute Resolution (1984) *Paths to Justice: Major Public Policy Issues of Dispute Resolution*. October 1983 panel.

National Institute of Law Enforcement and Criminal Justice, U.S. Department of Justice (1974) *An Exemplary Project, Citizen Dispute Settlement, The Night Prosecutor Program of Columbus, Ohio, A Replication Manual*. Washington, DC: U.S. Government Printing Office.

Palenski, Joseph E. (1984) "The Use of Mediation by Police." *Mediation Quarterly* (No. 5): 31–38.

Peachey, Dean; Snyder, Brian; and Teichroeb, Alan (1983) *Mediation Primer: A Training Guide for Mediators in the Criminal Justice System*. Waterloo, Canada: Community Justice Initiatives of Waterloo Region.

Pipkin, Ronald M. and Rifkin, Janet (1984) "The Social Organization in Alternative Dispute Resolution: Implications for Professionalization of Mediation." *The Justice System Journal* 9 (No. 2): 204–227.

Pruitt, Dean G. (1983) "Strategic Choice in Negotiation." *American Behavioral Scientist* 27 (No. 2): 167–194.

_____ (1981) *Negotiation Behavior*. New York: Academic Press.

Raiffa, Howard (1982) *The Art and Science of Negotiation*. Cambridge, MA: Belknap Press of Harvard University Press.

Rapoport, Anatol (1960) *Fights, Games, and Debates*. Ann Arbor, MI: The University of Michigan Press.

Richan, Anne (1984) "Developing and Funding Community Dispute Settlement Programs." *Mediation Quarterly* (No. 5): 77–86.

Rifkin, Janet (1982) "Mediating Disputes: An American Paradox." Paper presented at the NASPA Conference in Boston, MA.

Salem, Richard A. and Davis, Albie (1984) "Dealing with Power Imbalances in the Mediation of Interpersonal Disputes." Unpublished paper.

_____ (1982) "Community Dispute Resolution Through Outside Intervention." *Peace and Change: A Journal of Peace Research* 7 (No. 2/3): 91–104. (Now available from the Society of Professionals in Dispute Resolution.)

_____ (1982) "Getting to the Table." Paper presented at the Mid-Atlantic Conference sponsored by Society for Professionals in Dispute Resolution, Philadelphia, PA.

Santos, Boaventura de Sousa (1982) "Law and Community: The Changing Nature of State Power in Late Capitalism," in Richard Abel, ed. *The Politics of Informal Justice: The American Experience.* New York: Academic Press.

Sarat, Austin (1983) "Informalism, Delegalization, and the Future of the American Legal Profession." *Stanford Law Review* 35: 1217–1235.

Sheeran, Michael J. (1983) *Beyond Majority Rule: Voteless Decisions in the Religious Society of Friends.* Philadelphia, PA: Philadelphia Yearly Meeting of the Religious Society of Friends.

Shonholtz, Raymond (1984) "Neighborhood Justice Systems: Work, Structure, and Guiding Principles." *Mediation Quarterly* (No. 5): 3–30.

Simkin, William E. (1971) *Mediation and the Dynamics of Collective Bargaining.* Washington, DC: Bureau of National Affairs.

Sontag, Emily F. (1979) "A Study of the Effectiveness of the Mediation Versus the Adjudication Process in Resolving Disputes." Friends Suburban Project, unpublished paper.

Thatcher, Gary (1978) "From Lawsuits to Out-of-court Solutions." *Christian Science Monitor*, Nov. 29, 1978: 14–16.

Titmuss, Richard M. (1971) *The Gift Relationship: From Human Blood to Social Policy.* New York: Pantheon/Random House.

Tomasic, Roman and Feeley, Malcolm M., eds. (1982) *Neighborhood Justice: Assessment of an Emerging Idea.* New York: Longman.

Trubek, David M. (1984) "Turning Away from Law?" *Michigan Law Review* 82 (No. 4): 824–835.

Tyler, Tom R. (1984) "The Role of Perceived Injustice in Defendants' Evaluations of their Courtroom Experience." *Law & Society Review* 18 (No. 1): 51–74.

Useem, Ruth; Useem, John; Gibson, Duane L. (1960) "Men at Home:

Urban Neighbors," in Spradley, James P. and McCurdy, David W., eds. (1977) *Conformity and Conflict: Readings in Cultural Anthropology.* Third Edition. Boston: Little, Brown & Co.

Volpe, Maria R.; Christian, Thomas F.; and Kowaleski, Joyce E., eds. (1983) *Mediation in the Justice System.* Conference Proceedings May 20-21, 1982, John Jay College of Criminal Justice. Washington, DC: American Bar Association Special Committee on Dispute Resolution.

Vorenberg, Elizabeth W. (1982) *A State of the Art Survey of Dispute Resolution Programs Involving Juveniles.* Washington, DC: American Bar Association Special Committee on Alternative Means of Dispute Resolution.

Wahrhaftig, Paul (1982) "An Overview of Community-Oriented Citizen Dispute Resolution Programs in the United States," in Richard Abel, ed. *The Politics of Informal Justice: The American Experience.* New York: Academic Press.

_____ (1979) *Citizen Dispute Resolution Organizer's Handbook (revised edition).* Pittsburgh, PA: Grassroots Citizen Dispute Resolution Clearinghouse.

_____ (1979) "A Time to Question Direction." *Perspective* Fall/Winter 1979: 13–14.

_____ (1977) "Citizen Dispute Resolution: Whose Property?" Pittsburgh, PA: Pennsylvania Pretrial Justice Program.

Walker, Charles C. (1985) *Community Dispute Settlement: An Organizer's Notes.* Unpublished collection. Friends Suburban Project.

Wall, J.A., Jr. (1981) "Mediation: An Analysis, Review, and Proposed Research." *Journal of Conflict Resolution* 25 (No. 1): 157–180.

Walton, R.E. (1969) *Interpersonal Peacemaking: Confrontations and Third-Party Consultation.* Reading, MA: Addison-Wesley.

Wilensky, Harold L. and Lebeaux, Charles N. (1958) *Industrial Society and Social Welfare: the Impact of Industrialization on the Supply and Organization of Social Welfare Services in the United States.* New York: Russell Sage Foundation.

Witty, Cathie J. (1980) *Mediation and Society: Conflict Management in Lebanon.* New York: Academic Press.

Yaffe, James (1972) *So, Sue Me! The Story of a Community Court.* New York: Saturday Review Press.

The Yale Law Journal (1979) Introduction to special issue on dispute resolution. 88 (No. 5): 905–909.

Zion, James W. and McCabe, Nelson J. (1982) *Navajo Peacemaker Court Manual.* Window Rock, Navajo Nation: Navajo Tribal Courts.

Bibliographies and Directories

American Bar Association Special Committee on Alternative Means of Dispute Resolution. *Dispute Resolution Program Directory* (biennial).

Kilpatrick, Anne Osborne (1983) *Resolving Community Conflict: An Annotated Bibliography.* Athens, GA: Institute of Community and Area Development, University of Georgia.

Sander, Frank and Snyder, Frederick (1979) *Alternative Methods of Dispute Settlement—A Selected Bibliography.* American Bar Association.

Dispute Settlement Programs

The conclusions in this book are also based on interviews and materials from the programs listed below. Those with an asterisk were visited by Friends Suburban Project.

San Francisco Community Boards, CA

Mediation Services, Stamford, CT*

Neighborhood Justice Center of Atlanta, GA

Christian Conciliation Service, Oak Park, IL

Columbus Night Prosecutor Program, OH

Institute for Mediation and Conflict Resolution, NYC, NY

Center for Dispute Settlement, Rochester, NY

Community Mediation Program, Suffolk County, NY

Dispute Settlement Center, Chapel Hill, Orange County, NC*

Chatham County Dispute Settlement Program, NC*

Dorchester Urban Court, Boston, MA*

Children's Hearings Project, Cambridge, MA*

The Cambridge-Bridgeport Problem Center, Cambridge, MA*

UMass Mediation Project, Amherst, MA*

Mennonite Conciliation Service, Akron, PA*

Lancaster Mediation Center, Lancaster, PA

Philadelphia Human Relations Commission, Philadelphia, PA*

Philadelphia 4-A Program, Philadelphia, PA

Philadelphia Tenant/Landlord mediation project, Philadelphia, PA*

Community Association for Mediation, Pittsburgh, PA*

Brethren Conciliation Service, Harrisonburg, VA

Newham Conflict and Change Project, London, UK*

Ongoing contact with the following community mediation projects (all initially trained by Friends Suburban Project) provided additional information:

Dispute Settlement Plan for Chester County, PA

Community Dispute Settlement Program of Delaware County, PA

La Comunidad Hispaña, Kennett Square, PA

Lansdowne Mediation Program, PA

Dickinson Law School's Cumberland County Dispute Settlement, Carlisle, PA

Neighborhood Dispute Settlement of Greater Harrisburg, Harrisburg, PA

Lower Bucks County Mediation Service, PA

Community Alternatives in Criminal Justice, State College, PA

End Note

The difference between FSP and CDS may be somewhat confusing. For the sake of simplicity, in most places in this book we do not distinguish between the two programs.

Friends Suburban Project (FSP) is a program of the Philadelphia Yearly Meeting of the Religious Society of Friends, which since 1968 has worked on a variety of community peace and justice issues. FSP created the Community Dispute Settlement program and ran it from 1976 to 1982. Many other dispute settlement programs use FSP's consulting and mediation training services. FSP publishes *Peacemaking in Your Neighborhood: Mediator's Handbook.*

The terms *Society of Friends*, *Friends*, and *Quakers* are synonymous.

Community Dispute Settlement (CDS) was FSP's pilot project in community mediation. CDS incorporated in 1982 as an independent organization and moved into separate quarters. Its main purpose is providing direct services to disputing neighbors and family members. The official name is now Community Dispute Settlement Program of Delaware County.

More Resources from
New Society Publishers

A MANUAL ON NONVIOLENCE AND CHILDREN
compiled and edited by Stephanie Judson
foreword by Paula J. Paul, Educators for Social Responsibility

Includes "For the Fun of It! Selected Cooperative Games for Children and Adults"

Invaluable resource for creating an atmosphere in which children and adults can resolve problems and conflicts nonviolently. Especially useful for parents and teachers in instilling values today to create the peacemakers of tomorrow!

"Stephanie Judson's excellent manual has helped many parents and teachers with whom we have worked. An essential part of learning nonviolent ways of resolving conflicts is the creation of a trusting, affirming, and cooperative environment in the home and classroom. This manual has a wealth of suggestions for creating such an environment. We highly recommend it."

—Jim and Kathy McGinnis,
Parenting for Peace and Justice,
St. Louis, Missouri

160 pages. Illustrated. Large format. 1984.
Hardcover: $24.95
Paperback: $9.95

DESPAIR AND PERSONAL POWER IN THE NUCLEAR AGE
by Joanna Rogers Macy

Despair and Personal Power in the Nuclear Age is the first major book to examine our psychological responses to planetary perils and to lay the theoretical foundations for an empowering, personally centered approach to social change. Included are sections on awakening in the nuclear age, relating to children and young people, guided meditations, empowering rituals, and a special section on "Spiritual Exercises for a Time of Apocalypse."

This book was described and excerpted in *New Age Journal* and *Fellowship Magazine*, recommended for public libraries by *Library Journal*, and selected for inclusion in the 1984 Women's Reading Program, General Board of Global Ministries, United Methodist Church.

200 pages. Appendices, resource lists, exercises. 1983.
Hardcover: $19.95
Paperback: $8.95

Available from your local bookstore or, to order directly, send check or money order to **New Society Publishers**, 4722 Baltimore Avenue, Philadelphia, PA 19143. For postage and handling, add $1.50 for the first book and 40¢ for each additional book.